The Religious Studies Skills Book

ALSO AVAILABLE FROM BLOOMSBURY

A Beginner's Guide to the Study of Religion, Bradley L. Herling
Key Terms in Material Religion, edited by S. Brent Plate
The Study of Religion, George D. Chryssides and Ron Geaves

The Religious Studies Skills Book

Close Reading,
Critical Thinking, and Comparison

EUGENE V. GALLAGHER and
JOANNE MAGUIRE

BLOOMSBURY ACADEMIC
LONDON • NEW YORK • OXFORD • NEW DELHI • SYDNEY

BLOOMSBURY ACADEMIC
Bloomsbury Publishing Plc
50 Bedford Square, London, WC1B 3DP, UK
1385 Broadway, New York, NY 10018, USA

BLOOMSBURY, BLOOMSBURY ACADEMIC and the Diana logo
are trademarks of Bloomsbury Publishing Plc

First published in Great Britain 2019

A catalogue record for this book is available from the British Library.

A catalog record for this book is available from the Library of Congress.

ISBN: PB: 978-1-3500-3374-0
         HB: 978-1-3500-3373-3
       ePDF: 978-1-3500-3376-4
      eBook: 978-1-3500-3375-7

Typeset by Integra Software Services Pvt. Ltd.
Printed and bound in Great Britain

To find out more about our authors and books visit www.bloomsbury.com
and sign up for our newsletters.

For all our colleagues and friends with whom we've had the distinct pleasure of working at the Wabash Center for Teaching and Learning in Theology and Religion.

Online resources to accompany this book are available at: https://www.bloomsbury.com/cw/the-religious-studies-skills-book

Please type the URL into your web browser and follow the instructions to access the Companion Website. If you experience any problems, please contact Bloomsbury at: contact@bloomsbury.com.

Contents

List of Images

List of Figures

Acknowledgments

We would like to thank our mentors, teachers, and students for their insights on teaching and learning throughout the years. This book is the result of countless classroom interactions and conversations with colleagues at our institutions and beyond. Appreciation also extends to our families, who have learned to embrace our love for teaching as well as the time and energy required to do it well.

Thank you to Lalle Pursglove, Lucy Carroll, and the editorial and production team at Bloomsbury who helped see this book to press.

We thank especially Zannah Kimbrell, Jakob Zalman Breunig, and Ariana Shahinfar, all of whom read this book in draft form. Any remaining errors are our own.

Introduction: How to Use this Book

Teachers want you to succeed. They really do. College and university teachers generally devote a lot of time to devising syllabi, choosing readings, crafting assignments, preparing for class meetings, and evaluating student work. In a sense, they map out a path—sometimes multiple paths—that you can follow if you want to do well in a course. For some students, particularly beginning ones, that path may not be easy to see. It may even seem harder to follow. That perception can produce frustration, anger, and apathy. Unfortunately, none of those emotions is likely to lead you toward success.

We have written this book in order to help you succeed in the academic study of religion. We've tried to identify fundamental skills that will help you perform well in a variety of courses. Fortunately, those skills are not useful only in courses in the academic study of religion. They are also useful in all kinds of courses, but, importantly, they are useful in many dimensions of life after college. After you graduate and enter the work force, become part of a community, and exercise your rights and responsibilities as a citizen, you will continue to be able to call upon skills that you have learned and honed in college.

We have identified reading the syllabus, bracketing, close reading, critical thinking, and comparison as skills that are fundamental to the study of religion. Those skills are never practiced in the abstract. Rather, they are woven into the work of any given course. You will always be asked to perform a close reading *of something*, to think critically *about something*, and to undertake comparisons *between or among things*. All of that work takes place in the context of a particular course, especially in the work that is done during class sessions. The more you practice those skills in classes, the more likely you will be able to use them throughout your life after college.

All coursework is marked by a particular triangular relationship among the students, the teacher, and the material they have come together to study (see Figure I.1).

Students bring to the course their own interests, abilities, concerns, and experiences. So do teachers. Teachers largely have the responsibility for choosing the material on which everyone involved will focus. Students have the responsibility to learn.

What makes the classroom distinctive is the dynamic, triangular relationship among students, material, and teacher. If the relationship were only between the students and the material, they could study it on their own in a library, at home, or anywhere else. If the relationship were only between the students and the teacher, they would have to search for a common interest and it might not be substantial enough to constitute a college course. If the relationship were only between the teacher and the material, students would be superfluous and teachers could pursue their interest in any material on their own, without onlookers.

Any course needs all three elements, but that makes things complicated. A teacher must be aware of the full range of diversities that the students bring to the classroom, including their previous experience with the study of religion, their general attitude toward religion, their particular learning styles, how their social locations shape their work in college, and their general attitudes about the course and its subject matter, among many other things. You, as a student, need to be cognizant of your own motivations, your abilities, the degree of effort you want to invest in the course, and any constraints on your abilities to do the work of the course. The teacher needs to pick material appropriate to the announced topic and level of the course, accessible to the students, and capable of inciting their interest. You need to approach the material with an open mind, work to understand it, and be comfortable with

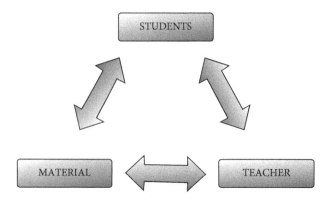

FIGURE I.1 *Relationships between students, material, and teacher.*

asking questions. As you can see, within the context of any course, there is a lot going on—much more than what we have briefly indicated.

But courses do not exist as independent entities. They are parts of various courses of study or curriculums. They can be part of a sequence of courses that define a major, concentration, or minor. But that is not likely to be a prominent concern for you when taking your first, and perhaps only, course in the academic study of religion. Courses can also be part of broader programs of a college or university. Courses in the study of religion are frequently parts of college- or university-wide programs of general education; sometimes they fulfill a particular category of distribution requirements which aim to give students a broad education in their first years. If you are undertaking the study of religion for the first time you are likely to end up in those introductory courses that fulfill distribution or general education requirements.

General education requirements are part of a program that will have its own specified goals. As a result, individual courses that are part of such programs will align their own goals with those of the broader program. The goals of such courses, thus, have a double function. They are both specific to the course and directly related to the broader program. Hence, you will benefit if you can understand such courses *in context*. The context of introductory courses in general education or distribution programs is important if you want to understand what the course is asking of you, and why. Throughout this book we will emphasize the importance of context in your understanding; both the requirements of a course and the way in which it is conducted. We can picture the importance of context by putting the previous diagram inside of another one (see Figure I.2).

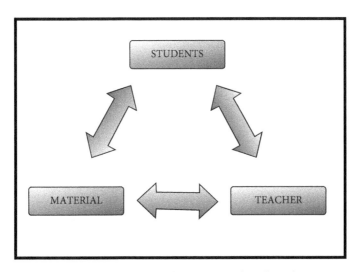

FIGURE I.2 *Relationships between students, material, and teacher in context.*

What you learn about syllabi, bracketing, close reading, critical thinking, and comparison is always shaped by a particular context. Institutional contexts shape what goes on in the classroom in many ways, some obvious and some less so. You, therefore, need to be able to "read" the context of the course you are taking for important clues about why it takes the shape it does and how you can perform to the best of your abilities in it. Fortunately, well-constructed syllabi provide multiple statements, or at least clues, about how to understand that context.

So, with that being said, how should you use this book? First, you should take it as a resource that is designed to help you succeed. Second, you should be aware that it is not about *what* you will be studying, but about *how* you will likely be asked to do it. Third, you can return to its explanations and illustrations at any time, but especially *when* you have questions about a task such as performing a close reading, offering a critical perspective on something, or making a comparison. You can also answer the questions and do the exercises that accompany each chapter and appear on the companion website for this book. If you get particularly interested in a specific topic, we also list further resources on that website. We hope that this book will be like an encouraging companion for you as you embark on the study of religion. It is aimed to support your efforts throughout the term and to be helpful in demystifying many of the things that you will have to do.

Online resources to accompany this book are available at: https://www.bloomsbury.com/cw/the-religious-studies-skills-book

Please type the URL into your web browser and follow the instructions to access the Companion Website. If you experience any problems, please contact Bloomsbury at: contact@bloomsbury.com.

1

Religion in Higher Education

That religion is an object of academic study surprises many new college students. Those who study religion in college often do so in their first or second years, frequently as part of a general education requirement. They thus embark on a distinctive form of academic inquiry at the same time that they are learning how to function in a new environment. The better you understand the particular environment of higher education, the more you will be prepared to succeed in all of your coursework, not just in the study of religion.

High schools work differently from colleges in several ways. For example, most college courses meet three times, twice, or even once a week. Students are expected to do a lot of their work outside of the classroom, with only twelve to fifteen hours total spent in the classroom each week. Instructors expect students to be independent and self-motivated. Students who grasp quickly how colleges and universities work will be better situated to succeed in their academic work, and those who understand how religious studies fits in the university curriculum will more easily adapt to disciplinary expectations.

The academic study of religion as a disciplinary focus in higher education is relatively new, although its roots go very deep. Religious studies is an interdisciplinary field, taught by scholars who are a diverse mix of anthropologists, historians, literary critics, philologists, philosophers, and sociologists, among others. The ways religious studies teachers are trained and the institutions in which they work have shaped their views about appropriate ways to study religion in courses and in the broader curriculum. Historical shifts have also affected the ways religion is integrated (or not) into the curriculum of colleges and universities.

There are many questions about how religion fits into higher education. You might be puzzled about the different ways faculty handle personal statements of faith in classrooms: some insist on complete "bracketing" of personal belief while others allow students to speak from personal experience. You might be surprised to find religion discussed at all in a classroom, in part because it is marginalized as a subject of study in K-12 education. There are many reasons for this state of affairs, not least the popular (false) perception that religion does not legally belong in public schools or that it is simply secondary to other studies (in some cases true).[1] Campuses have also expanded student services to include religious and spiritual support, a situation that makes the dividing line harder to discern.

Popular misconceptions about religion's place in college curricula have their roots in the ways religion is handled in public K-12 schools and in the history of higher education more generally. Your reaction to encountering religion in education stems from particular cultural norms. As intellectual historian Paul Boyer says, religion is the "Black Hole of American public culture."[2] This is a "black hole" into which most college students have fallen unawares prior to college. Most college students tend to think in terms of more well-known majors, such as English, history, and chemistry. We will begin by sketching the contours of the history of higher education and then describe the fraught relationship between the academic study of religion and public education.

A brief history of higher education

The words we use in higher education today—tuition, campus, prerequisites, convocation, freshmen—have their roots in a long tradition of education stretching back to the Christian cathedral and monastic schools founded during the ninth-century Carolingian Renaissance. Those schools, in turn, looked back to Christian religious institutions of the sixth century and before. Although informal learning and more formal schools flourished under the Greeks, Romans, Byzantines, and Muslims, it was not until the eleventh and twelfth centuries that true universities in the modern sense emerged. These earliest educational institutions were arms of the church: arithmetic was taught in order to calculate church finances; geometry was taught to enable the construction of cathedrals; astronomy was taught in part to allow an accurate calculation for the date of Easter.

The roots of the modern university are, then, in the Christian church, which monopolized education and focused primarily on training the clergy in church law, how to write and deliver a sermon, and how to manage church finances. In a world of widespread illiteracy, medieval universities produced rhetoricians and scribes, whose jobs rarely required individual thought. Indeed, much of the teaching and learning done in universities prior to the sixteenth century was by rote: students spent their time copying texts or devising commentaries on older texts, often on wax tablets if they could not afford parchment. All of this work was done in Latin, even in places where the colloquial language was not Latin. Knowledge of the official language of the church was a prerequisite for entry into higher education.

Unlike our highly structured institutions of higher education today, the earliest "schools" began as private agreements between teachers and pupils who met wherever and whenever it was convenient. There was no governing body over these relatively informal teacher–student relationships. Gradually such "schools" gained the support of secular or church authorities. By the fourteenth century, independent universities began to form when groups of local masters and students were given license to teach and learn by local civil or church sanction. All of those involved were men and all academic work was done in Latin, regardless of the everyday vernacular or common language of the students.

The next phase in the development of the university was the *studium generale*, arising in the thirteenth century as institutions opened to all men seeking higher degrees in law, medicine, or theology. Teaching duties were restricted to those who had earned master's status, an early model for faculty at today's institutions of higher education. Moreover, the status of master allowed a teacher to transfer those credentials to other schools without taking further qualifying examinations. Academic masters also acted as gate-keepers for their particular discipline, retaining the sole right to give examinations that qualified members to join the company of scholars.

Just as trade guilds maintained a hierarchy of apprentices, journeymen, and masters, universities maintained a hierarchy of students, bachelors, and masters. Particular institutions became known for specialization in certain fields in large part because of affiliated masters who excelled in those areas: one went to Bologna to study law, to Paris to study theology, and to Chartres to study music theory, for example. Thus an academic degree came to indicate admission to a particular profession such as law or medicine, just as completion of an apprenticeship in more applied fields allowed one to practice a particular trade.

The curriculum of the earliest monastic schools was initially based on a set progression of texts and meditation that required close, intense reading of the Bible and commentaries. These were studied alongside the great works of the seven liberal arts, divided into the preparatory *trivium* (grammar, logic, and rhetoric) and the more advanced *quadrivium* (arithmetic, geometry, astronomy, and music). Mastery of those subjects, which generally took about six years (with the bachelor's degree conferred after mastery of the *trivium*), allowed a student to depart with master's credentials or to go on to professional study in law, medicine, or theology. Students generally began their studies in their mid-teens and emerged with the most advanced degree by their early thirties.

Unlike in today's institutions, there was no required set of courses and certainly no set-aside "general education" requirement, as the liberal arts *were* a general education. Students took the courses that would allow them to pass the culminating examinations for whatever degree they wished to pursue. The original focus on liberal arts became overshadowed by the sciences under the influence of translations of Aristotle by Arabic and Byzantine scholars in the twelfth century, an emphasis that began to be balanced out in the late fourteenth and early fifteenth century with the reintroduction of classical texts. The last few decades have shown a swing back to sciences with the focus on STEM (Science, Technology, Engineering, and Mathematics) education.

Universities today share many characteristics with their ancestors, but the ways in which they differ are notable. University life for students was remarkably similar to today: medieval students regularly wrote home for money and tended to overindulge in alcoholic beverages.[3] Many found themselves overwhelmed by the work; others found the intellectual life to be energizing. What is perhaps most different is that the earliest universities were not places divided up into buildings for living and work. They did not have quadrangles and pathways busy with students as featured in glossy marketing materials. They did not have a central core or even share a campus. Originally, lectures were held wherever the master chose, whether that be his home or a rented space. Students lived in rented quarters as they found them, not in university-run residence halls. Some institutions, particularly in Italy, established student residential clubs, which were the earliest models for residential colleges in later universities. And instructors were not salaried professionals: they were forced to market themselves to their students in order to earn their wages.

Unlike the earliest universities, which tended to specialize in one professional area, *most universities today grant a range of degrees in undergraduate and graduate fields, while colleges tend to grant degrees only (or mostly) in undergraduate fields*. Universities are often made up of colleges, or groupings of faculty in related disciplines. Even the term "university" as used today does not match its earliest meaning for any group of people united in a common endeavor such as a guild.

Today's university is more like the medieval *studium generale*, a term that referred more to the student body in its geographical diversity than to the subjects being taught. The curriculum has changed quite a bit since the earliest universities, which put theology, the "Queen of the Sciences," at the center of the curriculum. Theology is now primarily taught in seminaries, divinity schools, and other denominationally affiliated schools primarily as training for ministry.[4] Today, students can read the same texts read by those earliest students *but they tend to ask very different questions as they engage in the relatively new academic study of religion*. For more on this distinction, see Chapter 3.

Student experience in the classroom today differs, too. The earliest universities tended not to quiz or otherwise assess their students in individual classes. The only assessment was a summative assessment at the very end of the education in the form of qualifying examinations. Until very recently, most students spent many hours hearing teachers read aloud and comment on standard texts. Classroom work consisted of lecture with little discussion. In today's world of immediate access to information of all kinds via the internet, it is hard to imagine a world where an academic library held fewer than 200 books, all uncatalogued (and therefore difficult to find) and often chained to lecterns and thus not circulating. Again, the goal of education in this system was not original research but, rather, the transmission and preservation of knowledge of previous generations. In fact, an emphasis on original research did not begin until the nineteenth century in Germany. That ideal took hold in the early twentieth century in the United States, when the government began providing grants to support research in science to help the war effort.

Both British and German models have shaped contemporary American colleges and universities. British models of residential colleges that teach through individual tutorials and seminars continue to shape American ideals, particularly in smaller liberal arts colleges. The German model that puts research at the forefront has distinctively influenced American research universities. This model puts highly specialized, original research in the center of university life, a model that necessitates academic freedom for faculty and students. The University of Pennsylvania is a fine example of the research model. Founded in 1740, the university began as a small colonial college and has become a research powerhouse. The university boasts an almost one billion-dollar annual research budget.[5] It is not alone in putting research at the-forefront of its agenda for both faculty and students. Many other institutions also mix the two models in providing a traditional "collegiate" experience even at large research universities.

Higher education has experienced tremendous growth in the last century, with religious studies growing alongside it since the 1960s. In 1900, there were approximately 1,000 colleges and universities in the United States. Today, there are more than 4,700 degree-granting institutions, including both two-year and four-year programs. Those institutions take many forms, from very small liberal arts and church-affiliated colleges to sprawling community college systems and state university systems enrolling tens of thousands of students.

Most private institutions are funded primarily through tuition and endowments, and public institutions receive some dwindling support from state taxes. Most educational institutions are nonprofit, although the last decade has seen a proliferation of for-profit and online enterprises. The key distinction here is whether the university is accountable to shareholders to make a profit or to a board of overseers that is not dedicated to maximizing profit. In general, non-profit colleges and universities are more likely to put student needs (and not financial gain) first, although solid finances are always crucial to student support.

The growth of religious studies departments and courses has paralleled the overall growth of higher education, with many departments of religious studies and religion coalescing in the 1960s. At first, many of these departments were joint departments of Philosophy and Religious Studies, and some remain joined in that way. The Department of Religious Studies at the University of North Carolina at Charlotte is a good example of this parallel growth of the university and religious studies. Founded in 1964 at a fairly new college for veterans, its Department of Philosophy and Religion began with a single faculty member. By 1971, when the departments of Religious Studies and Philosophy split, there were four faculty members in the new Department of Religious Studies. The department gradually expanded, moving from an early emphasis on New Testament and early Christianity to include the study of Hinduism and Chinese religions. The department currently houses fourteen full-time faculty members with specialties ranging from religion and sexuality to race and religion. Some faculty members situate their work in particular traditions while others focus on theory and method. This department, on a large state university campus, is in many ways typical of the kinds of growth seen in religious studies since its inception in the early 1960s.

Colleges and universities today continue to start programs or departments of religion or religious studies. They go by different designations: your institution might have a Department of Religious Studies, a Department of Religion, a Department for the Study of Religion, or a hybrid department with anthropology or philosophy. Some religious studies scholars reside in departments of interdisciplinary studies or as parts of programs or minors, rather than departments that offer major degrees. Religious studies has become one of many respected fields in the liberal arts or humanities, and departments of religious studies often employ faculty who work across disciplines. This is in striking contrast to the situation in K-12 schools.

Religion in public schools

Most college students have learned about religion all their lives, but that education has rarely happened in any intentional way in formal schooling. Religion is not a mandated part of public school education in the US, although it is a subject in many European countries prior to university. Many Americans believe this exclusion is justified by the establishment and free exercise clauses of the First Amendment: "Congress shall make no law respecting an establishment of religion, or prohibiting the free exercise thereof." The more commonly used term "separation of church and state" is found first in Thomas Jefferson's letter to the Danbury, Connecticut, Baptists in 1802, a text that is used by some to advocate for the complete separation of those spheres of life. A true separation of church and state, the argument goes, would make teaching religion in public schools unconstitutional.

This popular conclusion is false. It is entirely legal for teachers in public schools to teach, for instance, Bible as Literature or World Religions. The key is that teachers teach *about* religion and do not advocate a particular religious viewpoint. Yet, despite consistent decisions by the Supreme Court upholding teaching about religion in schools, relatively few schools nationwide choose to do so, and public schools are particularly wary of igniting controversy by sponsoring a class that might raise the ire of parents and the threat of a lawsuit. Very few US public school systems support stand-alone courses in religion.

Several scholars have worked to integrate teaching about religion in K-12 education. The American Academy of Religion issued a set of guidelines for schools in 2010. Spearheaded by the AAR Religion in the Schools Task Force, which was chaired by Diane L. Moore of Harvard University, the document aims to help schools assess the ways religion is taught as it is embedded in the curriculum. The report explicitly defines its mission as follows:

> These Guidelines support the ... constitutionally sound approach for teaching about religion in public schools—encouraging student awareness of religions, but not acceptance of a particular religion; studying about religion, but not practicing religion; exposing students to a diversity of religious views, but not imposing any particular view; and educating students about all religions, but not promoting or denigrating religion.[6]

This statement makes clear that schools are not expected to indoctrinate students but to educate them. As should be clear throughout this book, *religion is just one part of life that can be subject to study and analysis*. These guidelines were written to help teachers and administrators see how that can be done well.

Educators tend to agree that art, music, literature, and social studies are all enriched by understanding the effects religion has on individuals and cultures; nevertheless, religion itself is often considered too hot to handle. Religion is found here and there in K-12 textbooks, following a "natural inclusion" model, identified in the 1970s as a key methodology for teaching about religion and beliefs in K-12 schools.[7] The method behind natural inclusion is to fold religion into the curriculum where it fits most organically; for instance, a discussion of European wars over religion would be difficult to conduct without a consideration of the religious worldviews in conflict.

Many supported this effort, with historian of American religions Martin Marty, among others, critiquing the prevailing "unnatural exclusion" of religion that seemed to come from fear of legal missteps. Warren Nord, professor of the Philosophy of Religion at UNC Chapel Hill and founding director of its Program in Humanities and Human Values, notes that this approach to putting "religion in courses" rather than establishing "courses in religion" seemed a good fit for the K-12 curriculum. What these thinkers insisted upon was that religion be included, not ignored, even in secular American public schools. Yet the reality of teacher training and professional development shows that religious issues are consistently downplayed in American school systems. Natural inclusion helps to correct the sometimes egregious errors of the earliest generations of curricula and textbooks, but religion still seems to have been essentially ignored in American public education except as an historical or foreign concern.[8]

If you have encountered religion in school, you have likely done so in social studies. In the United States, social studies classes are arguably the most inclusive of subject areas in the K-12 curriculum, comprising anthropology, geography, political science, sociology, psychology, philosophy, history, and economics; in short, culture.[9] Social studies classrooms are where religion is most likely to arise (and thus to be considered or ignored), a situation that appears to have changed little since social studies began as a part of public school curricula in 1916.[10] A statement from the National Council for the Social Studies (NCSS) affirms that study of religion should be an essential part of the social studies curriculum, noting that "Knowledge about religions is not only a characteristic of an educated person but is necessary for effective and engaged citizenship in a diverse nation and world. Religious literacy (see Box 1.1 on the following page) dispels stereotypes, promotes cross-cultural understanding, and encourages respect for the rights of others to religious liberty."[11] That these positive outcomes ought to be fostered seems obvious, yet the American educational system has taken little action on implementing a religious studies curriculum.

According to NCSS, study about religion is essential to understanding both the nation and the world, and NCSS thus supports efforts on many fronts to brighten a rather dismal landscape of religious illiteracy. The body of educators issued a statement noting that "Omission of study about religion can give students the false impression that the religious life of humankind is insignificant or unimportant. Failure to understand even the basic symbols, practices, and concepts of the various religions makes much of history, literature, art, and contemporary life unintelligible."[12] Despite these idealistic statements, studies have shown that religion makes its way into history,

Box 1.1 One definition of religious literacy

"Religious literacy" helps us understand one another and helps us understand the world in which we live. A task force convened by the American Academy of Religion proposes the following suggested "religious literacy" outcomes for students in Two- and Four-Year Colleges.

Graduates of two- and four-year degree programs should be able to:

- Discern accurate and credible knowledge about diverse religious traditions and expressions;
- Recognize the internal diversity of religious traditions;
- Explain how religions have shaped and are shaped by the experiences and histories of individuals, communities, nations, and regions;
- Interpret how religious expressions make use of cultural languages and artistic representations of their times and contexts;
- Analyze the assumptions that people use to generate knowledge about religions, including the differences between confessional or prescriptive statements and descriptive or analytical ones.

From the draft AAR Guidelines, "What U.S. College Graduates Should Understand About Religion," January 19, 2018.

social studies, and literature courses, but it is taught as a secondary factor, not a focus for learning in its own right.

If you are taking a course in the study of religion at your college, the institution has decided that religion is worth studying as a primary focus and, likely, that it should be part of the general education in order to prepare you for the life you will lead in your communities, at your workplace, and as a citizen. In short, your institution has decided that religion is an important topic for inquiry that helps you learn valuable content and skills.

This "one course in religion" model is not the norm in many other countries. The United States system of education about religion is an outlier among other Western nations. Many other countries often require some broader form of "religious education" as part of public school under both more secular and more religious governments. In more religious environments, religious education usually involves explicit instruction in the doctrine and faith of one tradition; in more secular environments, religious education tends to be inclusive of multiple traditions. In Europe, it is common for students to encounter indoctrination in the state religion (if there is one) alongside a comparative religions approach well before they enter higher education. In

Britain, for example, students in primary education take compulsory Religious Education classes in which they study particular religious traditions around the world, including in-depth study of at least two traditions such as Buddhism, Christianity, Hinduism, Islam, and Judaism, among others. The curriculum also includes humanism alongside consideration of philosophical and ethical questions, and it focuses significantly on teaching doctrines of the Church of England as well.

This is not to say that students in the US know nothing about religion. In fact, you have been learning about religion all of your life, either through direct exposure or through more diffuse cultural channels. All teachers of religion have stories about student misconceptions about religious groups, ranging from simple factual to deeper conceptual errors. One category of misconception lies in stereotyping: "All X do or think Y" is a template for dismissing the complexities of the religions of others, even if students embrace parallel complexities in their own lives.

One example is that Buddhists are peace-loving, non-violent people. Buddhist foundational texts support this claim, but several historical and contemporary instances indicate that actual Buddhists have engaged in violent conflict despite the teachings of their sacred texts. To say that *all* Buddhists are non-violent is not an accurate description. Instead it is a theological statement that is not borne out in fact. Before taking a class about religion, you might easily make similar positive or negative claims about other groups. This reaction is based, in part, on a shared cultural assumption that religious thoughts and actions can be separated from people's actual lives. A life of learning uncritically about religion leads many students to just such assumptions and misconceptions. See Chapter 5 to learn more about critical thinking.

More importantly, this life of uncritical learning leaves American students and adults at a tremendous disadvantage, as religious illiteracy can lead to intolerance and conflict. As the US Supreme Court noted in *Abington Township School District v. Schempp*, "[i]t might well be said that one's education is not complete without a study of comparative religion, or the history of religion and its relationship to the advancement of civilization" (374 U.S. 203 [1963]). By these reasonable standards, very few American children graduate from high school with a complete education. And the systemic disregard for studying religion from a non-sectarian perspective also leaves many adults incurious and ignorant about religion's effects on the world.

Why does religious literacy matter? It matters because religion matters. Hate crimes prompted by religious bias have been increasing in recent years, a fact that comes, at least in part, from ignorance. It is easier to hate people one has never encountered personally. Much public discourse reflects a preference for evaluating others based on stereotype rather than on verifiable information. *In this, religion joins race, ethnicity, gender, sexuality, disability, and socio-economic status as one of the arenas in which shallow stereotyping passes for knowledge.*

Is there a solution to this widespread religious illiteracy, which encourages people to overlook context and complexity in favor of perilous simplicity? One solution, as mentioned above, would be more intentional teaching about religion in K-12 schools.[13] But college and university teaching about religion is equally important, as it is interdisciplinary and broad, analyzing religion from the perspectives of, for instance, history, economics, politics, culture, and psychology, with an emphasis on examining complexity and change through time.

Religious studies in American colleges and universities

If you are taking a course in religion, you are part of a discipline that is both ancient and new. Religious studies coalesces around several sub-disciplines, including anthropology of religion, comparative religion, history of religions, philosophy of religion, psychology of religion, and sociology of religion. It has its origins as an academic discipline in the nineteenth century, with the rise of biblical criticism and the translations of Asian religious texts. The earliest scholars of religion were allied with other fields, such as anthropology, philosophy, psychology, and sociology. Colonial conquests gave the study a tremendous boost, as scholars encountered new fields of study as explorers plundered new lands and encountered difference.

Many early private colleges and universities included some teaching about religion in an effort to form the character of their students. The earliest colleges in America were affiliated with particular Christian denominations. Seventeenth- and eighteenth-century (or Colonial era) colleges forthrightly put Christian moral instruction at the forefront of their missions, justifying the training of non-ministers through the Christian concept of vocation, which understands all meaningful work in the world is tied to God's will. For example, an advertisement in 1754 for King's College, which would become Columbia University, described its goals as "to teach and engage the children to know God in Jesus Christ, and to love and serve him in all sobriety, godliness, and righteousness of life."[14] For several centuries, that was still a prominent goal for many teachers in higher education. As one author put it, "We do not teach the Bible as an end but as a means to the end of Christian character and experience."[15] As those statements indicate, the study of religion was focused on the Bible, Christian history, and particularly Christian ethics.

Only gradually did the scope of the academic study of religion expand. Burgeoning knowledge of Asian, African, and other cultures beyond the US and Europe increased general awareness of the diversity of human experience. Also, the modern research university was dedicated to applying the processes of scientific reasoning to all fields of study, including religion. Over time, curricula began to include courses on topics such as Judaism, Islam, and the "religions of the East." The strongest impetus toward diversification of religion curricula, however, came in the wake of the Supreme Court decision in *Abington Township School District v. Schempp* in 1963. In that case, the Court ruled that Bible reading in public schools constituted the sectarian practice of religion and therefore violated the First Amendment of the Constitution. But the ruling also distinguished the academic study of religion, which it deemed permissible in public schools, from the practice of specific religions. The Court's distinction paved the way for growth of the study of religion in American higher education.

Along with the rapid growth of the study of religion in American higher education have come debates about the nature and scope of the field. Many of those arguments continue to this day. As the statement from King's College suggests, the goals of the study of religion in higher education remain contentious. Some teachers, and not only at religiously affiliated schools, continue to believe that the study of religion (and the liberal arts in general) can have a positive effect on the character of students. Such a sentiment, it seems, continues to lie behind general education and distribution requirements that direct students toward the study of religion. Other teachers are adamant that character formation or the promotion of inter-religious understanding and cooperation is not an appropriate goal for the academic study of religion.

These discussions likely fuel students' misperceptions about studying religion. Unlike English and psychology, religious studies is rarely considered as a major by entering students. Unlike history and biology, religious studies is rarely taught in high schools, so students have little background other than what they have learned through culture and family. Many who do adopt the major do so after happening upon a class or a teacher that opens up a world of thought. We might fairly ask what happens in religious studies classes to draw those students in, but the answers to that question would likely be as individualized as the students who populate religion classes. *Religious Studies is a discovery major, not a destination major, most often discovered only after arrival in college.*

One pervasive misunderstanding about religious studies is that the most common occupation pursued by graduates is in the clergy (see Box 1.2). This is not surprising, given the history of colleges in America. Most colonial colleges were founded to train ministers, and many colleges had strong denominational ties and considered theology and moral philosophy staples of any higher education. To put it simply, colonial colleges were overseen by clergymen who were tasked with educating future clergymen, and character education

Box 1.2 Who studies religion?

A study in 2009 showed that majors in religious studies had increased overall by 20 percent in the previous decade, to about 47,000 students in the United States, with the greatest increase at public institutions and more than 40 percent of community colleges offering courses in religion.[a] This number is still dwarfed by the number of students who major in business, psychology, and biology, to name a few other popular majors. Very few students adopt religion as their intended major in their freshman year: just 3 percent of incoming freshmen in the 2016 Higher Education Research Institution (HERI) study planned to declare religion (or the distinct but related field of theology) as their major.[b]

The number of religion majors in any department is generally quite small, ranging from single digits to the few departments that have 50 or more. Many students major in religious studies along with another major (commonly anthropology, communication, history, political science, psychology, or sociology).

A recent survey of religious studies alumni by the American Academy of Religion showed that about two-thirds of alumni of religious studies programs are employed in fields not related directly to what they studied. Twenty percent were employed by a religious organization and 13 percent were working as college faculty or administration. Others were working in K-12 education (9.6 percent), business and finance (8 percent), information technology (4.4 percent), law (5.9 percent), and non-profit work (8.7 percent).[c]

[a] https://www.aarweb.org/about/teagleaar-white-paper.
[b] https://www.heri.ucla.edu/monographs/TheAmericanFreshman2016.pdf, p. 29.
[c] http://rsn.aarweb.org/sites/default/files/PDFs/2015%20AAR%20 Survey%20Findings.pdf

was a key part of the curriculum. Despite colonial colleges' clear foundations in training clergy, most colleges and universities that were unaffiliated with a religious tradition had eliminated religion from the curriculum by the nineteenth century.

The assumption that learning about religion is only or even primarily a path to a religious vocation or personal fulfillment dies hard. This misconception is still repeated in older guides to college majors, and some online guides fail to consider religion as a major at all.[16] More recent editions tend to question outdated assumptions and describe religious studies as an interdisciplinary liberal arts discipline that prepares students broadly with transferable skills appropriate to many career paths. Chief among those skills are comparison, close reading, critical thinking, and writing, all of which are discussed in detail in this volume.

Perhaps the best indicator of the broader goals of religious studies within the liberal arts can be found in the "Learning Outcomes" or "Course Objectives" part of religious studies syllabi, many examples of which can be found in the collection maintained by the Wabash Center for Teaching and Learning in Theology and Religious Studies (www.wabashcenter.wabash.edu). We will be working with some of those syllabi again in the next chapter. Learning objectives are typically described separately from the course description, which usually outlines the major themes or content of the course. Learning outcomes enumerate the skills and knowledge that students are expected to develop over the course of a semester. The assignments given to students should match up to the skills being fostered in any given course.

The syllabus for a course on "Religions of Colonized Peoples (Africa)" offered at DePaul University by Dr. Teresia Hinga lists the following "Specific Objectives" for the course:

a   To familiarize the students with the phenomenon of religion and its implications for society.

b   To enable the students to appreciate and critically analyze the social-political role of religion in Africa.

c   To facilitate the creation of a context which allows and encourages students critically to appreciate the role of religion both in creating situations of oppression as well as in being a resource to resist oppression.

d   To create a forum in which the students can begin critically to analyze the social-political implications of religion in their own contexts.

The verbs used here are worth noting. This course aims to "familiarize" students with course content; to "enable" students to use analytical skills; to "facilitate" students' growth in recognizing and resisting oppression; and to "create" a forum that will enable students to reflect on their own contexts in light of what they have learned in the course. This teacher clearly wants students to put their knowledge and skills into action in the world. The goal is to foster self-reflective and even activist thinkers. This teacher encourages students to resist injustice in the real world, well beyond the classroom.

A course on the "Problem of Evil" offered in spring 2014 by Eric Nelson at University of Massachusetts, Lowell, also mentions promoting familiarity with the subject matter and critical reasoning. Professor Nelson adds the following clarification to the standard list:

1   The objectives of this course are for students to develop their ability
    and skills in:

    a   **Interpreting** texts by accurately and fully describing concepts
        and arguments and placing them in their social-historical
        contexts.

    b   **Reasoning** about ideas by (i) evaluating the content, structure,
        and strategies of philosophical and religious works, (ii) reflecting
        on their contexts by considering information and scholarship
        from the historical and social sciences, and (iii) applying
        concepts and arguments to contemporary issues and their own
        lives.

    c   **Collaborating** with other students, and presenting and
        supporting their ideas in public through class participation.

These are clearly skills that are needed in this class and in the job market.
Students are expected to learn skills of interpretation and analysis;
reflection and research; and application to current issues. Students in this
class are also expected to work with peers by presenting arguments in
class discussion, a set of skills that will likely be used in many jobs after
college.

Finally, a course on "Religion, Media and Hollywood: Faith in TV" by
Diane Winston at the University of Southern California Annenberg School for
Communication, lists the following course goals:

1   Exploring how media frames ethical issues, moral dilemmas,
    spirituality and the religious imagination.

2   Analyzing the function of religious and spiritual imagery in particular
    social locations.

5   [sic] Thinking critically about the role of the entertainment media in
    creating communities of discourse.

A student who reads this syllabus closely will be rewarded by seeing
the way the instructor defines and organizes content and skills throughout
the semester. Many instructors "scaffold" student learning by carefully
considering the stages by which students can best learn, first with careful
guidance and moving toward independence. As is the case with many lists
of learning outcomes, this one moves from skills specific to the content of
the course to a broader expectation of skills that can accompany the student
well beyond this course. This course should prepare students to be savvy,
thoughtful consumers of media who question what they see. As these

examples make clear, most often, the overall goal of religious studies classes is often to create reflective and independent thinkers. Each class will focus on a particular type and amount of content, but teachers generally think beyond that content to higher levels of learning and thinking.

You will likely find that work done in religious studies is solid preparation for graduate study or a variety of careers. Most majors find that their training in reading, writing, and communicating serves them well in whatever career they choose. Religious studies, in other words, prepares you for much more than religion or personal growth. Even a single course in religious studies will provide some preparation for many careers. The focus on close reading, comparison, and critical thinking, coupled with writing and speaking skills, will serve you well in future courses and your career. We will return to this in our final chapter.

Once you enroll in college, you will find yourself in interesting territory both physically and intellectually. Students enroll in institutions that are small and large; religiously affiliated or not; focused more on research or on teaching; catering more to a residential or commuter population; attended by students who have jobs or those whose only job is attending school. All of those factors affect what happens in the classroom. Particular departments are comprised of particular faculty members, each with their own commitments and expectations. Even classroom setup can affect the way classes are conducted: the medieval lecture hall is scarcely conducive to active learning, and unmovable chairs in any room make discussion with peers difficult. Many vestiges of the history of higher education continue to shape the lives of college students today.

The history of higher education and the role of religion within that landscape have shaped the ways religion can be discussed on college campuses. The ways religion is taught or avoided in K-12 education also shape the ways students perceive the academic study of religion in college. Depending on your institution and the expectations of your teacher in a given course, you might be given more or less liberty to discuss personal matters. Some faculty might take a genuine interest in your personal growth while others are all about the content and approach required in the course. Clues to these expectations can be found in the course syllabus and the wording of assignments, as described in the following chapter. You should take advantage of faculty office hours if you want more specific clarification from a particular teacher.

We have mapped some of the terrain that students who study religion in higher education will encounter. With a bit of observation and thought, you can situate yourself and your peers and teachers, as well as the subject matter of individual courses, within this terrain. Doing so will help you understand what is and is not expected of you, why teachers may say some of the things that they do, what is acceptable to say in the classroom and what is not. As noted above, this needs to be done for each individual course in religious studies, since faculty can differ as widely as students in their assumptions and expectations. Every course constitutes a new context in which you will need to figure out how to make your way.

Exercises and questions for further thought can be found at https://www. bloomsbury.com/cw/the-religious-studies-skills-book/skill-building-exercises/ chapter-one/

2

The Syllabus and Course Expectations

All teaching is local. That is certainly true about higher education in the US. The type of institution, for example two-year or four-year, research oriented or teaching focused; the size and composition of the student body; the mission of the college or university; its affiliation with religious groups or independence from them; and the size of its endowment are all among the factors that contribute to the distinctive contours of a college or university. And the contours of the institution shape how teaching happens.

Beyond general institutional factors, broad social forces distinctively shape teaching about religion in any institution. For example, many people have thought that the American political doctrine of the separation of church and state prohibited the teaching of religion in public institutions. That, however, is not the case, as described in the previous chapter. Some form of the study of religion has been present in American education from colonial times. But only in the later twentieth century did the study of religion grow at an impressive rate in public institutions.

Teachers and students enter the classroom with both explicit and often implicit goals for the academic study of religion. One researcher observed that there is a "great divide" between what faculty members want to accomplish in their teaching and what students want to get out of the religion courses that they take. Where faculty strongly emphasize "critical thinking" as a primary goal, students tend to focus on their own religious or spiritual development.[1] Teachers, students, and institutions may thus have rather different goals for what the study of religion will accomplish. It is therefore crucial for everyone involved to be as explicit as possible about their goals and to be aware of areas of convergence and divergence.

The default expectation that the academic study of religion would somehow lead to appropriate (Christian) character formation has also left an indelible mark on the curriculum. That expectation contributed to the formation of what some have called a "seminary model," in which introductions to the Bible, Christian history, and ethics dominated the list of courses. In that model Christianity served at least implicitly as the paradigm for "religion" in general. That position, however, has proven inadequate as a basis for comparison and generalization. As a recent report from the American Academy of Religion characterizes the field, the seminary model is gradually and unevenly being replaced by a "comparative" model for the curriculum that includes attention to multiple religious traditions, themes, issues, and theoretical approaches.[2]

For multiple reasons, then, the study of religion in US colleges and universities is characterized by diversity. Even within the same department or program, teachers frequently diverge in their understandings of their primary purposes. Students also differ in what they expect to learn, or be taught, in their courses. Course offerings also can vary widely from one institution to another. Even the definition of the object of study—religion itself—is open to substantial debate.

Probably the most widely shared underlying contention of the academic study of religion is that *religion is a human phenomenon*. Because it is something that human beings do, religion is observable. In the actions of people, including ritual performances, the making and using of religious texts and objects, and many other pursuits, religion becomes visible, even when figures such as gods, spirits, and other extra-ordinary beings are not. You can then study religion using many of the tools that can be employed to analyze other human actions, such as electoral processes, social movements, artistic performances, and many others.

The fundamental questions that preoccupy scholars of religion may appear too abstract and theoretical to interest many beginning students. But one place where they make a direct impact on your experience is in the syllabus. *The syllabus for any course embodies a series of decisions*. Teachers have to decide what to include and what to leave out. They need to decide how to approach the particular information toward which they will direct everyone's attention. They need to consider what they want you to learn and how to construct activities that will put you into a situation where you can learn. In most cases, the syllabus is created by the instructor, although sometimes it is a standard department syllabus developed by multiple teachers. In either case, it is a carefully fashioned document that repays your sustained attention.

The broader the topic of a course, the more decisions will have to be made about content, approach, and assignments, among other things. In particular, introductory courses, such as "Introduction to Religion," "World Religions," or "Introduction to the Bible," offer teachers substantial flexibility in devising a syllabus. In a single term it is simply impossible to include everything about such broad topics. As a result, such courses also challenge teachers to think carefully about what they are including and why. That process of thinking through the subject matter and approach of an introductory course inevitably draws upon a teacher's fundamental understandings of the nature and scope of the academic study of religion and its importance.

The syllabus, then, can be a very revealing document. Its descriptions of what you will study, how you will approach the material, and why it is important all offer significant insights not only into the specific course but also to the teacher's conceptions of why it matters and how it might fit into your broader education. For you, then, *developing the ability to read a syllabus for its full implications is an essential skill.* Beyond a list of class topics, required readings, and specific assignments, the syllabus offers a window onto the broader questions that animate the academic study of religion and connect it to other aspects of your college education. You should learn to read a syllabus not only for what it has to say about the nuts and bolts of a particular course but also for what it implies about the broader educational and social contexts and connections of the course. If you can do that effectively, you will be poised to bring a depth and clarity of insight to all of the work that you do for the course and beyond.

Syllabi have changed over time, most recently with the widespread implementation of electronic course management systems such as Blackboard, Design2Learn, and Moodle.[3] But whether they are printed on paper or exist only on the web, they can still be very revealing documents. *Reading the syllabus is a complex skill that can be improved, like any other skill, with practice* (see Box 2.1). Reading a syllabus carefully depends on the processes of close reading, critical thinking, and comparison that are foundational to the academic study of religion. To provide concrete examples of how syllabi can be read we will analyze three separate introductory syllabi from three different types of institution. We will pay particular attention to *what* is being included in the course, *why* it has been chose for inclusion, *how* you are supposed to pursue the work of the course, and *what* successful completion of the course is supposed to do for you. We will work with syllabi that are publicly available in the collection of the Wabash Center for Teaching and Learning in Theology and Religion.[4]

Box 2.1 Reading the syllabus

- What is the course about?
  - Consider the title, the description in the course catalogue or bulletin, and the description in the actual syllabus
    E.g. The Bible, What is Religion?, Introduction to World Religions
  - What has the instructor chosen to include and what is left out?
    The syllabus may have explicit statements about this topic. It will be easier to identify what has been chosen for inclusion.

- What level is the course?
  - Introductory, intermediate, advanced
  - Both the number and the title will provide indications

- What approach is the teacher taking?
  - Is there a particular theoretical perspective?
  - Is there a particular method of study, e. g. ethnography?
  - Pay particular attention to the first few class sessions, in which teachers frequently explain how they are approaching the material.

- What are the learning goals for the course?
  - Explicit goals
  - Implicit goals, while not be written down they may be implied or stated verbally

- How are the specific assignments connected to the goals and to the subject matter?
  - Some syllabi will do this explicitly
  - Teachers may explain their goals for assignments verbally, in class
  - If you have any questions, ask them in class or in a visit during office hours

- Is there a broader context for the course?
  - E.g. general education or the major
  - If so, are the connections between the course and that broader context made clear?

- What does the course require of each student?
  - E. g. attendance, participation, oral presentations, examinations, papers
  - How are the different requirements weighted?
  - Are clear about what you need to do in the course in order to succeed?

An introductory course at a private, regional university

Hofstra University is a private university located 25 miles east of New York City on Long Island. Of its nearly 7,000 undergraduates some 60 percent come from New York state and 42 percent from Long Island.[5] RELI 10, "What is Religion?," is the lowest numbered course offering from the Department of Religion. It is common for low-numbered courses to have the most general topics; courses get more specific at the intermediate and advanced levels. In some institutions all sections of such courses are highly regimented, with a common textbook and a common syllabus. But when they are not, the breadth of the topic virtually guarantees that each version of the course will differ from the others.

At Hofstra, multiple sections of "What is Religion?" are offered throughout the academic year. In general the course is explicitly designed as an introduction to the academic study of religion. As the course bulletin describes it, one of its general goals is to help "students gain concrete information about the way religious beliefs and practices shape the world."[6] Individual teachers determine the ways in which their specific versions of the course will be constructed to reach those general goals. Consequently, the individual sections show that there are many different ways to address the question, "What is Religion?"

Several things thus become apparent from the outset. The different sections of RELI 10 are the "same" course only at a high degree of generality. Each section will have a different thematic focus, use different examples from different religious traditions, and have different assignments. That is likely to be the case whenever multiple sections of a particular course are offered, particularly when they are taught by different people and do not have a common syllabus which all teachers must adopt. Students' experiences, then, will necessarily vary from section to section. Students in different sections will not read the same things, discuss the same issues, or tackle the same assignments. Students' experiences will also vary within each section according to levels of student interest, capacity, and engagement, and according to the ability of the teacher to communicate with and motivate individual students. In some ways, then, all students in RELI 10 are taking the "same" course. But in other ways each of them is taking a very particular course, shaped by their own interests and investments and their interactions with the teacher, with each other, and with the subject matter.

Another thing that the multiplicity of sections implies is that *there are multiple ways to pursue the same goal*. When a goal is phrased as generally as acquiring "information about how religious beliefs and practices shape the world," no particular path toward achieving that understanding is implied.

The specific information on which each section of the course focuses, then, represents an intentional selection chosen from a much broader field of possible examples. The analytical focus of the course is therefore less on mastering the details of the particular examples in themselves, though accuracy and precision are always necessary, than on understanding those details as specific demonstrations of more general processes. The examples are presented, at least implicitly, not as being meaningful in themselves, but as being meaningful in so far as they can be used to reveal more fundamental and general processes. In her section of RELI 10 Professor Ann Burlein, for example, uses elements of Judaism, Christianity, and Islam to address the theme of her course, "Religion and its Monsters." She certainly cannot teach her students *everything* about each of those religions. But she can use *specific information* from them to exemplify issues that bear upon her chosen theme.

Two important lessons can therefore be learned before even considering the details of a syllabus for a particular section of a multi-section course. First, there are multiple paths toward achieving such a broad goal as understanding how religious beliefs and practices shape the world. The topic can be investigated from many different angles, and lots of different information can be used to demonstrate how the shaping of a social world is accomplished. If you are alert to such implications you will have grasped something important about study in the humanities. It is open-ended; it draws upon a vast array of data; it focuses on constructing arguments about how specific data illuminate certain fundamental questions and topics. Consequently, it consists of developing, supporting, critiquing, and refining arguments rather than on the mastery or even memorization of discrete bits of information.

Second, there are no right answers. To study in the humanities in general and Religious Studies in particular is to enter complex conversations that have been going on for some time. It is not to seek the right answer that will settle things forever. College-level work in the humanities is primarily about argument and persuasion. To be sure, arguments need to be about something, and that something needs to be described as accurately and fully as possible. But that is only the beginning of a more complicated process. Arguments are about what something means, how it can best be understood. In Box 2.2 we provide a brief guide to generating arguments through the processes of description, analysis, and interpretation.

As arguments are fleshed out, they also address why one particular understanding of something is superior. It might be claimed that a particular argument is more comprehensive, sees more deeply, takes account of previously ignored factors or has some other noteworthy attribute. Arguments thus take the form of "X should be understood in this way because ... and this understanding is clearly to be preferred because ..." In that sentence "X" stands for the particular action, phenomenon, or belief under scrutiny.

Box 2.2 Generating arguments through description, analysis, and interpretation

- What do you want or need to know?

  - How abstract is your question (e.g. what is truth?)
  - How general is your question (e.g. why do so many people believe in God?)
  - How can you focus your question (e.g. time period, cultural area, social group, etc.)

- How can you find out about what you want or need to know?

  - What resources are available (e. g. scholarly books, journal articles, newspapers and news magazines, encyclopedias, web resources, fieldwork, etc.)?
  - Which resources are most likely to be helpful?
  - What are the primary sources (*from* the group/person/etc. under consideration)?
  - What are the secondary sources (*about* the group/person/etc. under consideration)?
  - What is the authority of a secondary source (author, author's credentials, etc.)?
  - What is the hierarchy of secondary sources, i.e. which will be most important for your work, which less so?

- What will you do with what you have found?

  Description (what is it?)
  - Have you collected sufficient information?
  - What is the nature of the information you have collected?
  - What is its specific relevance to the question/issue/problem at hand?
  - Do you have the right kind of information to answer your question?
  - Do you have the right amount of information to answer your question?

  Analysis (how does it work?)
  - What do I have here?
  - Where does it come from?
  - What distinctive language does it use?
  - How is it structured?
  - Who is speaking?

o On whose authority is the argument made?
o What's its point or point of view?
o What kind of evidence does the material offer to support its point?
o What, if any, argument, is being opposed?
o What are the opposing arguments' purported weaknesses?
o How is this information helpful for your specific purposes (guide, foil, footnote, etc.)?
o On what implicit or explicit theory is the argument based?
o How generalizable is the argument?

Interpretation (what does it mean and why does it matter?)
o What do you want teach people?
o Who is your audience?
o How can you best make your point?
o What is your thesis?
o How does your thesis lead to a structure for your argument?
o Are the overall structure, individual sections, and transitions clearly marked?
o Do you summarize your argumentative points as they accumulate?
o Do your conclusions extend your argument beyond the original thesis?

Examples might include the Muslim pilgrimage to Mecca, the *gohonzon* shrine in Nichiren Buddhism, or the prohibition of the worship of other gods in the first commandment in the Hebrew Bible (see Exod. 20:2–3). What follows the first "because" would entail a careful description and analysis of the material under consideration. The phrase "should be understood in this way" encapsulates the argument. What follows the second "because" provides the reasons why one's own interpretation is superior to others. It makes the case for why an interpretation is persuasive.

Clearly, the construction of persuasive arguments is a complex intellectual process. We will have more to say about the processes of argumentation throughout this book. At this point, we are asserting that every syllabus constitutes a particular argument. Especially when teachers have broad latitude to choose what to teach and how to approach it, their choices cumulatively make up, or at least imply, an argument about what is important to learn about religion, and why. When you read through the syllabus to discover the decision-making that has produced it, you can learn a lot where the teacher is coming from, where the course is supposed to be going, why it is asking the questions it does and not others, and what types of attitudes, investments, and practices will help you perform well in the course. *A careful reading of the syllabus can help you be successful in any course.* Students do not always read the syllabus with the care and attention to detail that they should. After all, the syllabus is very often much more than a list of class topics and due dates. It is an argument about what is important to learn—and why.

Take, for example, the specific section of RELI 10 at Hofstra, taught by Professor Burlein. Professor Burlein's syllabus opens with a description of course goals. Acknowledging that students come to the course for various reasons, the syllabus states which general education goals and also which departmental learning goals the course fulfills, including critical thinking, analytical reasoning, written communication, oral communication, and attention to "global issues." Assuming that the course is actually aligned with those broad goals, students can thus expect that they will be expected to think carefully and analytically, to write persuasive prose, and to be able to present their ideas orally during class sessions. They can also expect to address topics and issues that are not limited to personal and local significance but that somehow are "global" in their scope.

Beyond that, the statement of goals for RELI 10 devotes considerable effort to characterizing the academic study of religion. That is particularly important because the academic study of religion is encountered much less frequently in K-12 education than subjects like English or History. Most students encounter the academic study of religion for the first time in college. They therefore cannot be presumed to be familiar with the conventions of that intellectual pursuit, as they might be with some of the conventions for the study of English or History.

Professor Burlein uses the metaphor of a wager throughout her description of course goals. She writes that "The wager of religious studies is that you learn something worthwhile if you stand back and study, not just particular religions, but 'religion' in general."[7] She then stipulates that the specific information for the course will come from the religions of Judaism, Christianity, and Islam. Of course, she could just as easily have chosen Hinduism, Taoism, and Shinto, or any other combination, for that matter. She signals that the goal of the course is not to learn about those religions in isolation from each other, but to use the data they provide to construct tentative generalizations and ask "larger questions." As she puts it to her students, Professor Burlein's broad goal is "to open up a space where you think analogously, migrating back and forth between different concrete situations." She stresses that the kinds of questions that a student or scholar of religion asks are very different from those asked by someone who stands within the perspective of a specific religion.

The syllabus thus announces several fundamental assertions that characterize the academic study of religion. First, studying the human phenomenon of religion is distinct from practicing a specific form of religion. Accordingly, students' religious commitments, or lack of them, are not the focus of the course. Professor Burlein directly tells students that she "will not grade you on your personal beliefs or non-belief." Her stance implies that studying religion involves putting some distance between one's own convictions and those of the people being studied. She asks, "What kind of thing can you learn if you try to understand different worldviews?"

Second, the study of religion is inherently comparative and generalizing. It aims to move from particular data to broader generalizations about them. The instructions for one of Professor Burlein's assignments argue that "The point of comparing AND contrasting different religions is to get yourself to think something NEW."

Third, the study of religion has developed a range of intermediate categories that facilitate the organizing of vast amounts of data. Professor Burlein specifically focuses on ritual communication. She asks "how do embodied practices communicate religious beliefs and feelings, perceptions and ideas." She also introduces the concept of episteme, "the shared rules by which different logics or worldviews get formed." The focus on those categories also has the effect of excluding certain things—such as myths, systems of purity, or many other things that could be viewed as elements of religion—from consideration and thus focusing students' attention.

Fourth, the study of religion is frequently thematic. As noted earlier, Professor Burlein announced an overall theme for the course, namely "Religion and its Monsters." That choice of a theme further tightens the focus of the course and thereby makes it more manageable for students. It identifies very specific "concrete situations" that will then be subjected to analysis, comparison, and generalization.

A close and careful reading of the syllabus for "What is Religion?" can in itself yield insights into how the teacher conceives the academic study of religion, the specific approaches that she will adopt, and the practices and habits of mind that you will have to develop in order to succeed. Before the course is even fully underway, the syllabus serves as an introduction to the course, the field of study in which it is embedded, and a vision of what the study of religion can contribute to an individual's education. Virtually any syllabus can teach a lot, especially when it is read with care.

An introductory Bible course at a religiously affiliated college

Gustavus Adolphus College is a liberal arts college of some 2,200 students in St. Peter, Minnesota, affiliated with the Evangelical Lutheran Church in America (ELCA). Because of the institution's religious affiliation, the mission of the Department of Religion includes not only promoting "a better understanding of religion as a basic aspect of human experience" but also an understanding of "the Christian heritage and its contemporary expressions."[8] As an expression of its longstanding religious commitments, Gustavus Adolphus requires that every student take "one regular semester course substantially in the Christian tradition."[9] While those distribution requirements overlap in many ways with those at Hofstra, they are distinctive in their inclusion of a required course focusing on Christianity. That emphasis also decisively shapes the department curriculum, which can be located toward the middle of the continuum between the seminary and comparative models.

REL 110, "The Bible" is the lowest numbered course in the department. It is offered every semester and is taught by multiple members of the department in rotation. It is one of the courses that satisfies the specific distribution requirement for a course "substantially in the Christian tradition." Although the purview of "The Bible" is narrower than a course which takes the whole of religion as its subject, it is still very broad. Consequently, teachers of REL 110 face similar decisions about what to include in the course, what to leave out, and how to approach the material they want to consider.

Professor C. D. Elledge situates his sections of REL 110 at Gustavus Adolphus as general introductions to the study of religion. The opening phrase of the course description characterizes the course as "an introduction to the study of religion through an exploration of the Bible."[10] That way of describing the course brings it closer to Professor Burlein's "What is Religion?" even though the materials used in both courses vary significantly. The stark differences emphasize again that there are many ways to undertake the study of the human phenomenon of religion. Students in "The Bible" can expect not only to learn about the Bible itself but also about how the materials in the Bible exemplify general aspects of the much broader category of religion. To reinforce that impression, the course description also claims that the Bible addresses "fundamental problems of meaning and value."

The syllabus for "The Bible" pays particular attention to how the course is related to a category of the distribution requirements at Gustavus Adolphus. As the college catalogue puts it, "The requirement of one regular semester course substantially in the Christian tradition is a curricular expression of the College's long-standing institutional commitments, as articulated in its Mission Statement to develop students' mature understanding of the Christian faith."[11] The syllabus for "The Bible" elaborates on that statement by stressing that the course will focus on "what the human sciences can teach us about the Bible" in four specific areas. The course examines what types of literature are represented in the Bible, the historical events that shaped the production of the Bible and which the individual books of the Bible interpret, the theological and religious ideas that occur in the Bible, and the contexts in which the Bible has been read and used.

At a religiously affiliated college such as Gustavus Adolphus teachers can reasonably expect many of their students to have at least a passing familiarity with the Bible. But students are much more likely to know some (random) things about the Bible than to have devoted serious thought to the question of what constitutes religion. Because of the current construction of K-12 education in the US they most likely have not encountered the Bible in an academic context. The knowledge that students bring to the classroom thus constitutes a particular challenge in a course such as "The Bible." Accordingly, Professor Elledge stresses in his syllabus that students need to become self-reflective. He asks them to consider "what are *your own* presuppositions and habits of mind when you read the Bible?" (his emphasis).

Professor Elledge is encouraging his students to think not only about *what* they are learning but also *how* they are learning it. In the particular case of the Bible, students who have had religious education or worship experience within a particular tradition have learned to understand the Bible in certain ways. That prior experience with the Bible may facilitate or impede the type of academic enquiry that characterizes REL 110, "The Bible." Students will have a better chance to succeed in the course if they can become aware of how their prior experience shapes their presuppositions and expectations about what a college course on the Bible might actually entail.

The ability to be self-reflective is an important skill for performing well in any college course on religion. Students who have their own religious commitments, students who may be suspicious of or actively hostile toward religion, and even those who profess neutrality or indifference toward the subject all can benefit from considering the presuppositions and expectations that they bring to the classroom. When Professor Burlein encouraged students "to ask questions that you could not ask if you stand within the situated perspective of an actual life," part of what she wanted them to do was to recognize whatever presuppositions about religion that they had and to attempt to hold them in abeyance or "bracket" them in order to undertake the type of thinking that characterizes the academic study of religion. You can learn more about bracketing in the next chapter.

That kind of self-awareness is not always easy to accomplish. But such thinking about your own thinking—what educational theorists call "metacognition"—can help **you** become aware of **your own** strengths and weaknesses in all areas of your work as a learner. Identifying strengths and weaknesses makes it easier to target specific areas for reinforcement and improvement.[12] Such metacognitive abilities are certainly not specific to the study of the Bible or to the study of religion in general. They are essential skills for learning in any classroom and in all other arenas of life. Professor Elledge suggests some of that when he writes that "the Bible course hopes to equip students with a valuable tool for examining larger issues in the liberal arts."

Professor Elledge's syllabus also emphasizes the development of specific skills. Introductory courses that fulfill distribution or general education requirements are frequently tasked with focusing on skills that are deemed to be essential elements of a college education. You can find the emphasis on skills disconcerting or somehow beside the point. Why would a religion teacher focus on "cultivat[ing] reading and writing skills," as the syllabus for "The Bible" puts it? You might think that they should be graded solely on your ideas, not on how effectively they are expressed, either orally or in writing. Such attitudes, however, are founded on a fundamental misunderstanding that relegates writing, for example, to specifically designated composition courses. If they have to take required writing courses, some students might conclude that "writing courses" deal with mechanics and refinement of skills but other courses in the humanities, for example, deal with ideas.

Ideas, however, are only accessible through the language in which they are expressed. They cannot be separated from it. Muddled language, either orally or in writing, communicates muddled thinking. The development of reading and writing skills, among others, is thus an essential component of any course in a college curriculum, especially introductory courses. Accordingly, courses like REL 110, "The Bible," frequently have a dual focus. They aim, as the syllabus states, "to increase students' knowledge of the content of the Biblical text," but they also aim to refine, through practice and correction, skills that students can employ in all of their coursework and in their lives after college.

Once you understand the dual function of any course, which most often is clearly outlined in the syllabus, you will be well-situated to benefit from everything that the course offers you. Introductory courses such as "The Bible" and "What is Religion?" are self-consciously embedded in a broader institutional curriculum and the view of education that it enacts. They are explicitly designed to help students develop foundational skills for the rest of their education. Rather than being an inappropriate imposition on a course that should be devoted to other things, attention to writing mechanics and strategies in an introductory religion course is both essential to deeper understanding of the subject matter and foundational for work in other courses.

Two features of introductory courses to which you should pay particular attention are the ways in which they make *connections* and depend upon *selections*. Courses like "What is Religion?" and "The Bible" are connected to broader programs of general education and through them to the mission of the institution through the learning goals that they emphasize. That is one of the reasons why they frequently emphasize the development of skills such as persuasive writing. An awareness of such connections between individual courses and broader programs of study helps you to understand each as part of a programmatic effort to shape your education. The selections that such courses make from the rich array of information about religion that is available to them decisively shape each course and each section of a course. Such selections give you clues about how the teacher conceives of the subject under discussion and how the teacher wants you to channel your efforts.

An introduction to the Old Testament at a public university

Missouri State University, located in Springfield, enrolls nearly 20,000 undergraduate students, largely from Missouri, in addition to graduate students. In 1995, the university was granted a statewide mission in public affairs by the state legislature. The university identifies the "three pillars" of its mission as ethical leadership, cultural competence, and community engagement.[13] Those pillars are woven into a carefully articulated program of general education. The university states that "The aim of general education at Missouri State University is to develop people capable of making choices that lead to thoughtful, creative, and productive lives and to responsible participation in society."[14] The program of general education is designed to help students to gain (1) intellectual and practical skills, (2) knowledge of human cultures, (3) knowledge of the natural world, (4) knowledge of public affairs, and (5) integrative and applied learning skills.[15]

A syllabus for an Honors section of Religious Studies 101, "Literature and World of the Old Testament," a course that is offered in multiple sections each year, strives to make the connection between the subject of the course and the mission of the university very clear. Professor Victor H. Matthews writes that the course's "application to the Public Affairs Mission of the University can be found in its efforts to educate students about the past so that they can build upon this heritage in making informed decisions about their own culture and the future direction of society."[16] With that description, students are primed to expect that they will be asked to consider not just the "literature and world of the Old Testament" itself but also its continuing and potential future impact.

The syllabus explicitly acknowledges the distance between contemporary readers and the subject matter under consideration. Professor Matthews states that the course will focus on reconstructing what the text might have originally have meant to its ancient audience in the Ancient Near East, but he also stresses that such an effort will encourage students "to take seriously, state accurately, and evaluate thoughtfully positions other than their own and cultures other than their own." That statement echoes ideas expressed in the other two syllabi.

In each syllabus examined in this chapter, the goal of the Religious Studies course *as a general education course* is to get students to make connections between the specific subject matter of the course and broader questions about human life. Students thus encounter one of the intended functions of general education. In each course, they are being asked to *generalize* by connecting their specific learning in the course to what they know from other sources. The specific information in the course is presented as *providing examples* of questions, issues, or topics that have broader, general, relevance. Since most students who take a college course in the study of religion will be taking it in order to fulfill general education or distribution requirements, understanding how courses are designed both to introduce their subject matter and to serve the goals of a broader curricular program can help you prepare yourself for success in such courses.

General education programs also very frequently describe the skills that they are designed to help students acquire and hone. Well-articulated general education programs connect the development of skills to the general outcomes that they promote. At Missouri State, for example, the general education program aims "to develop people capable of making thoughtful choices that lead to responsible participation in society."[17] Making thoughtful choices and participating responsibly entail certain skills which Missouri State describes as both intellectual and practical. The university asserts that they include being able to:

1) Gather, organize, and evaluate information and ideas,
2) Develop and explore new ideas, perspectives and approaches,
3) Express yourself clearly through writing in social, academic and professional contexts,
4) Listen critically and speak well to all audiences,
5) Reason and solve numerically-based problems, and create and communicate logical arguments based on such evidence,
6) Identify a need for information, then locate and responsibly share the information, and
7) Work in collaboration with others to solve problems and make decisions.[18]

No single course in a general education program can meet such a broad array of goals. But students should be aware of how the skills required by each course that they take are related to the full array of skills addressed by general education. In the case of "Literature and World of the Old Testament," several general goals receive particular emphasis. For example, students' acquisition of information (#1 above) is based on the fundamental process of close reading, in which "the biblical text will be carefully followed to determine and explain what the authors are saying." Evaluation of ideas (#1 above) comes to the forefront in an assignment where students are required to read and assess in writing two different articles concerning the Hebrew Bible/Old Testament. In those essays, which give students the opportunity to refine their expressive abilities, students are directed to identify the article's thesis and to assess how it has improved their understanding of the course material, among other things. Students are also encouraged to practice their skills of oral presentation (#4 above) in classroom discussions and in reports on their reading of scholarly articles.

Like the course on "The Bible" at Gustavus Adolphus, Professor Matthew's syllabus also tries to move students in the direction of self-reflection. Professor Matthews carefully distinguishes the study of the Old Testament at a state university from the study of it within a particular religious group. He directly addresses students, arguing that "You do not have to have a faith commitment in this course, nor will you be asked to abandon your faith." Holding one's own commitments at least temporarily in abeyance is a crucial aspect of taking seriously, stating accurately, and evaluating thoughtfully the actions and beliefs of someone in a culture different from one's own. Similar statements appear in the other two syllabi considered here.

The frequency with which such statements about students' religious commitments are encountered on Religious Studies syllabi signals both a basic characteristic of the academic study of religion—that it is devoted to the analysis and understanding of religious phenomena rather than to the personal evaluation of them—and a challenge that teachers frequently encounter. That challenge derives at least in part from two contexts.

First, as mentioned earlier, the academic study of religion is still rarely a part of the curriculum in K-12 education. As a result, you have likely not had the prolonged exposure to the study of religion that you have had to English or History, for example. Many students encounter the academic study of religion for the first time in college. Second, if you have previous experience with, for example, the study of the Bible, you are most likely to have acquired that experience in the context of specifically religious education; that is, education sponsored by individual religious groups for others in that group. Not surprisingly, religious education of that sort has different goals than college and university education.

Because the academic study of religion is new to so many college students and because other kinds of study of religion take place outside of the classroom, it is essential for you to work on becoming a self-reflective learner. As each of the syllabi discussed in this chapter indicates, it is crucial that you become aware of the preconceptions, expectations, and even biases that you may bring to courses like "Introduction to Religion" or "Introduction to the Bible." Becoming aware of such "pre-understandings" is a crucial requirement for being able to understand, as Professor Matthews's syllabus puts it, "positions other than [your] own and cultures other than [your] own."

The syllabi of introductory Religious Studies courses thus provide not only a glimpse into how individual teachers conceive of the field or its broad sub-fields, such as biblical studies, but also opportunities for reflection about how the academic study of religion can contribute to the general education of students. Typically, that contribution comes in two forms. Introductory Religious Studies courses frequently offer intensive training in written and oral expression, in the skills involved in close reading for deep comprehension, and in the gathering, organization, and evaluation of information. But such courses also frequently address the broad questions of human meaning that are at the heart of programs of general education.

The appropriateness of Religious Studies courses for general education also suggests that the learning in such courses is designed to be *transferable*. Religion intersects with many other areas of human activity, including politics, literature, and the arts, among others. Students who become familiar with the academic study of religion will be prepared to develop broader and more sophisticated understandings of those phenomena. Also, the skills on which Religious Studies typically focuses, including close reading, written and oral expression, analysis of primary information, and the evaluation of arguments, are eminently useful in other areas of study.

The extent to which such knowledge and skills are transferable, however, depends on your self-conscious awareness of the broader implications of what you are actually learning. In any course, the syllabus can be a trustworthy guide to that process of developing self-awareness by connecting the specific activities that make up a course (e. g. reading, writing, test-taking, discussion) to other dimensions of your education (e. g. how general education courses connect to each other and to your major) and broader contexts of meaning (e. g. living as an informed citizen).

Assignments

The sections of the syllabus that carry the highest stakes for you are the ones that detail assignments on which you will be graded. In some syllabi, grade-bearing assignments are simply noted and are explained in detail elsewhere. In other syllabi, the explanation of graded assignments is included. Wherever the description of grade-bearing assignments is found, you have multiple reasons for reading them very carefully.

In this section we will examine assignments from two of the syllabi previously discussed. Careful reading of assignments is a first step toward success in fulfilling them. The more precisely you know what is expected of you, the more effectively you will be positioned to meet those expectations. As with syllabi in general, we will see that assignments frequently address both the skills that they will demand and the subject matter on which they will focus.

For one of the writing assignments in his "Introduction to the Bible" course, Professor Elledge gives students a choice of three topics. Each option involves an element of comparison, focusing on two different texts. Students are directed to read and re-read each of the texts, and in the body of their five-page papers to respond to a series of questions that Elledge provides for them. In this case, the teacher's instructions focus the students on a particular topic and a set of analytical questions. In effect, the instructions structure the students' responses for them. Students are relieved of the necessity to pick a topic for themselves and to decide on an analytical approach to it, a set of skills that might well be expected in an upper-level class.

Professor Elledge also provides general guidance for writing papers. He underlines the importance of carefully following his directions by stressing that "the most basic form of evaluating a paper in this class concerns whether or not the paper has followed the assigned directions." He also stresses that the papers must have a thesis. As we have previously noted, the academic study of religion involves making arguments, proposing, defending, and adjusting interpretations, and making a point. *A thesis is an argument in a nutshell.* It is not a description of a topic, but rather, as Professor Elledge puts it, "your own personal claim about the topic."[19] The difference between a topic and a thesis is essential for students to grasp. Most often they will be asked to write persuasive or argumentative prose, rather than simply reproduce information.

In a persuasive essay, everything flows from the thesis. Since the thesis constitutes an argument, it has to be an argument about something. Specific evidence that supports the thesis is an absolute requirement. The essay can also consider evidence that might potentially undermine or contradict the argument. The examination of evidence needs to be well organized, so that the relationship of each individual bit of evidence to the overall argument and to each other bit of evidence is abundantly clear. In effect, the thesis determines the structure of an essay. It is articulated in the introduction, applied and supported in the body, and summarized and extended in the conclusion. Through the questions and assertions included in them, assignments like the ones described by Professor Elledge give students substantial help in structuring their essays, if only those instructions are read carefully.

The "semester project" in Professor Burlein's "What is Religion?" course is more elaborate, but it has several similar features.[20] Like Professor Elledge's assignments, it too focuses on comparison. As Professor Burlein counsels students, "comparison and contrast is one way to get yourself to think something new about religion." Professor Burlein's assignment also demands close reading of texts, but it adds the elements of observing of a ritual, interviewing a practitioner, and engaging directly with specific theoretical perspectives. The assignment unfolds in two phases. In the first, students attend at least two rituals from a religion that is not their own. During one of those occasions they are directed to interview one of the participants. Like Professor Elledge, Professor Burlein provides a partial list of questions that students might want to ask their interviewees. Students must then write a paper that includes both analysis of the ritual and analysis of the interview. You can read more about argumentation and writing in Chapter 7.

In the second phase, students are directed to compose another paper that explicitly relates what they have learned to a set of theoretical readings from the course. As with the first phase of the assignment, Professor Burlein provides a set of detailed guidelines for issues that students should address. For example, she provides this guidance about comparing and contrasting religions: "do NOT make a list of similarities and differences. **The point of comparing/contrasting is to help you see something—about each religion or maybe even about religion in general—that you did not see (or see as fully) before you started comparing and contrasting.** You MUST draw conclusions from the comparisons and contrasts that you note."[21] Both that statement and the typographical clues that Professor Burlein provides indicate what is most important for students to do. You can read more about comparison in Chapter 6.

Both Professor Elledge and Professor Burlein display an evident interest in helping their students succeed. They provide detailed instructions for completing assignments, breaking them into their constituent parts, and suggesting sequences of questions that need to be asked. They also give ample indications of how students' performance will be evaluated. Both teachers offer a map for success. But you need to develop the skills in reading such maps. It is not sufficient to gain a general sense of an assignment before embarking on it. Like anything crafted with care, descriptions of assignments repay equally careful consideration.

Though it may not always look that way, your teachers want you to do well. Teachers have spent years of time and effort mastering their subjects and honing their classroom abilities. Syllabi and their component parts are hardly ever dashed off haphazardly. Instead, they are carefully thought through. Their structure and language are designed to communicate important ideas. They are designed to encourage and support you in the enterprise of learning.

Recognizing that will help you get out of those documents everything that your teachers have striven to put into them—and more.

In this chapter we have focused on the syllabus and the assignments it contains. Teachers typically put a lot of thought into constructing both the syllabus and individual assignments. The ways in which teachers describe a course in a syllabus provide insight into how they see the course fitting into the discipline of Religious Studies and into your broader education. A syllabus or a description of an assignment will also provide you with a map to success. Such maps can help you channel your energies, structure your time, and organize your work to meet the requirements of the course to the best of your ability.

We have emphasized that the syllabus can be read as embodying *a series of decisions*. Teachers decide what to include and what to leave out, how to put course topics in a sequence, how to make the relations among different topics as clear as possible, among many other things. In addition, there are many other decisions that teachers have to make, and they, too, repay your careful consideration. For example, teachers need to decide how to use the time allotted to actual class sessions. Over a fifteen-week semester, three 50-minute classes per week or two 75-minute classes per week will amount to 27.5 hours of contact. Students and teachers will therefore spend a little more than a full calendar day together. Teachers need to decide how that time can best be used.

Whether teachers lecture, hold discussions, engage students in role-playing or simulation exercises, or do anything else during class is not random. Teachers generally try to match what they do in the classroom with what they want you to learn or learn how to do. There is a point to *what* happens in a class session and to *how* it happens. If you bring the same type of questions to individual class sessions that you bring to syllabi and descriptions of assignments, you will have a better understanding of *what* you are expected to do, *how* you are expected to do it, and *why* it matters for that particular class session, for the course as a whole, and for your education generally.

Exercises and questions for further thought can be found at https://www.bloomsbury.com/cw/the-religious-studies-skills-book/skill-building-exercises/chapter-two/

3

Learning Through Bracketing

An upbeat *Newsweek* article on religious studies ends with the following grand claim: "For students earnestly interested in the Meaning of Life, religious studies is the way to go."[1] This journalistic view captures a long-standing tension in religious studies. Some faculty teach primarily for "religious literacy" while others are far more invested in teaching critical thinking. That is, mastery of specific content is a primary focus for some and a secondary focus for others. Some faculty are more open to your personal religious beliefs and concerns, while others aim to establish a climate of objective, academic inquiry. Some teach with the "whole student" in mind, while others feel more comfortable with straightforward scholastic pursuits. As a whole, faculty who teach about religion represent a hodgepodge of approaches and commitments. You and your classmates come to class with a similarly eclectic mix of approaches and commitments. Research shows that college students today are more focused on spirituality and personal identity formation than past generations, which makes the *Newsweek* headline above work for its audience.[2]

As shown in the syllabus examples in the previous chapter, all religious studies classes balance content literacy and critical thinking. One key skill for all religious studies students, beyond the acquisition of content knowledge, is *bracketing*, or the ability to suspend judgment in examining phenomena. In order to understand the complexities of religions, you need to adopt as neutral a stance as possible, at least temporarily. That allows you to openly consider alternative ways of viewing the world, to see how they make sense to other people. This also necessitates that you recognize your own biases and assumptions so you can factor them in as you think through an issue. Bracketing asks that you leave aside some fascinating but ultimately unanswerable questions. Is reincarnation real? Does God exist? Did the death of Jesus Christ atone for the sins of humankind? Those questions can be— and are—answered by insiders. However, it is not appropriate for the student of religion to evaluate truth claims.

In actual practice and among scholars, bracketing is a messy business. The extent to which scholars are called upon to judge what they study is an open question in the academy, but it is not such a live question in undergraduate classrooms. Although some teachers will be open to personal anecdote and statements of faith, most will require you to adopt a temporary neutrality and overall openness to the work at hand. The first step in this process is learning the facts about religions, which depends, in part, on defining "religion." The second step is thinking through the implications of those facts with the help of intellectual bracketing.

Defining religion and religious literacy

Scholars often debate what it means to call religious studies a "field" or a "discipline"—a question that reveals assumptions about what students of religion do. Robert Orsi ponders a curious situation in "The 'So-Called History' of the Study of Religion." He sets out wondering why scholars of religious studies are so minimally interested in the history of their own field. Among other questions, he asks if "Maybe it's because there is no such thing as religious studies, a discrete discipline with distinctive habits of heart and mind, but instead a cluster of methods and theories drawn from many disciplines, so that its past dissolves into fragments of other histories?"[3] Unlike more established disciplines, such as English, religious studies is relatively new to higher education and the interdisciplinary nature of the faculty in departments can make the field appear scattershot.

Orsi's point is expressed by others as well, many of whom question how religious studies can define itself clearly against its theological past. Such thinkers are wary of approaches that privilege Western conceptions and push scholars to consider how they justify their place as a separate, definable academic discipline. With a definable object of study—religion—scholars then parse what that means and how it should be studied. Students thus find several approaches at play if they take more than a few courses in religion. They might also find several approaches in a single course.

Those debates aside, it seems to go without saying that students of religion study religion. Yet that claim invites several questions. Comparing definitions of religion is a staple activity in many introductory courses, and these courses often make the issue of multiple definitions the focus of study. This perennial exercise can frustrate students who want a definitive answer, but even scholars disagree about the definition of "religion" as it is studied in the academy.[4] Most faculty members have a working definition of religion with which they delimit what they study, although many will not share this particular definition with students. It is common to ask students to grapple with definitions of religion, particularly in courses in theory and method.

A simple comparison of a Merriam-Webster definition of religion ("The belief in a god or in a group of gods") and a definition that is more functional and used in a popular textbook ("Religion is that system of activities and beliefs directed toward that which is perceived to be of sacred value and transforming power") can help students see the ways definitions include, exclude, and invite comparison.[5] For instance, some definitions of religion put deities as essential characteristics, thereby excluding some forms of Buddhism, while others focus more on social interactions, which marginalizes those who consider religion an individual pursuit. Comparing definitions of religion is a staple activity in many introductory courses.

Comparing definitions from different thinkers can invite discussion about power, categorization, and authority. It is also a good touchpoint for cultural and historical contextualization. Karl Marx's definition of religion provides an interesting comparison to that of Rodney Stark and William Bainbridge. Marx calls religion "the sigh of the oppressed creature, the heart of a heartless world, as it is the spirit of spiritless conditions. It is the opium of the people."[6] Rodney Stark and William Bainbridge consider religions "systems of general compensators based on supernatural assumptions."[7] These definitions invite comparison and analysis based on real-world evidence. Students of religious studies are often asked to consider the assumptions and biases that underlie such definitions. They are also asked to use examples and evidence from religions in the real world against which to test these definitions.

One assignment that brings these ideas to the fore is "Invent Your Own Religion." Babak Rahhim includes this sort of assignment in "Religion 101: Tools and Methods in the Study of Religion," taught at University of California, San Diego in spring 2015. As one of the "methodological experiments" built in to the class, students write a 1,000–1,500 word essay describing and justifying the structure of their own religion. "Your religion, which should have a name, could be anything as long as you explain, based on the reading assignments and lectures, various features of it."[8] With parallels in other fields, such as "create your own government" or "design a utopia," this sort of assignment allows students to put what they have learned into creative application. Students should learn from this exercise that definitions matter. *"Religion" is always defined in a particular way for a particular purpose*.

However religion might be defined, it is apparent to many that the study of religion is needed now more than ever. This should be obvious to anyone who reads local, national, or international news or pays attention to local, national, or international politics. Several recent studies have shown that Americans are remarkably ignorant about basic facts about religions. The Pew Forum's 2010 "U.S. Religious Knowledge Survey" showed that Americans are at once very religious and ignorant of facts pertaining to beliefs and practices.[9] The results show that Americans can, on average, answer 16 of the 32 survey questions correctly, with the strongest showing on questions about Christianity.[10] Other polls show that six in ten Americans rate religion as "very important" in their lives. Four in ten report attending weekly worship. Yet the average American cannot pass a test about the history, leading figures, and beliefs and practices of the world's major religious traditions.

This Pew survey comprises multiple-choice questions that span a range of religious traditions, focusing on texts, beliefs, and rituals (see survey at http://www.pewforum.org/quiz/u-s-religious-knowledge/). Sample questions include "Which Bible figure is most closely associated with leading the exodus from Egypt?" and "In which religion are Vishnu and Shiva central figures?" alongside questions about the role of religion in public life. Religious affiliation did not necessarily help the original 3,412 survey takers with their answers: atheists, agnostics, Jews, and Mormons tended to outscore mainline Christians and Roman Catholics on some questions related to their faith traditions, even after controlling for levels of education. As uncovered in this quiz and explored in more detail in Chapter 2, *Americans tend to think legal restrictions on teaching about religion are stricter than they actually are.*

In *Religious Literacy: What Every American Needs to Know—and Doesn't*, Stephen Prothero makes several trenchant observations about Americans' simultaneous ignorance of, and passion for, religion. On the very first page of the introduction, he remarks, for instance, that "[in America] faith is almost entirely devoid of content." It is content—facts—that are the focus of Prothero's manifesto and of a 15-item quiz he gives to students in his classes.[11] The quiz includes prompts such as "Name the holy book of Islam" and "Name the Four Noble Truths of Buddhism" and "What are the first five books of the Hebrew Bible or the Christian Old Testament?" The results from his classes are disappointing for those who believe religious literacy is cultural literacy.[12] As these two studies show us, ignorance about religion—even one's own religion—is the rule rather than the exception in American history.[13]

This issue of basic illiteracy about religion is not just about lack of knowledge. That Americans don't know who celebrates Diwali (Hindus, Jains, and Sikhs) or even who wrote the synoptic gospels (Mark, Matthew, and Luke) is telling but not debilitating. Isolated instances of ignorance are relatively quickly solved with a good search engine. Yet ignorance of basic information can breed other problems.

One problem is that such widespread illiteracy about religion feeds a culture of stereotyping and misconceptions. One telling example of this phenomenon is a common misperception of Muslims, often depicted in textbooks and in the popular press as camel-driving nomads. In fact, the country with the world's highest population of Muslims is Indonesia; few Muslims own camels or live nomadic lives in the desert. This is just one example of how people tend to fall back on personal knowledge that is abstracted, universalized, and calcified; in other words, they rely on simplified stereotypes rather than wrestling with complexity. Without new and accurate information, old and inaccurate conceptions are hard to replace.

Another problem is that lack of knowledge makes more complex thinking about religions more difficult if not impossible. No discipline can continue without its practitioners holding in their heads certain bodies of knowledge and habits of mind. No chemist can do her lab work competently if she has to pause to Google formulas or safety procedures. No historian can weave a story about the past without a grasp of the broader context. And no student of religious studies can think broadly and deeply about religion without some basic knowledge of particulars.

It is the task of students of religion to gain both religious literacy and new habits of thought from their work in the discipline, even if they are also on a quest to find the meaning of life. In a way, we are all students of religion, receiving and interpreting messages about religion from daily life and popular culture, but we aren't always aware of the religious messages imbedded in our culture. Indeed, religion and culture are interwoven in ways most people never recognize. Reading a newspaper or watching a news program is challenging without a basic understanding of the stories being told. An article about the Rohingya in Myanmar is enriched for the reader who understands the geography, the history, and the most fundamental worldviews of the Buddhist majority and the Muslim minority in that country. Without that background, the article can be hard to decipher. "High Holy Day Shuttles" signs by a temple during Rosh Hashanah or Yom Kippur are more easily understood by those who know about significant Jewish holidays. Evangelical preachers on television make more sense when one has seen them before and has a sense for the messages they tend to give. Even better is knowledge of the texts from which those preachers work.

Religion also suffuses film and television entertainment. Bollywood movies often take their plots and messages from Hindu epics, and films based on the Bible are legion. Television shows such as *Futurama* and *South Park* parody religion by inventing new or satirizing existing religions. Yoga DVDs for Western audiences include spiritual messages along with physical instructions, and elimination-style reality television shows lean heavily on religious themes, such as ritual, hierarchy, and doubt about outcomes. Hip-hop and rap music often refer to religious myths and ideas. In other words, religious ideas and values are often brought before us in the form of entertainment. As a student of religious studies, you will learn to see and be able to analyze those messages more readily than one who takes entertainment at face value.

Religion is everywhere, even where we least expect it. The formal study of religion in college provides a necessary critical perspective. The ways this is accomplished vary by institution, course, and instructor, but some broad outlines of common practices can be useful in conjunction with the specific guidelines given in syllabi and assignments. Many religious studies courses require something like bracketing of their students, in part due to the muddling of borders between the study of religion and the practice of theology.

Religious studies and theology

Many guides to college include the religious studies or religion major on a spectrum from the academic study of religion to training for religious vocations. This reflects the historical roots of religious studies in theological studies. Many guides to college majors put church-related training and careers at the forefront, to the dismay of many faculty at secular institutions. Clerical ordination is not always or even most often the goal of the religious studies student, and it is likely that some guides to college majors turn potential students away from religion classes.

The Princeton Review is a popular destination for prospective college students. It lists common reasons for choosing a major (earning potential as well as "subjects you love") alongside a list of the top ten majors. Their searchable majors guide brings up no results when one searches for "religion." A search for "religious studies" shows the pervasiveness of the link between religious studies and theology:

> Some people mistakenly think the only reason you'd want to major in Religious Studies (or just Religion, as it's called at some schools) is to have a career as a priest, minister, or rabbi. We hope you aren't one of those people. It's true that Religious Studies is a very good major for students who want to go on to seminaries for further training as religious professionals.[14]

Perhaps the most interesting part of the quotation above is the line "We hope you aren't one of those people." We hope this isn't meant to discredit those who want to pursue a career in the clergy; indeed, many who do aim at that kind of career know the importance of understanding other religious traditions. Yet the line speaks volumes about the ways people perceive the academic study of religion. To its credit, the guide goes on to describe how useful such a major can be to developing writing and speaking skills, and it notes that interviewers will "invariably" find the subject interesting.

This guide is an advance on earlier portrayals of the field. An older print guide does not even list religious studies as a separate discipline (the popular *Complete Idiot's Guide to Choosing a College Major* also fails to consider it as a separate major). Instead, it locates it within philosophy and notes that

"While there are philosophers and teachers of religion and theology, the most common occupation associated with religion is member of the clergy or Imam."[15] The guide goes into some detail about work as a pastoral leader, noting the low pay clergy receive. Such old guides are out of touch with the expectations of the workforce today, in which those who hire often rate "critical thinking skills" as a top requirement for recruitment.[16]

In the more popular College Board *Book of Majors*, "Religion and Theology" are not listed under humanities disciplines but as a separate category in the table of contents. Subsections to this category include Bible Studies, Islamic Studies, Judaic Studies, Preministerial Studies, Religious Studies, Sacred Music, and Theology.[17] Despite this inclusion of those more theological subjects, the guide asks: "Did you know … that most religious studies majors do not intend to pursue careers as priests, imams, or rabbis? This major is mostly taught as an interdisciplinary liberal arts field that prepares you for many different career paths."[18]

The content of these guides is often at odds with the websites of most departments of religion or religious studies, which make great efforts to distance themselves from theological roots of the discipline. See Box 3.1

Box 3.1 Comparing confessional/apologetic statements with academic statements

Confessional/apologetic statement	Academic statement
Karma explains the path of each human life.	Hindus believe in karma, the sum of a person's past choices and definer of future lives.
Eight million kami inhabit Japan.	Those who practice Shinto believe in kami, or spirits.
Christianity is the one, true religion.	Christianity is one of many major religions.
The Bible is the Word of God, written by Moses.	The Bible is a library of texts from multiple authors and different contexts.
Thetans occupy many bodies through many lifetimes.	Scientologists believe humans are spiritual beings (thetans) inhabiting temporary bodies across time.

to get a sense for the difference between theological and academic points of view. The academic study of religion is not meant to be partisan, and the ways in which a department situates itself in relation to a faith tradition has much to do with the institutional mission and the particular faculty within a department. Many note that religious studies does not require any level of faith commitment nor does it ask students to engage in questions about truth and falsehood relating to any particular religious tradition. That is what is commonly meant by "bracketing."

What is bracketing?

In your classes in religious studies, you will encounter expectations similar to those in other humanities and social science courses. You can generally expect a mix of lecture and discussion, with reading done outside of class and papers or exams for assessment. Some of the texts read and questions asked can overlap significantly. For instance, in the syllabus from "Classical and Contemporary Sociological Thought," taught at Oberlin College in spring 2016, students are assigned selections from Émile Durkheim's *The Elementary Forms of Religious Life* and asked to consider the following questions on three consecutive class periods:

- What is religion, and what can it tell us about social life? How should religion best be studied, and what concepts describe its characteristics? What are the differences between magic and religion? What is the human meaning of religion, and what is religion's role in conceptual thought?

- What is the relationship between the totem, the divine, and the people of the clan? What is mana? What is a social force, and its relationship to force in general? What are souls, the high god, and ancestral spirits?

- What are cults, rites, asceticism? What does [the author] mean by positive and negative cults? What is the relationship between the sacred and profane? How is science dependent upon religion? What is the function of piacular rites?[19]

It would not be surprising to have those questions appear on a syllabus or in a discussion in a religious studies class. The same sorts of questions about vocabulary, meaning, and the interaction of human and proposed supernatural forces can animate the reading in both contexts.

Assignments in other disciplines can also be similar. Anthropology classes can include fieldwork, in which students go out to a field to conduct, for instance, a "thick description" of an hour in a local McDonald's or ethnographic interviews of people living in a homeless shelter. Psychology classes, too, can require interviews of individuals, and political science classes might require attendance at local political events, with students reporting back what they observed. Religious studies teachers sometimes assign similar tasks, such as site visits to local religious spaces or interviews with adherents of particular faith traditions, as discussed in more detail in Chapter 7.

As in many humanities and social science disciplines, students of religious studies do self- and peer-evaluation of writing, short writing assignments, fieldwork, site visits or field trips, group projects, case studies, structured debate, open-ended discussion, simulations or role-playing, brainstorming, viewing of videos, small group discussions, and interviews. Sources for reading include textbooks, monographs, and primary sources on websites and in anthologies; other sources include films, podcasts, and video games. Students use clickers or other polling technologies in religious studies classes, too. Assessment and grading are based on essay exams, objective short answer essays, multiple choice exams, research papers, class presentations, quizzes, journal entries, oral presentations, and participation in class discussion. And the major rites of passage, such as the introductory theory course and capstone course or senior seminar, are hardly unique to this field.

What, then, distinguishes religious studies from these other disciplines from the student perspective? "Religion" is a capacious category, and you will likely study a very broad range of questions and topics. Religious studies syllabi, department mission statements, and common structures for majors all argue for a certain domain of knowledge taught and learned with a particular set of ends in mind. One major difference between religious studies and other humanities disciplines is the place of prior commitment in a given classroom. You have learned about religion all your life, and some of that learning has resulted in fixed positions that can sometimes interfere with the kind of learning that college courses demand. Notably, the legacy of theological studies in religious studies departments and the complexities of student expectations can cause a divide between students' and teachers' understandings of the entire enterprise.

The landing page of the University of Alabama's Department of Religious Studies notes: "You don't have to wear a toga to study ancient Rome. And you don't have to be religious to study religion."[20] This seems fitting for a large public institution, which rightly distances itself from theological pursuits. By contrast, the landing page for the Religion Department at Hope College stakes itself squarely within the broader institutional mission: "When we say 'religion' we mean things of the head and heart. We mean shared religious observances as well as personal faith and spirituality. We mean something that is intensely private, yet shapes society and politics, culture and family—church, temple, synagogue and cyberspace."[21] Being aware of these dispositions in any institution and department can help you better anticipate teachers' expectations. Confusion reigns when expectations are not clarified.

In some contexts in both the broader world and in institutions of higher education, the study of religion and theology can be seen as at violent odds, while in others they can be considered inextricably linked. Despite some inevitable overlap, the assumptions behind each discipline are starkly opposed. Theologians are most often insiders or practitioners speaking to an audience of co-religionists. They are often driven by personal conviction about matters that may or may not be provable to others. Those involved in the discussion are seeking very different types of proof than those demanded by an outsider. Religious studies, as the academic study of religion, aims to make arguments based on evidence for an audience of outsiders (even when the scholar or the reader is an insider as well). Religious studies classes also make extensive use of theological materials, studied analytically rather than for constructive purposes. This can confuse students at times.

The academic study of religion is an academic rather than a religious exercise. From the perspective of the liberal arts, the academic study of religion is not theological or confessional, nor is it the search for eternal truth. It does not look at religious ideas or actions in terms of "right" or "wrong" and "true" or "false"; rather, it investigates critically the ways in which religious ideas and practices develop within specific historical and cultural contexts and the ways in which religious ideas and practices shape history and culture.

Put another way, those who study religion engage with it as one among many human creations. Therefore, as a student of religion, you should not make claims (in your academic work) about "truth." *You must seek to understand rather than to endorse or judge.* Your job is to do the work from an academic (some would say "objective") perspective rather than to measure those sources based on your own personal criteria (e.g. whether the text accords with what you understand to be biblical ethics or your own political point of view).

Bracketing in the classroom

The academic study of religion as pursued today in the US often traces its roots to a key Supreme Court decision in 1963, although that origin story may not be so clear cut.[22] *Abington Township School District v. Schempp* pitted a school board against a family of non-believers who wanted their children exempt from daily prayers. The decision favored the non-believers, who should be free from unconstitutional religious indoctrination in public school. Justice

Clark, on behalf of the majority on the court, wrote that "education is not complete without a study of comparative religion or the history of religion and its relationship to the advancement of civilization."[23] Faculty across the spectrum of institutions of higher education tend to hold some version of this as a chief value, regardless of their research specialties.

Federal and state laws shape behavior at private and public schools in different ways. Any government body (in this case, a public college or university) is bound by the First Amendment of the US Constitution, which explicitly prohibits the establishment of religion. This clause restricts taxpayer-funded, but not private, institutions from preferring one religion over any other. The same amendment grants all individuals freedom from government interference in religious belief and practice. A public institution must remain neutral in regard to religion, and it must not sponsor or hinder the practice of religion.

Public universities, which are funded in part by taxpayer money, have occasionally experienced criticism from private citizens and state legislators for their sponsorship of art installations, theater productions, and classroom assignments. One signal example came from the University of North Carolina at Chapel Hill, the faculty of which chose Michael Sells's *Approaching the Qur'an: The Early Revelations* as a common freshman reading in 2002. The uproar that ensued was focused on possible indoctrination and violations of the First Amendment. The court found in favor of the university, citing curricular and pedagogical relevance.

Private secular and religious institutions are not controlled in the same way by the US Constitution, although they are often subject to particular state restrictions. Private institutions enjoy freedom from government interference in matters of religion. In general, faculty and students at denominationally affiliated institutions can speak freely about personal faith, as long as they do not offend the sensibilities of the controlling body of the institution.

The US-based First Amendment Center has expressed the difference between secular teaching about religions in public schools and confessional teaching in six clear statements. Denominationally affiliated schools will permit devotional approaches to religion as part of their institutional mission. Some such institutions will require a faith statement from students and faculty. Some private institutions will permit prayer or meditation in college classrooms as part of instructional time, while public schools are legally prohibited from sponsoring that sort of display. The fourth through sixth items are perhaps most interesting to students: teachers trained to teach about religion in public institutions are to teach about religion in respectful, inclusive ways. The same expectation goes for students in classrooms in those institutions. A situation in which a political science professor can give higher grades to those in her party of choice would be unjust. The same goes for religion: the more "religious" students do not have an advantage in doing the sort of work expected in religious studies courses. In short, expectations should be academic, not confessional, a legal requirement that protects all parties.

Faculty are protected by academic freedom in the classroom when they speak about subjects in their area of specialization when relevant to the topic at hand. This means that faculty in chemistry, for instance, are permitted to speak about controversial issues in chemistry from their informed point of view. Faculty in other disciplines have the same privileges within their disciplines. But academic freedom does not extend to teachers or researchers who speak outside of their area of specialization. A chemistry teacher who aims to convert her students to Jainism through graded work or even casual mention is outside of the protections of academic freedom. According to these guidelines, religion can be discussed freely in a course about religion, because the key element is relevant to the subject at hand. The faculty member must be neutral in doing so, without evidence of either coercion or punishment in any form for not adhering to a particular viewpoint.

These legal issues can trickle down to the classroom when, for instance, students object to certain assignments that they believe impinge on their religious faith. Students are ordinarily permitted accommodations on religious grounds, for either absences or substitution of assignments. Most faculty members will consider permitting students to complete alternate assignments, depending on the circumstances of the request. Some cases come down to a question of the teacher's motives. A 2004 case in Utah, *Axxon-Flynn vs. Johnson*, ruled in favor of the university in a case brought by a student who would not say lines in a play that she found offensive. As a Mormon, the woman in question made it clear that she would not say words that offended her beliefs. The court decided in favor of the university for its embrace of "school-sponsored speech," arguing that pedagogical decisions fit the course goals and did not violate this student's rights. The conclusion here indicates that curricular decisions by faculty that are not motivated by prejudice are not in violation of the First Amendment clause of the US Constitution. Faculty trained in a particular discipline have freedom to make pedagogical decisions based on that training. *In all cases, faculty and students can shield themselves from critique by being very careful to note when they are expressing personal opinion.*

Several studies have shown that there can be a gap between what faculty aim to accomplish in their introductory classes and what students want from those same classes in both religious and non-religious institutions. A study by Barbara Walvoord, *Teaching and Learning in College Introductory Religion*

Courses, surveyed 12,000 students at a range of institutions. That study and others show that students tend to take religious studies classes in order to explore their own spiritual life or to bolster their already held commitments and investments. They want basic religious literacy as well as opportunities to discuss big questions, and they want guidance about how to live a good life. Teachers tend to be far more interested in teaching critical thinking skills (the subject of Chapter 5 of this volume).

One example of where these two perspectives can come into conflict is the Bible course. This standard course in many departments aims to help students read biblical texts in academic ways often not sanctioned by religious authorities. The emphasis is most often on historical context and close reading of an often-familiar text. A few examples can be found in the Wabash Center syllabus collection. An honors religious studies course by Victor H. Matthews at Missouri State University, discussed in Chapter 2, includes a clear disclaimer in the syllabus. After noting the *Abington Township School District v. Schempp* decision, Matthews notes that "the approach here is different from that taken in a religious group."[24] The goal of the course is to reconstruct the original meaning of the text in its original context "rather than on what the text means for us today." Matthews notes that students will not need to have a faith commitment nor will they have to abandon any faith they hold. "You will earn a good grade in this class the same you do in other courses, not by being more religious."[25] Students should recognize this as the standard in all humanities courses.

This recognition of student faith perspectives comes across in a different way in a syllabus for a New Testament course by James Kelhoffer at St. Louis University in spring 2007. The first page of the syllabus includes a "Special note: Like all courses offered by the Department of Theological Studies, this introduction to the New Testament is open to students of all faith traditions and is a serious and rigorous academic course." The teacher here aims to dispel the notion that this course will be an exercise in spiritual development. The syllabus goes on to note that "Having a background in Scripture through your church or religious high school does not in any way constitute a substitute for studying for this class." This informs students who may think that they have a strong background in the Bible that the academic expectations might well be challenging for them. The note ends by assuring those who have never read the New Testament that "you will have every opportunity to learn and excel in this course."[26] This course, offered in the Theology Department of a Catholic university, makes it clear that the academic study of ancient texts requires academic rigor and focus, not prior faith commitment.

Syllabi for introductory courses often present an argument about acceptable approaches to the material. Joseph Adler's "Religious Studies 101" at Kenyon

College in spring 2014, titled "Encountering Religion in Global Context," introduces students to the idea of bracketing:

> This combination of critical analysis and intuitive understanding [in the academic study of religion] requires, as a crucial first step, that we attempt to set aside, or "bracket," our own beliefs and assumptions about the meaning of human life, the existence or non-existence of gods, and the truth or untruth of particular religious traditions. Only then can we attempt to understand other religious traditions on their own terms, in their own frameworks of beliefs, and in their own social and historical contexts. To do otherwise, i.e. to bring our own religious assumptions to the material we study, would be valid or meaningful only within the context of our own religious tradition and community.[27]

This syllabus takes a clear stance that a "global and pluralistic approach" requires "as much objectivity as possible." That said, Dr. Adler is aware that full bracketing is difficult and that other issues might be at stake: one should bracket or be objective "while also attempting to develop and maintain sensitivity to subtle and sometimes inexpressible levels of human meaning."[28] This tempering of the more hard-line stance seems like a reasonable nod toward student expectations while maintaining rigorous academic standards.

Aside from Introduction to Religion, perhaps the greatest number of disclaimers can be found on courses focused on Christianity, because it is so pervasive in our culture. For instance, the syllabus for Religion 256: Christianity, taught by James B. Wiggins at Syracuse University, includes a common refrain: "[This course] will not presuppose you are familiar with 'Christianity' nor committed to being a Christian; it will not confirm any particular form or expression of Christianity as the only true or correct version; thus, it will privilege no particular form of Christianity."[29] Less pointedly, a clause in the syllabus by Alan Altany for RST 305 at Marshall University reiterates the academic, non-sectarian, unbiased requirements of inquiry while also noting the following after the list of course objectives: "This can all serve to encourage students in their quest for meaning, understanding, compassion and wisdom."[30] The objectives of both teachers and students can be met, although a student's progress on the path toward personal fulfillment cannot be measured in grades.

These kinds of disclaimers can be very helpful to students who wonder how much of their own perspective is permissible. Students who struggle in the academic study of religion are often paralyzed by prior confessional learning: they are "insiders" who find it difficult to situate themselves as "outsiders" to the matter at hand. It can be difficult to set aside the religious or theological lens a student has been trained to use, as if it were the only one available. For many students, this is a stretch that allows them to grow academically in ways few other fields can match. Again, awareness of each teacher's expectations as described in the syllabus can inform students about the boundaries they are expected to respect.

To cite particular examples, students with Christian backgrounds tend to read the first few chapters of Genesis as a story about the first humans being tricked by Satan. The consensus of modern scholarship holds that this common interpretation goes beyond the original intention of the author of the text, who likely understood the serpent (*nahash* in Hebrew) as a trickster figure, eager to sow doubt and confusion about God's word in the allegorical first humans. Teachers often provide reading questions focused solely on the text at hand in an effort to dispel this common misunderstanding.

For example, a course at California State University, Northridge, provides students with reading questions that ask them to probe more deeply into the text in order to help them think beyond what they believe they know. "Is the Serpent the 'Devil'? What actual evidence is there in the story itself for believing that he is? Does the Serpent ever actually advise the Woman to DO anything? Does the Serpent ever SAY anything which is not true?"[31] Students who read the text closely while bracketing any previous knowledge or belief will see that there is no necessity to interpret "the serpent" as "Satan." Sometimes this is made quite explicit on an assignment. One of the study questions for "Sex and the Bible" at the University of North Texas are more pointed: "What does the serpent represent (Hint: NOT Satan!)?"[32] These sorts of questions and assertions encourage students to look beyond long-held assumptions.

Another example of the ways teachers of religious studies approach course material might involve ritual. The adherents of a tradition will often make claims about what a ritual does that cannot be verified by an outside observer. If a practitioner of Haitian Vodou asserts that a spirit (*loa*) Kouzin Zaka responds to offerings by encouraging agriculture to grow, an outsider might well disagree and offer a scientific explanation for any apparent change. A scholar might determine that what the ritual "does" is establish community and group identity. You, as a student in a class on Vodou, might well be asked to examine that ritual closely. What actions do the participants take? What objects seem important? Is there music or other important sounds? Do the people speak? Is there a clear hierarchy of any sort? Here the focus might not be on what the practitioners say is happening; rather, you might be responsible for crafting as objective a description of the ritual as possible, bracketing your own judgment about actions and outcomes. You might have gone into class thinking that Vodou is evil or least not a legitimate religion. Your job as a student is to suspend judgment and think critically about the phenomena before you.

Yet another example involves the Roman Catholic and Eastern Orthodox rites of transubstantiation, in which a priest is understood to transform bread and wine into the literal body and blood of Jesus Christ, with the appearance of bread and wine intact. Protestants and Catholics disagree on the meaning of Jesus' words "For this is my body," and their disagreements have led to bloodshed and schism. There are many ways of understanding the Christian Eucharist, with Lutherans maintaining a doctrine of "real presence" in the Eucharistic host and those that see the Eucharistic meal as a symbolic memorial.

Outside of denominational schools, and often not even there, you would not be asked which interpretation of the ritual is correct. Teachers of religious studies would more likely focus your thought on the logic behind each interpretation within each context. What factors might have led a particular group to a particular interpretation? What difference might a particular interpretation make in the lives of those who agree with it? What is at stake in one particular theological stance over another? You might be asked to assume that interpretations are each valid in their own way, in their own contexts. This assumption needs to stand even when that recognition causes discomfort or a desire to judge based on previous knowledge.

Part of the difficulty—and the fun—of religious studies is that it considers natural and supernatural phenomena side by side. Religious studies is uniquely situated to think about human responses to what they posit to be supernatural in ethics, geopolitics, literature, history, and language, to name only a few areas of life. Students—both those who are religious and those who are not—often struggle with questions about making appropriate judgments about religious ideas and practices. Must one believe stories of possession or mysticism that seem to bend or break natural laws? Or is belief not at issue? Should one avoid questions of belief or truth in order to understand the views of another individual or group, even if those views conflict directly with one's own views?

Scholars of religion do not assume that religion is divinely inspired; rather, they study what they can observe and analyze academically, such as the historical, social, economic, and political origins and implications of religious traditions. Religious studies scholars and students apply the methodological tools of several disciplines in the liberal arts (such as historiography, sociology, anthropology, philosophy, and literary theory) to religious phenomena in the same way those tools are applied in other fields of study. Religious studies encourages you to practice both detachment and engagement in their approach to and handling of questionable claims made as truths. The kind of suspension of judgment is somewhat similar to that practiced by lawyers, who might well disagree with their clients but who are bound to advocate for them nevertheless.

Practicing bracketing through reading, observing, and discussing

Box 3.2 Examples of primary, secondary, and tertiary sources

Research question	Primary source	Secondary source	Tertiary source
How did Barack Obama use the word "change" in the 2008 election campaign?	Transcript of Obama's Democratic National Convention speech	*Essays in The Obama Presidency and the Politics of Change*, edited by Edward Ashbee and John Dumbrell (Palgrave-MacMillan, 2017)	Dictionary definitions of "change"
Why are most Rastafari black?	*The Holy Piby* (aka *The Blackman's Bible*)	*Becoming Rasta: Origins of Rastafari Identity in Jamaica*, by Charles Price (New York University Press, 2009)	Related articles in *The Encyclopedia of Caribbean Religions*
How are Shinto ideas expressed in popular culture?	*Princess Mononoke*; manga comics; *Cool Japan Guide: Fun in the Land of Manga, Lucky Cats, and Ramen*, by Abby Denson (Tuttle, 2009)	*Regionalizing Culture: The Political Economy of Japanese Popular Culture in Asia*, by Nissim Otmazgin (University of Hawai'i Press, 2014)	Short article in The Forum on Religion and Ecology at Yale (http://fore. yale.edu/religion/ shinto/)

Reading

Students in religious studies courses read texts, as do students in most humanities disciplines. Reading is a complex activity that can be strongly informed by the ideas and assumptions we bring to it. Reading a text that makes a claim with which you strongly disagree can produce an emotional reaction that leads you to reject (and thus not seriously consider) the text. The word "read" is understood quite broadly and in particular ways, as explored in Chapter 4 of this volume. The word "text" in religious studies is also expansive: it can mean a traditional written document, such a legal document or diary, or it can mean a film, an image, music, clothing, an artifact, architecture, or a sound, as well as other aspects of what is known as "material culture," or the study of the objects and spaces people define as part of their cultural world.

The types of texts listed in Box 3.2 are most often treated as "primary texts," and they are the most direct source for original research. Primary sources provide first-hand evidence of the topic under study but they can also be aggregate information, such as census data or public opinion polls. Secondary sources interpret primary sources for the reader. They provide second-hand evidence. Rather than presenting a text itself, they describe, interpret, or comment on a text or group of texts. Ideally, a student research paper is a secondary source that uses primary sources (and other secondary sources) to make its case.

Some define a third category—"tertiary" sources—although others just lump those sources in with secondary sources. Tertiary sources curate information from reliable secondary sources into condensed summaries of the current state of knowledge. Textbooks are classic tertiary sources; however, some textbooks include primary sources as illustrations or in a companion volume. Reference books provide useful introductions to broad topics and can be a good first stop for bibliographical information. *Wikipedia* is perhaps the most widely used tertiary source, as it is a compendium of primary and secondary source information interpreted by many authors.

To return to a previous example, you could learn more about the doctrine of transubstantiation in Roman Catholicism in several ways. You can go directly to a tertiary source such as *Wikipedia*, which will provide a simplified overview of the issue from, potentially, many authorial perspectives. You can use the bibliography in the *Wikipedia* article to find secondary sources that delve into the topic in more scholarly depth. In this case, you would find two sources in English—a scholarly monograph and a book chapter—as well as several links to online sources, some of which are primary sources. There are, of course, many other secondary studies of the Eucharist than are listed in this *Wikipedia* article. If you are interested in doing a research paper on the subject (a popular question for students revolves around parallels with cannibalism), you would do well to seek out more secondary sources and to focus on several primary sources for your own close study. Some of those will be found in translation in anthologies of primary sources and others can be found online, albeit often in antiquated translation. Primary sources, again, are those originating from a particular time and place as "first-hand" documents.

These distinctions are somewhat artificial, as any one piece of evidence could be a primary source in answering one question and a secondary or tertiary source in addressing another research question. Look through a newspaper. It is a collection of articles, opinion pieces, and advertising, arranged in topical sections that might change with the day of the week. An article about a notable sporting event is usually a secondary interpretation, but many papers also provide "raw data" that is not featured in any particular article. The newspaper is read by most people as a secondary source: its interpretations trusted because its journalists are trusted. But any newspaper can also be read as a primary source (such as in the weather data, which is a daily index of information) that is interpreted differently for different purposes. The same weather data might make one person conclude "umbrella" and another conclude "monsoon season has begun."

Historical newspapers are often used as primary evidence for scholarly study. How they are read depends on the questions the researcher asks. "Do certain baseball statistics reflect changes in the stock market?" can be answered through analysis of several consecutive editions of the newspaper. "Does the ratio of perfume ads to pharmaceutical ads increase in the weeks approaching Valentine's Day?" can be answered with a smaller sample of papers, perhaps over several years. Those questions are driven by the researcher's curiosity, a lens that narrows down the evidence to be examined.

Newspapers and magazines cover religion regularly, so they can be good sources for answering students' questions. A newspaper article reporting on debates in Germany over the classification of Scientology as either a religion or worldview would be considered a primary source in a paper about defining religion. An article in *People* magazine about Tom Cruise and Scientology can also be a primary source in a paper about celebrities and religion. But both can also be secondary sources, if they comment on or editorialize about the subject beyond reporting the facts. And both can fail to bracket judgments and give a skewed view of the subject.

The ways texts are classified can also change by discipline. The Oxford English Dictionary is a tertiary source for a reader wishing to find the definitions or etymology of a particular word. The same text becomes a primary source in a study of the change in dictionary standards over time. An accounting textbook can be a secondary source to the accounting student and a primary source to an historian writing a history of accounting textbooks. An encyclopedia article about religious conversion is a secondary source, except to the observer interested in the ways conversion has been described in different studies over time.

Film works the same way. A documentary that uses original footage is a secondary source, while the original footage is a primary source. But the same documentary can be read as a primary source if the research question is "How have documentary films changed in structure in the late twentieth century?"

You will be asked to read all sorts of texts in college classes. You might find reading a text more arduous than watching a video, but reading well in any medium requires the same attention to detail: you must always be willing to question sources, assess logic, come at the text from multiple perspectives, and continually ask critical questions of whatever source you are examining. In fact, a video of a ritual can be much more difficult to interpret than a descriptive text because of its complexity and strangeness. The nuances of gesture or the particulars of the setting can be lost on or misinterpreted by the outsider. Only close observation and careful questioning, while keeping yourself from making value judgments about the material, can help you focus on interpretation and analysis.

Classes which include primary documents are especially helpful in showing you how to query a text (see Box 3.3). Objective questions that help you situate a text and understand its internal logic can help you avoid following your own interests or biases. The following questions focus on textual documents, but they can be expanded to include the kinds of primary and secondary sources listed above.

Box 3.3 Querying a text

- What is the date of the document? If there is no definite date, can one be estimated? What else is known about the cultural context of the document?
- Who is the author and what is/was his or her place in society? What is known about the author? What might have motivated the author to write this particular text?
- What kinds of rhetorical strategies does the author use in this piece? How does the text make its case? What is the intended audience of the text? How might this influence its rhetorical strategy?
- What arguments or concerns does the author respond to that are not clearly stated? Provide at least one example of a point at which the author seems to be refuting a position never clearly stated. Explain in detail what this position may be.

- Is the author credible and reliable? Use at least one specific example to explain why. Make sure to explain the principle of rhetoric or logic that makes this passage credible.
- What kind or genre of document is it? Is it a letter? A poem? An op-ed? An obituary?
- Who is the intended audience? Can the reader know or imagine why it was written?
- What is the thesis or what are the main themes, if any? Is there a core message? How can you identify it?
- What presuppositions, assumptions, or values are apparent in the text? What is left unsaid? How do the ideas and values in the source differ from the ideas and values of our age? Are there portions of the text that we might find objectionable but that contemporaries might have found acceptable? How might the difference between our values and the values of the author influence the way we understand the text?
- What makes the document significant? Is the document meant to be an eyewitness account or a later interpretation of an event?

Note that none of these questions gets at questions of value, such as whether a particular text is true or false. Structuring your queries can provide the distance necessary to see a text for what it actually says, not what you wish it would say to agree with your worldview. Answering all of these questions is rarely necessary, but a full view of any text often requires knowledge of context as well as some research into secondary sources. Any reliable research or close reading paper will delve into many of these questions.

Observing

You will likely be asked to observe religion in various ways. Good observation requires attention to detail as well as solid note-taking skills. It also involves bracketing in several ways: bracketing of assumptions about appropriate conduct, about truth and falsehood, and about what particular gestures or words might mean in another context. Many introductory religion classes include some sort of first-person or hands-on experience, either through actual site visits or mediated through videos that allow students to experience more than they can in a written text. Site visits to local worship spaces or even to worship services help students to encounter difference and sameness in their own local area. Videos or virtual visits to online museums can simulate that sort of "real-life" experience. Many students are energized by experiencing new things while others are more comfortable reading about things in books. Site visits are a way to help many students venture out of their comfort zones.

This sort of assignment is akin to ethnographic research, which is a common method that anthropologists use to study people in their own environments. Ethnographers engage in fieldwork that takes them to the group they wish to study to enable them to observe life in all of its complexity. This sort of work requires a keen sense of observation, an attention to detail, and an ability to describe and analyze those observations in clear prose. The writing involved in fieldwork begins with notes and observations and/or transcriptions of conversations.

Fieldwork and site visits also raise some interesting ethical questions. Is it right to observe human beings from an outsider perspective? How much latitude does one have to interpret an experience in one's own terms? Good ethnographic projects choose locations or groups that help answer particular questions. Good ethnographers allow life to go on around them to allow meaningful observation. Fieldwork must always attend to questions of empathy for and fairness to the group under study. Part of being fair is to strive to present the group in a way that it could agree with. When you are observing, ask yourself, "am I presenting this group, action, or object in a way with which those for whom it has religious meaning might agree?" Bracketing your own opinions and convictions makes it easier to understand what things might mean to other people.

The types of questions a student is expected to ask for an observation assignment often mirror those asked of standard written texts. Imagine, for example, that you have an assignment to visit a cemetery in a class on death and the afterlife. In this case, the cemetery itself is used as a primary text. You are prompted to begin with basic information. What is the name of the cemetery? How big is it? How old is it? Is it still accepting burials? Is it private or run by a town or corporation? A basic description of the cemetery surroundings can help the reader get a good sense for the place and its place in history. Some description will require judgment: is the cemetery well landscaped and maintained? Is it a pleasant or unpleasant space? What lends it those qualities?

You should be careful to note any other details, such as type and number of buildings and style of grave markers. This will require examining the tombstones, statues, crypts, and artwork. Are the markers above ground or at ground level? Can an observer read any significance into any patterns of markers? Is the cemetery divided into special sections, such as a section for veterans or family plots? If so, what might this tell you about the people who use the cemetery to bury their dead?

Some teachers might prompt you to think about the site's history and symbolism. What are the dates and names on the oldest and newest gravestones? What kinds of symbols are used on the gravestones, if any? Are there any common symbols or sayings among the stones? You might want to do some research in secondary sources about those symbols to get a broader sense for how and why symbols systems change.

Other teachers might be more interested in living religion and how people interact with the cemetery space. You might be asked to examine any decorations around the graves. Are they fresh? Plastic? Is it apparent that the plots are tended beyond mowing the grass? Is there a ritual going on or any individuals or groups visiting a plot? If so, what are the people doing? Some teachers will ask you to think about your own presuppositions about such places. Are there things you might not feel like doing in this space? Are there things you absolutely would not do in this space? Why or why not?

Still other teachers might ask you to extrapolate from your experience in the cemetery. Sometimes this takes the form of imaginative but informed guesswork. What does this cemetery tell you about our culture or about the culture of its builders? What might a complete stranger make of the place? Would he or she know it as a place of burial? Would he or she know where the place begins and ends? What evidence might support any conclusions a stranger might make about the cemetery?

This sort of assignment is designed to help you learn to read a site as if it were a type of text. This is a skill that can be used in real life as you become attuned to the meaning of symbolism in built spaces. Other fieldwork assignments require more interaction and attention to human behavior. These trips especially help students experience the strangeness and familiarity of "the other," and they require the observer to look as much as possible with fresh eyes and to hold in abeyance any preconceptions about how things "should" be. Sometimes these visits are done in groups and sometimes they are an independent project; almost always they are designed to open students' minds to lived religions.

With that in mind, many such assignments require you to attend a religious service outside of your own experience. You might be required to do preliminary research about the group, both in standard secondary sources and by calling the site to make arrangements for the visit. That research is often complemented by more research after the visit to help you understand things that were puzzling or interesting during the visit. This process is essential as you learn how to approach your studies as neutrally and empathetically as possible.

Some teachers are very clear about etiquette during visits, and some will assign a particularly useful guide: *How to Be a Perfect Stranger: The Essential Religious Etiquette Handbook*. Many will provide a series of questions to answer, all of which are aimed at helping you hone your skills at observation. The list of questions is rarely exhaustive, so you might be encouraged to pay attention to other things that interest you. You should also be able to take notes in an unobtrusive way. These notes will help jog your memory for any later writing task.

As in the cemetery description assignment above, site visit assignments often involve extensive description. You will likely be asked to describe the setting. What type and size of building is it? What kind of seating plan, decoration, placement of important objects, symbols, and furnishings that may be used in worship (or the absence of ritual objects etc.)? What is the general age and number of people attending?

Some questions get at the type of liturgical or sacred time the group follows. What type of service is it? Regular weekly worship? Holiday? Weekday early morning or evening? Wedding, baptism, or other initiation ceremony? All of these are clues to the types of rituals that one might encounter. Other questions involve the atmosphere or feeling of the space. Is there a musical component? What type, amount, and style of music? Was it performed or created by the congregation? Are there decorations? Of what sort?

Still other questions might get at issues of authority or hierarchy. What kind of clothing did attendees wear? Did participants in the service wear special clothing or vestments? Were they placed in a particular place in the worship space? Did they move through the space? If so, how? Are both women and men involved in the proceedings? Did attendees participate and how? Are there distinctions of gender, race, or age in worship leadership or attendance?

As in the cemetery example, some questions will require some judgment or guesswork alongside the specifics. Some teachers will expect you to reflect on your own experiences in any unfamiliar worship space. For instance, you might be asked to consider how welcoming the congregation was. Some might ask you to compare the service directly with other services or ceremonies you have attended. A series of questions can help you answer those questions. How formal or informal was the service? What elements lead the observer to that conclusion? Was the service primarily scripted or spontaneous? How can you know? Description sometimes involves specific timekeeping. How much time was spent in various activities, such as group singing, spoken prayer, scripture reading, and preaching? What was the style of prayer or preaching? Was there a central message? Was it written and read? Prepared but not written? Spontaneous? What might those elements tell you about the group being observed?

Some of this fieldwork will also require a small amount of research beyond observation. Some teachers will ask for a map or drawing of the place, for instance. All of this work is a way for teachers to help you learn to describe and then "think with" a particular place, in the same way you learn to describe or summarize and then "think with" written texts. This can be challenging but it can also be immensely rewarding. Such assignments can help you see the world around you in new and interesting ways, as unencumbered as possible from the comparisons you might make to what is most familiar to you.

Discussing

Few students learn well through lecture alone. Many studies have shown the cognitive benefits of discussion to promoting both basic comprehension and metacognitive thought.[33] As James Lang describes in *Small Teaching: Everyday Lessons from the Science of Learning*, the kinds of self-explaining that go on in class discussion are essential to developing problem-solving and critical thinking skills. *We often only understand what we think when we say or write what we are thinking.*[34] And we gain tremendously by explaining difficult concepts to others, including our peers. This is why some lecture classes have separate discussion sections led by teaching assistants, as such smaller sections allow students to ask questions and talk about the lecture and reading material in a way not possible in the larger class (see Box 3.4). In all cases, discussion can help you learn bracketing in real time.

Box 3.4 How to get the most out of discussion

Read or listen carefully to the prompt. Some discussion leaders will begin by soliciting very general feedback ("What did you think about this reading?" or "What struck you in this reading?"). If your teacher does this often, you would be wise to think of an answer in advance of each class. Some discussion leaders will be far more pointed in their prompts ("Where can we find the thesis in this piece?" or "How does this work compare to the poem we read for last class?"). Annotating your reading will help enormously with more detailed prompts. Coming prepared to class will help you participate more fully.

Listen to your classmates. A productive discussion can only take place if all parties are paying attention to each other, not just to their own ideas.

Refer back to the reading as a focus for discussion. If the discussion moves toward personal anecdote rather than textual evidence, be the one to steer it back.

Make connections across the course. Find commonalities or difference among the readings for the course, and see what your teacher and classmates think about those.

If you are frustrated that one or a few students continually monopolize discussion time, speak to your teacher about it. Remember that sometimes this happens because other students are unwilling or unable to speak up.

Some students perceive class discussion as useless at best. They have a partner in Vladimir Nabokov, whose character Clements in *Pnin* decries the newest teaching techniques, including discussion, as follows: "letting twenty young blockheads and two cocky neurotics discuss something that neither their teacher nor they know."[35] Some discussion might well fit this description, but a discussion led by a skilled teacher with students who have done the reading in advance offers invaluable opportunities for furthering understanding. Discussions can go badly for several reasons: students are not prepared, the instructor does not provide sufficient guidance, or the subject does not lend itself to discussion. It would be a waste of time to discuss a timeline of dated events leading up to the Thirty Years' War. It would be fruitful, however, to discuss in depth how various events might have contributed to the war.

Discussions go well when they are focused and directed and when they return to a common text or subject around which the questions turn. You will benefit most from discussion by developing skills of attentive, respectful listening to others with whom you might strongly disagree. Discussions require intellectual (and sometimes emotional) agility from all participants. They allow you to engage in nuanced consideration of complex issues and to practice patience, respect, and empathy. The ability to listen and let others speak, especially about contentious issues, is a valuable life skill.

Teachers often assign student discussion leaders during the semester. This requires the discussion leader to do extra work in preparation, well beyond the close reading required for daily assignments. Usually, a discussion leader provides context, presents a brief summary of the reading, and then suggests questions for discussion. The best discussions stick close to the text and are specific: prompts such as "what struck you in this reading?" or "does anyone have any questions?" don't indicate depth of thought to the professor or one's classmates. Carefully considering several focused questions will pay dividends in any discussion.

One of the most difficult parts of participating in discussion is staying focused on the topic. It is tempting to connect what one is discussing to a personal experience or a connection to another class, but often those connections are not interesting or useful to anyone else in the room. You might be afraid to ask questions, but that is precisely what discussion forums are for: asking a question that relates to the material shows a teacher that you are wrestling with the assigned material. Making connections to other readings in the course can also show the teacher that you have read well and thoroughly. This is why it is so crucial to read well in advance of any discussion. Those who do not prepare cannot benefit as much as those who do.

Another difficult part of discussion is dealing with controversial subjects, particularly those that are close to the experiences of students in the room.

A teacher can lecture about race relations in the 1960s with little disturbance in the classroom, but peers speaking up about their own experiences or making divisive comments can quickly inflame any discussion. A skilled teacher welcomes these sorts of "hot" encounters within limits, and students and the teacher must always remember the rules of civil discourse. Emotions can help or hinder learning, and managing one's emotions can be challenging. Students who are able to consider the other side of any issue are often better at learning from discussions.

Finally, more and more courses are integrating online discussion into class work. Online discussion can be synchronous (students post on a subject at roughly the same time) or asynchronous (students post at different times), but most online discussion is meant to be interactive. Many teachers will require responses to other students' posts as part of the online discussion grade. In general, students tend to want to provide brief reviews of the reading (e.g. "I didn't enjoy this reading"), while teachers are looking for engagement with the reading (e.g. "The passage from the Bhagavad Gita makes an interesting comparison with last week's reading from the Book of Genesis"). Online discussion can be more thoughtful than in-class discussion, because students have time to collect and edit their thoughts. It is worth taking the time in online discussion forums to engage with the material rather than to provide a passing review of your initial reaction to it. This bracketing of your own uncritical response fosters more meaningful discussions for you and your classmates.

Both in-person and online discussion serve the same end: to help students engage with the material to understand it and their own ideas. Speaking aloud in groups is also a necessary skill in many jobs, and learning how to present one's ideas and listen to critique is critical to contributing meaningfully in any discussion. Listening carefully to others and questioning your own assumptions are essential to any meaningful civil discourse. Bracketing even long-held assumptions can be scary but liberating. Imagine taking off a pair of tinted glasses that made the entire world look blue. You have been wearing those glasses for 20 years, and you assume the world is blue. Imagine the new thoughts you might have were you to trade those glasses in for another shade or no shade at all. You would see differently. *Religious studies, in part through bracketing, helps you to see the world differently.*

Students of religion are in a field unlike any other. The field has interdisciplinary breadth and global and historical depth that can't be found elsewhere on campus. Many students come to the academic study of religion expecting personal spiritual development. Although that might be an accidental outcome of exposure to ideas in any course, teachers tend to be strongly interested in developing students' skills and knowledge, goals achieved in part by reading, observation, and discussion that brackets personal judgment and biases. Most teachers will expect academic approaches to the material, so learning the difference between "academic" and "confessional" is essential for many students. If a single introductory course in religious studies teaches nothing else, it will at least show you that there are many other ways to understand the world.

Exercises and questions for further thought can be found at https://www. bloomsbury.com/cw/the-religious-studies-skills-book/skill-building-exercises/ chapter-three/

4

Close Reading

Any student who enrolls in college will be expected to have some ability in reading. But each person's educational training can vary widely and not everyone will be prepared for the type of reading required in college courses. Courses in the study of religion are frequently reading-intensive. They generally include readings from two types of sources. *Secondary sources*, such as textbooks, other books on specific subjects, and essays from scholarly journals, are generally produced by scholars who describe, analyze, and interpret materials from individual or multiple religious traditions. *Primary sources*, such as scriptures, commentaries, hymns, and prayers, are generally produced by individuals within religious traditions (see Chapter 3 for more extensive discussion of types of sources).

Either type of reading material may well prove daunting when encountered for the first time. Textbooks may be chock full of unfamiliar terms. They may articulate a point of view that is challenging or they may include presuppositions that are difficult both to identify and to grasp. The same goes for scholarly books and articles. Scholarly writing has its own forms, patterns, and ways of expression. Becoming familiar with such conventions can help you make sense of what you read. In addition, scholarly writing in one discipline, such as Chemistry, will differ in its characteristic modes of presentation from scholarly writing in another field, such as the study of religion. For beginners, there is a lot to get used to.

Those challenges are compounded when reading primary texts. First, the vast majority of those texts are presented in translation. Neither the Hindu Bhagavad Gita, nor the Muslim Qur'an, nor the Christian or Jewish Bibles, nor the works of Maimonides (Judaism), Thomas Aquinas (Christianity) or Chaitanya (Hinduism), for example, was originally written in English. Consequently, teachers and students alike must rely on translations.[1] And translations can vary substantially. A painstaking amount of work goes into producing a translation, and the rendering of a text in one language into English, for example, is not a simple process. Encountering multiple, differing, translations of the "same" text can thus be perplexing or troubling. But it can also be illuminating.

Second, most primary sources have origins that are distant from our world in both space and time. For example, the Bhagavad Gita, which is part of a vast Indian epic called the Mahabharata, is anywhere from 2,200 to 2,500 years old and comes from a culture very different from the contemporary US. Similarly, the Qur'an was recorded in the seventh century of the Common Era in a desert, tribal culture very removed from our own. Also, the Bible, which is at least as much a library of diverse books as it is a single book, includes individual books composed over a period of centuries in very different social and cultural settings. While translations can mask some of the profound differences that separate contemporary readers from ancient, or even relatively recent, religious texts, they cannot overcome them. As a result, reading, and making sense of, religious texts on anything other than the most superficial level is a skill that has to be learned and frequently practiced.

In this chapter we focus on a process called "close reading." The modifier "close" is particularly important. It describes a type of reading that is not content with achieving a general sense of what a piece of writing conveys. Rather, it depends on a disciplined focusing of attention on the details of a particular piece of writing in order to achieve broad and deep understanding (see Box 4.1). It looks for the meanings and nuances of individual words, patterns of vocabulary and expression, connections between one word or phrase and another, the structure of a particular piece of writing, and any other clues from which the reader may construct meaning from the text. Close reading is a particular way of *paying attention to details* in whatever is under consideration. Close reading is therefore a complex intellectual process that takes time and effort. It also requires practice. It cannot be accomplished at a glance. It ideally requires *re-reading*, going back over the impressions gained during a first encounter to check them for accuracy, deepen and extend them, and to discover things that may not have been immediately apparent. Close reading is essential to the process of making meaning. It involves not only the ability to grasp at a deep level the sense of a particular item but also the ability to *use that understanding* in multiple ways.

As a particular way of paying attention to details, close reading can also, metaphorically, be applied to things other than texts. Particular objects, such as flags or candles, can also be subjected to close reading. So can pieces of music, with or without words. Ritual actions, such as rites of initiation, offer particularly rich fields for close reading since they include words, gestures, other actions, and many other details. Virtually anything can be subjected to

Box 4.1 Close reading

What is entailed in close reading?

On the level of *language*, close reading involves the ability

- to recognize the meaning of individual words
- to find out the meaning of unfamiliar words
- to identify the meaning of foreign words and phrases
- to recognize and understand technical vocabulary, such as vocabulary specific to a particular discipline
- to recognize or be able to find out the meaning of various textual conventions, including
  - abbreviations (such as, i.e, e.g., cf.),
  - textual effects (such as, italics, underlining, bold print, superscript numbers)
  - phrases from languages other than English (such as, from Latin, *sic, mutatis mutandis*)
  - footnotes, endnotes, or other forms of citation.

On the level of *structure*, close reading involves the ability

- to recognize the relationships among
  - words
  - sentences
  - paragraphs
- to understand the meaning and implications of headings and sub-headings and other ways of breaking a text into sections
- to recognize how material is introduced and arranged
- to form hypotheses about what the structure of the material at hand might indicate
- to distinguish, for example, expository prose from poetic language.

On the level of *making meaning*, close reading involves the ability

- to distinguish what is central from what is peripheral
- to identify the central point or argument
- to identify the ways in which the central point or argument is supported, deepened, extended, defended
- to identify assumptions and presuppositions
- to summarize the reading in one's own words
- to formulate analytical questions about the reading
- to formulate a tentative interpretation of the reading.

close reading. Its broad applicability is what leads us to identify close reading as a key skill in the study of religion. In many ways it is *the* foundational skill. *The more you practice close reading, the easier you will find other aspects of your courses, in religious studies and beyond.*

In this chapter we will undertake close readings of three brief examples of primary texts and one very brief example of scholarly writing. Our focus will be on how the process of close reading sustains and deepens description, analysis, and interpretation. We are not so much concerned with the persuasiveness of particular interpretations of each of the examples, but rather with the process of close reading itself. Close reading slows down the movement from description of an object or event to its interpretation. It focuses and disciplines the eye, and hence the thinking, of the observer. When undertaken with rigor, it leads to description of an accuracy, comprehensiveness and complexity that you may not have experienced before. It gives you more to think about and more to say. Complex description then can serve as the basis for creative analysis and interpretation.

A short text

The Qur'an is the central scriptural text of Islam. In Arabic, *al-quran* means "the recitation." Islamic tradition holds that the prophet Muhammad received the Qur'an over a period of twenty-three years from Allah (God) through the angel Gabriel. Muhammad then recited the revelations that he received and those around him recorded them in writing. After Muhammad's death in 632 CE, those written records were compiled into the Qur'an. The processes involved from Muhammad's initial experience of being called to be God's prophet through the compilation of the Qur'an were complex and scholars differ on their reconstructions of what is likely to have happened.[2]

For our purposes those scholarly concerns, important as they are, can be left to the side. We want, instead, to use the first chapter of the Qur'an as an example for the processes of close reading. Strictly speaking, Islamic tradition asserts that the Qur'an itself cannot be translated, since it was delivered to Muhammad in Arabic.[3] In deference to that position an influential English translation adopted the title *The Koran Interpreted.*[4] Nonetheless, translations of the Qur'an abound, even as they frequently acknowledge their inability to capture adequately the beauty and power of the Arabic Qur'an.[5] Most undergraduate students must use a translation if they are to study the Qur'an at all. That introduces another element of complexity to the process of close reading.

For our example, we will start at the beginning, with the short first chapter, or *sura*, of the Qur'an. With the title, *Al-Fātiḥa*, "The Opening," the *sura* has been identified as communicating the "essence of the Qur'an."[6] It is the most frequently recited *sura* of the Qur'an, being used not only in prayers and liturgy, but also at the closing of business transactions where both parties recite it as a sign of their good faith and their commitment to mutual responsibilities.[7] We will work with two recent translations, though many more could, of course, be considered.

Michael Sells prints his translation in this way:

> In the Name of God
>   the Compassionate the Caring
> Praise be to God
>   lord sustainer of the worlds
> the Compassionate the Caring
>   master of the day of reckoning
> 5   To you we turn to worship
>   and to you we turn in time of need
> Guide us along the road straight
> the road of those to whom you are giving
>   not those with anger upon them
>   not those who have lost the way[8]

Arthur Droge prints his translation in this way:

1   In the Name of God, the Merciful, the Compassionate.

2   Praise (be) to God, Lord of the worlds, 3 the Merciful, the Compassionate, 4 Master of the Day of Judgment. 5 You we serve and You we seek for help. 6 Guide us to the straight path: 7 the path of those whom You have blessed, not (the path) of those on whom (Your) anger falls, nor of those who go astray.[9]

What can close reading tell us about the first *sura* of the Qur'an? Since close reading focuses on the details of the material at hand, we might well ask first why the two renderings of the text look rather different. Sells's translation occupies twelve lines of print, while Droge's occupies five. The twelve lines from Sells are short and unpunctuated. Six of them are indented and six are not. Sells puts the number 5 next to the seventh line. Droge's translation includes punctuation marks. After a break between the first line and what follows, he sets off phrases and sentences with numbers, reaching number 7 before the end. If the formal layout of the text is not simply the result of a translator's or typesetter's whim, what might it indicate?

If you have experience reading poetry, you might well notice the similarity between the layout of Sells's translation and poems you have seen in the past. In fact, through his arrangement of the text Sells is trying to convey some of the poetic nature of the Qur'an. Although standard poetic indicators like rhyming and meter are absent in Sells's English, the short lines and internal repetitions convey the idea that the passage is a specific kind of language. Although Droge's translation does not adopt the same strategy of presentation, his interpolation of numbers also achieves the effect of breaking the text into its constituent parts. In his rendition, the seven verses of the *sura* can be more clearly identified than they can in Sells', where only the number 5 serves the reader as a guide to breaking the text into smaller parts.

Each translator, then, has made choices about how best to convey both the sense, and the much more elusive "feel," of the text. In addition, each translator implicitly acknowledges the difficulty of reading the text by providing brief clarifications and commentary in the notes to their translations. Each set of choices has benefits and drawbacks. Sells's presentation suggests to the reader that the text is poetic, and should be expected to have qualities, such as rhythm, allusiveness, and figurative language, that poetry typically has. Droge opts instead to focus on rendering the sense of the passage, in part by adding punctuation marks to indicate the relationships between one phrase and another. Each translator aims to make the text available to those who cannot read Arabic so that they can apprehend, at least in part, what it conveys. Decisions that shape the layout of a text, even the numbering of verses, can thus be an important clue to how the translator understands its meaning.

Although meaning may not be entirely independent from form, it can nonetheless be grasped in different formats. Attention to the details of the text, specifically the language it uses, can help the reader construct a sense of its meaning. It is best to start at the beginning. Both Sells and Droge translate the very first words of *Al-Fātiḥa* in the same way. The text identifies itself as being in the name of God, who is then further qualified as Compassionate and Merciful or Caring. From the start, then, it is clear that we are dealing with a text that is in some way religious. Whatever one's preferred definition of "religion," the reference to God would seem to locate the *sura* within that sphere of human activity.

We also learn in the world implied by this text that God has a specific character. Sells and Droge differ on whether the appropriate English equivalent of an Arabic term is "Merciful" or "Caring," but the three terms, including "Compassionate," have overlapping ranges of meaning. The importance of those qualifiers is underlined when they appear again in the third verse of the *sura. Repetition is a clue to significance.* When something is repeated twice in such a short text, it is bound to be important. Similarly, repetition also shows that the character of "God" in the text is important. The second and fourth verses provide additional information about the nature and character of the God in the text.

First, God is presented as being worthy of praise, presumably from human beings. Both Sells and Droge translate the beginning of the second verse in similar fashion. Then Sells adds "sustainer" in his translation, where Droge has the more terse "Lord of the worlds." In either translation, some relationship is being asserted between God and plural worlds. Sells reads the text as implying that the Lord is the "Creator deity."[10] At any rate, in English the word "Lord" connotes the ability to exercise power over or to rule over. In this case, then, the Lord has power over multiple worlds. What those worlds might be remains unclear. In an analogy to other passages in the Qur'an, Droge suggests that it might mean either "Lord of the heavens and the earth" of "Lord of all peoples."[11] At any rate, the Lord is depicted as having extensive ruling power, perhaps that of the creator of the worlds.

Beyond that, the Lord is also claimed to have substantial power to make certain unspecified determinations. Either individual or communal history is implicitly described as moving toward a certain point in time, a day of reckoning or of judgment. As of verse 4, it is not yet clear precisely who will be judged and on what basis, but the text definitely asserts that God has the power to serve as judge.

All of the terms and phrases that have been used to describe God up to this point have another dimension to them as well. They each imply some sort of relationship between God and an as yet unspecified audience. God is merciful, compassionate, and caring toward someone or some group. God is praiseworthy. God rules over and sustains worlds. God will act as a judge on a day of reckoning that will occur at a time that is not yet disclosed. In all of those ways, God is portrayed as being in a relationship.

The relationship becomes a little clearer in verse 5. God is addressed in the second person by a group only identified as "we." The translations differ slightly, although Droge acknowledges that "serve" could also be "worship," as Sells has it.[12] For English-speaking readers, "worship" would likely imply some sort of ritual or liturgical relationship between God and the unidentified group. What makes the God of *Al-Fātiḥa* worthy of worship or service would likely be found in the characteristics previously attributed to God. Those characteristics, particularly compassion, caring, and mercy, would also connect logically to why people would turn to God in time of need or seek God's help. Through its ascription of attributes to God and characterization of human responses to God, *Al-Fātiḥa* is describing a particular form of relationship between humans and God, part of a religious system.

That theme continues with the plea in verse 6, for God to guide humans along the "straight path" or "road straight." As Droge notes, that image is typically taken to be a reference to the religion of Islam, the religion through which God guides humans along the straight or correct path, rather than, as the final verse puts it, leading them, or allowing them to go, astray.[13] The image of the straight path can also be connected to the previous mention of a day of judgment or reckoning. Those who follow the straight path are implicitly likely to be judged approvingly and those who go astray will be the ones on whom God's anger will be unleashed.

Close reading of a single short text of seven verses can thus produce a fragmentary but substantial picture of a religious system. The religious world implied by *Al-Fātiḥa* is focused on a single God who created and rules over the world and who will judge it on a day sometime in the future. That God is involved in a caring relationship with an unspecified group of humans who provide worship to God and who seek God's guidance for their lives, particularly in light of the future judgment. While compassionate, that God can also be angered by people who fail to follow the path set out for them.

Although more could be said about what a close reading of *Al-Fātiḥa* can produce, it might be helpful at this point to draw together some of the implications from this first exercise in close reading. First, *close reading is an iterative process, or one that requires repetition*. No one discovers everything about a text on first reading. Re-reading can uncover layers of meaning, connections, and questions that were missed initially. Second, *form and structure matter*. Whether something is printed in stanzas or paragraphs, at the beginning or end of a collection, as prose or in verse, as an argument or a metaphor, or in some other identifiable way can provide important clues to what it is trying to communicate. So, too, will the internal organization of any text. Third, *language repays careful scrutiny*. When certain terms are repeated or when they are combined with other terms that have a similar range of meanings, their frequent appearance is a key to their significance. If it is repeated, it is worth sustained attention. The connections between terms are also worth careful consideration. Those connections form a web of relationships as they do in *Al-Fātiḥa* among the characterizations ascribed to God and those ascribed to human beings and between each set of attributes and the other. The system of relationships implied in a text may also serve as a model of or model for a system of relationships among a group of human beings, between one human group and another, or between a group of humans and a god, group of gods, or other extraordinary figures.

An object

As we suggested earlier, written texts are not the only things that repay the careful attention that produces close readings. Other things can, and should be, "read" just as carefully with similarly productive results. The possibilities are virtually endless. One could read carefully the colorful sequin-and-cloth spirit flags used in Hatian Vodou, the exterior and interior of a Hindu temple or *mandir*, the clothing of a Shinto priest, the eight-pointed cross of the Church of Scientology, or any other physical manifestation of a religious culture. As our example for the close reading of an object, we have chosen an item that is widespread throughout Jewish cultures, the menorah (see Image 1).

That virtually schematic presentation of the menorah captures its essential elements. It is a lampstand with three branches on each side of a central column topped by a seventh lamp. The cups at the top of each branch were originally filled with olive oil that could be burned to provide light. Similar oil lamps have been used throughout history. Though the menorah's general function appears clear, the object itself does not give a clue to the context(s) in which it was used. As is often the case with other religious objects, there is substantial textual evidence that describes both the construction and uses of the menorah. Reviewing the textual evidence can help the observer read the menorah in context.

According to the Hebrew Bible or Old Testament, the origins of the menorah go back to the time of Moses. Exodus 24 continues the narrative that culminated with Moses' reception of the Ten Commandments from God on Mount Sinai. In it, the people who followed Moses out from Egypt ratify the covenant between themselves and their Lord, proclaiming that "All that the Lord has spoken we will do, and we will be obedient" (Exod. 24:7). After that solemn affirmation, Moses returns to the mountain where he encountered God and stays there for forty days and forty nights.

Exodus 25 details some of what Moses learned. He was told what kind of offerings the Israelites should make to their God, and to build an ark of the

IMAGE 1 *Drawing of a Hanukah menorah.*
From Wikipedia Commons.

covenant, a table for the bread of the presence, and a mercy seat. He was also told to craft a lampstand. The text goes into substantial detail about its materials and appearance (see Exod. 25:31–40). Moses is told to make sure that the lampstand conforms to the divine specifications (Exod. 25:40). The lampstand itself, therefore, is not simply a pedestrian object that provides light but one that has religious significance.

Exodus 27:20–21 reports that the lamp should be fueled by pure olive oil and that Aaron and his sons should keep it lit from evening to morning each day, just outside of the curtain that veils the tabernacle or portable shrine that the Israelites maintained during their time in the wilderness. When the Israelites eventually settled in the land of promise and built a temple in Jerusalem, the menorah occupied a prominent place in the new temple where it was kept continually lit.

The menorah ceased to play a role in temple ritual when the second Jewish temple was sacked and destroyed by the Romans in 70 CE. The commemorative Arch of Titus in Rome has an interior relief that shows the triumphant Romans making off with the menorah and other spoils from the temple (see Image 2).

IMAGE 2 *Menorah in the arch of Titus.*
Still image from the Khan academy video.

In the left center the image shows the seven-branched menorah being borne on the shoulders of the Roman troops along with other booty.

In many ways the form of the menorah follows from its function. It is a lampstand, designed to illuminate other religious objects in its near vicinity. Scholars and members of the Jewish community over time have tried to propose specific meanings for the seven branches of the candelabrum.[14] But no particular theory has carried the day.

Whatever else might be said about it, the menorah is saturated with history, particularly ancient history. As our brief references to the story of the exodus from Egypt, Moses' encounters with God, the erection of the first temple in Jerusalem, and the destruction of the Second Temple in 70 CE suggest, for anyone familiar with such events simply seeing a menorah conjures up major turning points in the history of the Israelite and Jewish people. The menorah functions as a touchstone of memory, a guide to understanding the fortunes of a specific community in relationship to its God and to other people.

As an object, then, the menorah does not stand on its own. It is embedded in multiple contexts. From the first mentions of it in the Hebrew Bible, it is presented as part of a web of relationships with other religious objects, God, and a specific community. Thus, as with *sura Al-Fātiḥa*, close attention to the menorah reveals at least fragments of a complex religious system. Since the menorah packs so much significance into a single object, it has also proven to be very adaptable. For example, it occupies a prominent place on the emblem of the contemporary state of Israel (see Image 3).

In a sense, then, the menorah can stand for Israel itself. It is an object through which multiple symbolic meanings are refracted. Depending on the

IMAGE 3 *Emblem of the state of Israel.*
From Wikipedia, "Emblem of Israel."

uses of an actual menorah or an image of one, it can stand for different things, for different people, in different contexts. Its range of meanings is malleable and adaptable but not exhaustive: there are limits to what a menorah might represent.

That adaptability becomes particularly clear in another depiction of the menorah. Strikingly, menorahs do not only come with seven lights or candles (some menorahs are now electric). The menorah used in the celebration of Hanukkah (called a *hanukiah*) actually has nine lights or candles (see Image 4).

As with the so-called temple menorah, the key to the nine-branched menorah lies in ancient history. The Jewish festival of Hanukkah commemorates the rededication of the second Jerusalem temple in 165 BCE. The original temple in Jerusalem, built by King Solomon in 957 BCE, had been destroyed by the Babylonians in 586 BCE. When the Persian king Cyrus issued his edict that allowed Jews to return from captivity in Babylonia, re-building the temple was something they wanted to do as soon as possible. The rebuilt temple was dedicated c. 516 BCE. Work continued on the Second Temple over the ensuing years.

In 168 BCE, the Seleucid King Antiochus, who led one of the empires that had formed in the wake of the death of Alexander the Great, extended his political and military control into the land of Israel. He sacked the temple in Jerusalem, massacred many Jews, and outlawed the practice of Judaism. The next year he ordered a statue of Zeus to be erected in the temple. That

IMAGE 4 *Drawing of a menorah.*

act of profanation sparked a guerilla rebellion against the forces of Antiochus, led by a Jew named Mattathias and his five sons. In 165 BCE the rebellion successfully regained control of the temple and it was rededicated.

The Books of First and Second Maccabees, considered by scholars to be "extra-canonical" rather than a part of the Bible, recount the story of the rededication of the temple after the successful Maccabean revolt. (One of Mattathias's sons, Judah, had been nicknamed, "Maccabee," "the Hammer," and the revolt took its name from him.) They tell of an eight-day period of celebrations to mark the restoration of worship in the temple. Another source, in the compilation of rabbinic legal opinions called the Talmud, recounts that when the celebrants were searching for pure olive oil to use in the menorah, they could only find enough oil to burn for a single night. Miraculously, however, the oil lasted for all eight nights of the celebrations. To commemorate that event, the Hanukkah candelabrum has nine branches, four on each side of the center post whose flame is used to light the other eight on each consecutive night of the holiday.

The Hanukkah menorah thus adds another layer of meaning to the history of the menorah. The variation in the number of lights and branches evokes another turning point of Jewish history. Evoking its early description in the book of Exodus through its use in the first and second temples in Jerusalem, to its multiple contemporary uses, the menorah condenses significant episodes of Jewish history into a single material object. For those familiar with its multiple connections to events, places, figures, and practices from Jewish history, the menorah functions as a compressed expression of multiple meanings.

"Reading" an object like the menorah demonstrates the importance of linking a given "text" to its context(s). Since the construction and use of the menorah are described in multiple texts that were composed over a long period of time, reading this particular object is a dynamic and iterative process. As with *sura Al-Fātiḥa*, each successive reading of the menorah and the texts about it yields additional information. Also, as with *Al-Fātiḥa*, the form and structure of the menorah matter, most notably in the comparison of the seven- and nine-branched versions. But the form of the menorah also gives some clue about how it most likely was used, which leads to further consideration of its roles in a complex and evolving ritual system. Also, the "language" of the menorah can be considered in two ways. First, the object itself has a distinctive articulation that occurs in many variations, not unlike the variation that occurs in different translations. Some menorahs are plain, for example, and some are very ornate; some present themselves as "traditional" while others are distinctively modern. Second, the object is modeled on a linguistic description in the book of Exodus.

As the variety of menorahs shows, the biblical guidelines for the construction of a menorah are frequently understood to be suggestive rather

IMAGE 5 *Menorah with Christmas bulbs.*
Source: https://www.dreamstime.com/royalty-free-stock-images-menorah-3d-garland-image1575299.

IMAGE 6 *Menorah created by the Temple Institute, Jerusalem.*
Source: http://www.templeinstitute.org/vessels_gallery_11.htm.

than rigidly determinative. A simple side-by-side comparison underlines that point (see Images 5 and 6).

The menorah on the right was made at the Temple Institute in Jerusalem. As its website puts it, the Institute

> is dedicated to every aspect of the Biblical commandment to build the Holy Temple of G-d on Mount Moriah in Jerusalem. Our short-term goal is to rekindle the flame of the Holy Temple in the hearts of mankind through education. Our long-term goal is to do all in our limited power to bring about the building of the Holy Temple in our time.[15]

If a third temple is to be built, all of the paraphernalia of the original temple will have to be constructed as well. Builders associated with the institute have striven to follow the guidelines in the Bible with unfailing accuracy. The Institute's website reports that "The conclusions upon which the construction of the menorah was based took into account archeological evidence and, of course, the halachic (Jewish law) requirements of materials, dimensions, ornamental affects and manner of manufacture as first delineated in the book of Exodus, and further explicated by Jewish sages throughout the millennia."[16]

The menorah they have produced is massive. According to the Institute, it weighs a half-ton and used some 45 kilograms of twenty-four carat gold. It is approximately five feet tall.

The menorah on the left looks quite different. Though functionally similar, it is very different in design. It uses electricity instead of oil lamps; it also has colored lights instead of uniform candles or oil lamps. If the Temple Institute focused on exacting conformity to the biblical descriptions, the contemporary creation takes much more latitude with the traditional form of the menorah. In size, composition, and design it could hardly be more different than the monumental piece produced by the Temple Institute. But while they are very different, they are still similar in their function and in their connections to Jewish history.

Undertaking a close reading of an object raises some of the same challenges as performing a close reading of a text, but also some distinctive ones. With *sura Al-Fātiḥa* we were able to focus primarily on the text in isolation and still make some meaning from its distinctive language. Although the menorah provided some clues to how it might be understood through its particular design and structure, it yielded much more when it was linked to its textual and ritual contexts. In each case, we noted variability. English translations of *Al-Fātiḥa* produce at least somewhat different impressions of the structure and sense of the *sura*. Similarly, each construction of a menorah, as the final example shows in particular, produces an object that is both like other menorahs and distinctively different. Such variation demands comment. It suggests that multiple readings of the "same" thing are not only appropriate, but necessary.

A ritual

Like other religions that have continued over a long period of time and taken root in places beyond their place of origin, Buddhism has been expressed in diverse forms. For our third example in this chapter, after examining a passage of the Qur'an and comparing menorahs, we will focus on a particular practice within a school of Buddhism that developed in Japan and has diversified since its founding.

The Japanese religious reformer Nichiren (1222–1282 CE) saw himself as living at a crucial juncture of history. He was convinced that the third and final cycle of Buddhist law was unfolding. In the first cycle the True Law of the Buddha had flourished, in the second cycle Buddhism had become formalized, and in the third cycle it had degenerated. He was particularly critical of the dominant schools of Buddhism in thirteenth-century Japan, arguing that they had all gone astray and were misled.

In the style of many reformers, Nichiren claimed only to be re-emphasizing what the Buddhist tradition had always taught. He claimed that in his own teaching, he was simply letting the traditional religious texts, or *sutras*, speak for themselves. At the heart of Nichiren's religious program was devotion to a particular text, the Lotus Sutra, which he believed best captured the true message of the Buddha.

The central practice that he encouraged was the chanting of praise to the wisdom of the Lotus Sutra in the phrase "*nam-myoho-renge-kyo*," which can be roughly translated as "devotion to the Mystic Law of the Lotus Sutra." The central ritual object for Nichiren was the *gohonzon*, a *mandala* or graphic symbol inscribed with the title of the Lotus Sutra among other things. It would serve as a focal point during the chanting of praise to the Lotus Sutra.

One group that vigorously espouses Nichiren Buddhism is Soka Gakkai International (SGI). Born during the difficult years of the Second World War, it quickly captured a substantial following through its aggressive efforts at recruiting members. SGI grew out of an educational reform movement begun by Tsunesaburo Makiguchi and Josei Toda in 1930, but it evolved into a religious movement when Toda experienced enlightenment while reading the Lotus Sutra.

Soka Gakkai sees itself as continuing the practice established by Nichiren in the thirteenth century. Although members do hold meetings with each other and also try to bring their message of Buddhism to others, the central practice remains chanting *nam-myoho-renge-kyo* and excerpts from the Lotus Sutra in front of a *gohonzon* at home. *Gohonzons* can range from simple scrolls to extremely elaborate altars with the scroll as the focal point. Image 7 shows an example of a scroll, which is frequently displayed within a simple wooden box, but which also could be part of a much more elaborate altar.

As with texts and other religious objects, the structure of this item gives a clue about its meaning. In this scroll, the characters for *nam-myoho-renge-kyo* occupy the center, running from top to bottom. As the website for Soka Gakkai International puts it, "*Nam-myoho-renge-kyo* is written down the center of the *gohonzon* in bold characters. *Nam*, meaning devotion, signifies the intent of summoning or harmonizing with. It expresses a vow to believe in our Buddhahood and take action in alignment with this vow."[17] The phrase that the practitioner chants focuses the devotee's eye at the same time that the sound of the chanted phrase reaches the ear. Engaging multiple senses enhances concentration.

Around the central portion of the scroll "are characters that represent the various positive and negative tendencies and energies within life. All such energies are intrinsic to life, but harmonized by the law of Nam-myoho-renge-kyo, all reveal an enlightened aspect and function to create value and happiness."[18] In the scrolls that he himself inscribed, and in their

IMAGE 7 Gohonzon *scroll.*
From Wikipedia, "Soka Gakkai."

reproductions, Nichiren's name appears below the central invocation. In his writings, Nichiren underlined the importance of the *gohonzon*, claiming that "I, Nichiren, have inscribed my life in sumi ink [special ink used in East Asian calligraphy], so believe in the Gohonzon with your whole heart. The Buddha's will is the Lotus Sutra, but the soul of Nichiren is nothing other than Nam-myoho-renge-kyo."[19] As with the menorah, religious texts help to contextualize the meaning of a religious object.

Anyone who chants in front of the *gohonzon* is aligned with both the practice of Nichiren himself and with what he identified as the fullest and clearest expression of the teaching of the Buddha, the Lotus Sutra. Just as the menorah can be read as evoking multiple key events of Jewish history, so also does the *gohonzon* link those who chant before it to each other, to Nichiren, and through him to the Buddha. In its own way, the *gohonzon* also functions as a touchstone of memory that links the present to the past.

SGI practitioners also chant selections from the second and sixteenth chapters of the Lotus Sutra, in a practice known as *gongyo*. The Soka Gakkai International website offers a selection of videos to help practitioners learn how to chant properly, including a "karaoke-style" guide to pronounciation of *nam-myoho-renge-kyo* and another for *gongyo*.[20] Videos are also available on a dedicated Soka Gakkai YouTube channel.[21]

The six-minute "How to Chant" video[22] notes that members of SGI strive to chant in both the morning and the evening, facing the *gohonzon* altar in their homes. Two young members of the multicultural group featured in the professional video provide detailed instructions for beginners. They emphasize that individuals need not visualize anything, nor should they try to empty their minds. They should simply focus on their hopes and dreams. The unseen narrator breaks down the meaning of each syllable in the chant. One of the featured SGI members describes chanting as a "spiritual workout" that revitalizes her and gives her "the strength not to be defeated by [her] problems." The process of chanting is presented as both relatively simple and immensely rewarding.

For practitioners seeking a fuller understanding of the *gohonzon*, Soka Gakkai provides a detailed diagram with commentary on each section.[23] That teaching aid suggests that the *gohonzon* repays repeated readings, just as other religious texts and objects do. The scroll lays out a web of textual relationships, between the central affirmation of praise for the Lotus Sutra and the founder of the school of Buddhism that Soka Gakkai claims to continue, between the title of the Lotus Sutra and multiple other aspects of its teachings, and between practitioners, the founder of their school, and the founder of Buddhism. The deeper one's understanding of the *gohonzon*, the Lotus Sutra, and Buddhism, SGI suggests, the more one will be able to benefit from the practice of chanting, on the way to recognizing their own Buddhahood.

Chanting *nam-myoho-renge-kyo* is a simple ritual, but deceptively so. When that ritual action is read closely, the careful observer can discern layers of significance that might not have been immediately apparent. Close reading shows that there is always more than initially meets the eye. As with our other examples, the practices of close reading—repeated re-readings, relentless focus on details, careful attention to form and structure, awareness of the nuances of language, and connection to context—enable an observer to develop deep and broad understanding of the material at hand. That processes of making sense *of* a particular example supports the subsequent processes of making sense *with* it by relating a particular item to others through comparison or relating it to generalizations or theories under which it might be considered. That is why we identify close reading as a foundational skill. It lays groundwork for other, more complex, forms of intellectual inquiry.

A definition of religion

We do not have the space in this chapter to work through a close reading of a scholarly article, let alone an entire book. But since the same procedures of close reading that we have identified in our examination of the three primary sources also apply to secondary sources, a very brief example should suffice. The problem of defining religion has occupied a prominent place in the academic study of religion. You may recall that one of the syllabi examined in Chapter 2 was entitled "What is Religion?" Many courses will address the issues involved in defining religion, while others may simply stipulate a definition that students can work with throughout the term.

Such definitions of religion are not simple common-sense propositions with which virtually everyone could easily agree. They do not simply name what exists in the world. Instead, they are arguments about what is important, and what is not. They are designed to direct observers' eyes to certain things and not to others. That is, they serve scholarly purposes. Reading such definitions closely, therefore, helps students identify the particular scholarly purposes involved, consider them analytically, and use them effectively in their efforts to make meaning of particular religious texts, objects, and processes.

We have chosen a definition for purposes of illustration that, even though it is more than a hundred years old, remains influential. Since it also articulates a strong stance on several perennial issues, that makes it worth our consideration. In 1901–1902 the Harvard philosopher and psychologist William James delivered the Gifford Lectures at the University of Edinburgh. They were first published in 1902 as *The Varieties of Religious Experience*. They have remained in print ever since.

To circumscribe his subject, James writes, "religion, therefore, as I now ask you arbitrarily to take it, shall mean for us *the feelings, acts, and experiences of individual men in their solitude, so far as they apprehend themselves to stand in relation to whatever they may consider the divine.*"[24] As with our other examples, we can direct some attention to the form of James's statement. Part of it is in italics. That section is, in fact, the actual definition that he is proposing. But the part that comes before it is equally important. In the opening section James acknowledges that his definition is arbitrary. He suggests that other definitions are certainly possible. Perhaps the most important part of his introduction is the simple phrase, "for us." With that qualification, James signals that he is asking his audience to follow him as he articulates a definition of religion for specific purposes. His definition is presented as useful. It will help him, and those who follow his thinking, to see and understand certain things. It will focus their attention and direct their analytical and interpretive efforts.

A careful examination of James's language provides further indication about where James wants his audience to direct their attention. His object of investigation is "feelings, acts, and experiences." He is as interested in emotion as in action; he is also interested in the inner lives of religious people, their experiences. In the definition itself, he does not lay out the actual or potential relationships among feelings, acts, and experiences. That is deferred until a later time, but a careful reader would be alert to the need to make such connections.

The next phrase reveals a distinctive emphasis of James, through repetition. He intends to study not only individuals, but individuals in their solitude. The unit of analysis for James is the individual person, rather than, for example, the religious community. Throughout the lectures that make up *The Varieties*, James makes extensive use of biographies and particularly autobiographies. Above all, James is interested in the extraordinary experiences of exceptional individuals; he is convinced that they tell him much more about religion than the pedestrian experiences of "your ordinary religious believer" whose "religion has been made for him by others, communicated to him by tradition, determined to fixed forms by imitation, and retained by habit."[25] That strong and narrow focus is announced clearly in his definition.

The final phrase in James's definition revolves around his focus on the individual in a different way. James removes himself from making any definitive statements about "the divine." Instead, he aims to understand what the individuals he is studying have to say about the divine. His focus is on what others think, or "apprehend," rather than on what is actually true or real. What counts is what *they* consider to be divine, not how any individual's perception conforms, or not, to what James thinks about "the divine." James is thus firmly committed to making descriptive, and analytical, statements about others. He does not intend to make prescriptive statements based on his own perceptions.

James's definition reveals not only a characterization of the phenomenon of religion, but also an agenda for research. He acknowledges that his definition is arbitrary, which gives careful readers the opportunity to work with his definition to see what it will yield. But he does not demand that his definition be accepted as the final word on the nature of religion. In effect, he is inviting his audience to entertain the intellectual possibilities that such a definition opens up. He directs their attention *toward* the religious feelings, acts, and experiences of individuals. As a result, he directs their attention *away from* other things, such as communal rituals, ethical guidelines, theological speculation, or community life.

A close reading that attends to the structure and particular language of James's definition of religion can produce important information about not only the definition itself, but also about the program of research that it implies. The definition suggests the types of phenomena that James will investigate, the types of evidence that he will focus upon, and even the types of conclusions that he may draw. The definition implies a series of choices that James has made about what is important to investigate and how that investigation should be undertaken.

The same type of close reading that we have done with James's brief definition can definitely be used on a larger scale. Analysis of the structure and language of scholarly articles or books can provide important clues about the author's presuppositions, goals, and research agenda. In reading larger pieces, it is wise to begin at the beginning. Look for statements that circumscribe the subject matter, articulate an analytical perspective, sketch out a research field, and otherwise indicate what an author intends to look at, what an author proposes to look for, and what an author hopes to find.

Close reading and academic practice

Close reading is a component part, actually an essential prerequisite, of many forms of academic work in which you can be expected to engage, such as class discussions, written or oral examinations, and the writing of various forms of essays. Close reading is also a crucial component of critical thinking, something on which we will focus in the next chapter. Before we move on, however, we will address the connection between close reading and a standard form of academic discourse, the critique.

In academic practice, being "critical" has a distinctive meaning that can differ from the way the term is used in common language. When someone is described as being critical of a friend, sibling, or stranger, for example, the implication is that the person is being negative or derogatory. Criticism in that sense implies finding fault or identifying something negative. Critique, on the other hand, ideally involves an even-handed assessment of strengths and weaknesses, negatives and positives. In academic practice critique involves taking things apart, but not in order to tear them down. Academics take things apart in order to see how they work, to achieve a fuller understanding of them.

Taking something apart, however, can seem threatening. Especially when someone has strong emotional ties to the object of critique, which can definitely happen when the topic is religion, critique can seem more like attack. When something is taken apart analytically, but not put back together, it can appear to have been destroyed rather than understood. The emotional investments that students have in, or against, religion, therefore, can hinder their ability to do the kind of work that is required in college courses.

We think that a fuller understanding of what the process of close reading can entail can help you overcome any hesitance you may have to engage in academic critique. We take our cue from Peter Elbow, who has written with uncommon insight about teaching writing, but also about teaching and learning in general. Elbow has acknowledged that the academic fondness for critique can sometimes spill over into the type of criticism that dwells only on the negative. He argues that academics excel at the "doubting game."[26] Consequently, they strive to increase their students' mastery over that game's characteristic moves.

Doubt, however, can be corrosive. Doubt can shake or weaken religious convictions. If the learning goals for a particular class session or course do not include such a direct assault on (some) students' personal beliefs, then doubt can distract them from the task at hand. Though Elbow admits that the systematic application of doubt has produced substantial academic insight, he argues that the doubting game should also be balanced by what he calls the "believing game." For him, the believing game involves "the equally systematic, disciplined, and conscious attempt to believe everything no matter how unlikely or repellent it might seem, to find virtues and strengths we might otherwise miss."[27]

Elbow's description of both approaches as games is important. It suggests that both are provisional approaches that can be tried out on the material at hand or temporary stances that can be adopted to see what they might yield. In short, they can be played with. Both games invite their participants to entertain, seriously but for a limited time and without necessarily making a personal commitment, a range of possibilities for making meaning about a particular body of evidence.

We think that Elbow's seriously playful approach to making sense and meaning of any kind of evidence could be particularly productive in the religious studies classroom. Rather than directly challenging students either to state and justify their own convictions and practices or to wrestle personally with the convictions of others that may initially challenge and affront, Elbow's approach entices students to entertain a variety of "what if" questions that can provide multiple points of entry into the religious worlds of others. That process of entertaining seriously how others make meaning of the world is an important element of the academic study of religion.

In terms of the examples we have used in this chapter, someone playing the doubting game might ask how *sura Al-Fātiḥa*'s description of God as compassionate and merciful might square with the subsequent statement that God's wrath would be directed against those who stray from the straight path. Someone playing the believing game would ask how believing that God has determined a path that individuals should follow in their lives would shape the lives of Muslims. Someone playing the doubting game might raise questions about whether the Lotus Sutra actually does express the core of the Buddha's teaching or whether Soka Gakkai accurately understands what Nichiren taught. Someone playing the believing game might rather focus on trying to understand how chanting before the *gohonzon* actually could revitalize a practitioner's life. All are valid and important questions. Elbow argues—and we agree—that both types of approaches can be employed in the academic study of religions in colleges and universities.

To relate that discussion of Elbow's doubting and believing games directly to our treatment of close reading in this chapter, we distinguish different ways to read. The fundamental purpose of reading is *reading to understand*. Such reading involves the effort to grasp the fundamental point as accurately and comprehensively as possible. Many different intellectual processes are involved in that effort, as we outlined in Box 4.1.

You should ask yourself why you are reading the item in question, that is, what are you supposed to be able to do with what you have gleaned from the reading. You should also ask what is the context in which you are supposed to be reading something. Does it serve, for example, as an introduction to a particular topic, or should it deepen your knowledge of something with which you are already familiar? Will you be expected to be able to compare what you are reading with something that you have already read? Being aware of such questions helps you understand what you are supposed to look for. In college courses, reading is rarely undertaken for its own purpose. Rather, it is undertaken in order for students to be able to do something further, to discuss the reading in class, to use the reading to inform their responses on an examination, to integrate elements of what they have read into an argument in a paper. To get a sense for the elements of close reading for particular purposes, see Box 4.2. Reading to understand implies being able to *read to use* what one has learned in some other activity.

Following Elbow, we highlight two distinct approaches to reading. The first is the time-honored academic reading to critique. It involves identifying assumptions, elaborating their implications, and evaluating them. It focuses on pointing out strengths and weaknesses. It entertains alternatives. The complementary process of reading to believe or endorse asks in what ways the argument or presentation makes sense. It looks for the presuppositions that one would have to accept in order to accept what the material has to

Box 4.2 Close reading

Forms of Close Reading

- *Reading to understand* involves
  - getting the point
  - separating central from peripheral
  - grasping context
  - identifying arguments
  - identifying evidence on which arguments are based
  - uncovering assumptions that shape arguments
  - identifying and interpreting conventions of presentation.

- *Reading to critique* involves
  - assessing strengths and weaknesses
  - elaborating implications of assumptions
  - testing theory against data, either those provided by the author or others
  - comparing alternative arguments
  - assessing whether an argument actually accomplishes what it claims to.

- *Reading to endorse* involves
  - asking about the ways in which the argument makes sense
  - temporarily suspending disbelief
  - avoiding premature negative criticism
  - determining the criteria or assumptions on which it makes sense
  - provisionally accepting the argument
  - determining how acceptance of the argument entails acceptance of other arguments, premises, or ideas.

- *Reading to use* involves
  - asking what the argument allows you to do or see
  - considering how would you extend the argument to cover other cases/data/examples
  - determining how would you situate this argument among others on the same or similar topics.

say. It pursues implications, asking if the premises of a particular reading are accepted, what other premises or conclusions will also have to be accepted.

Exercises and questions for further thought can be found at https://www. bloomsbury.com/cw/the-religious-studies-skills-book/skill-building-exercises/ chapter-four/

5

Critical Thinking

The character William of Baskerville in Umberto Eco's medieval murder mystery *The Name of the Rose* challenges received wisdom when he announces that "Books are not made to be believed, but to be subjected to inquiry. When we consider a book, we mustn't ask ourselves what it says but what it means."[1] The same can be said of art, music, literature, and film; the same can be said of actors, politicians, teachers, and lawyers. And the same can be said of ideas and behaviors of all sorts, including ideas and behaviors related to religion. Although some students resist this and remain credulous in the face of all sorts of information, *the goal of a college education is to learn how to take care in examining one's own thinking and the thinking of others.*

Most departments of religious studies and many universities include "critical thinking" in their stated outcomes for students and majors in the discipline. Critical thinking has taken an expected place alongside other standard outcomes, such as familiarity with fundamental terms and concepts, exposure to key methodologies and theoretical approaches, and competence in communication. This is true at all levels of higher education, from two- and four-year programs to large state schools to small liberal arts or church-affiliated institutions. All teachers strike some balance between teaching "the facts" or "content" and teaching how to think.

Critical thinking is mentioned at the department level and above on many colleges and university websites. Grinnell College, a small liberal arts institution in the Midwest, presents the following in its mission statement: "The College aims to graduate individuals who can think clearly, who can speak and write persuasively and even eloquently, who can evaluate critically both their own and others' ideas, who can acquire new knowledge, and who are prepared in life and work to use their knowledge and their abilities to serve the common good."[2] Likewise, a large public school, the University of Nevada, Reno, presents the mission of the College of Liberal

Arts this way: "The college provides students with the knowledge, critical thinking skills and creative experience they need to navigate in a complex global environment."[3] Three Rivers Community College in Connecticut "provides a well-rounded and rewarding educational experience with an emphasis on critical thinking, effective communication, and the College's institutional values."[4] As a phrase, "critical thinking" has weight in higher education, but how the phrase is defined and how it can best be taught are open questions.[5]

This lack of clear definition has fed a sense of despair in some circles. Several recent studies have questioned how effective colleges and universities are in teaching critical habits of mind. Standardized tests devised to evaluate critical thinking have been the target of criticism by faculty if not by administrators. One such test is the backbone of a study published as *Academically Adrift: Limited Learning on College Campuses*, which surveyed more than 2,000 students at a range of institutional types, finding that more than one-third of college students did not show improvement in learning (particularly understood as skills in critical thinking) over four years of college education. Many faculty members viewed *Academically Adrift* with either suspicion or a sense of defeat, wondering what has or has not been happening in their classrooms when they are teaching "critical thinking."

Despite such studies, teachers in many disciplines tend to consider teaching critical thinking as they understand it to be absolutely central to their work in the classroom. Teachers see critical thinking skills as transferable well beyond academia. Students who are critical thinkers are useful in many jobs, and they tend to be lifelong learners who are adept at formulating questions, gathering evidence, and reaching conclusions. As Ken Bain notes throughout *What the Best College Teachers Do*, the most effective teachers make intellectual development through critical thinking a staple of their courses.[6] His follow-up book, *What the Best College Students Do*, argues that the best students learn how to make connections across disciplines and engage in deep learning.[7] Critical thinking can be the key to interesting, engaging employment well beyond college and, in general, interesting engagement with the world.

Critical thinking is considered characteristic of college education, as it is a step well beyond the lower order learning that is characteristic of much K-12 education. Students in primary education often learn through rote memorization rather than more holistic thinking. For instance, one reason that history is often disliked by students is that it is associated with the boring memorization of names, dates, and events that are easily assessed on standardized exams. If you excelled at social studies in K-12 education, you are likely skilled at memorization. To excel at history in college, you will need to engage in deep learning that involves critical thinking. You will need to ask good questions. You will need to sift through evidence. You will need to make connections. And you will need to go beyond "the facts" to deeper meanings.

One lamentable result of this state of affairs in primary education is that you may not be in the habit of asking "why?" Why is this the way it is? How could it be otherwise? How does what I'm learning fit in with what I already know? Why does that matter beyond the classroom? Asking questions in the search for answers is a habit that is not generally rewarded in primary education, but it is essential to success in college. Asking questions will help you go beyond personal opinion to consider evidence and counter-arguments. Developing structured habits of questioning, classifying, comparing, and considering will open the door to new ways of thinking.

Like the term "religion," "critical thinking" admits of many definitions and no consensus across disciplines. It can mean something rather vague, such as developing interpretive distance and learning to take multiple perspectives, or it can mean something very specific, such as mastering deductive logic. It can be defined very simply as "disciplined analysis" or more extensively as shown below. The term is capacious but not inclusive of all types of thought. "Critical thinking" generally excludes other types of higher-order thinking, such as certain kinds of problem solving and creativity.[8] Figuring out how to fix a car engine does not require the kind of critical thinking discussed here, nor does imagining and following through on painting an abstract triptych.

A critical thinking framework seems fitting for a discipline such as religious studies that seeks neither to promote nor undermine particular ways of understanding the world but seeks, above all, to analyze and understand them. As described in Chapter 3, religious studies demands a certain emotional distance from the subject that allows analytical, comparative, and even evaluative work. For many departments of religious studies and most faculty members, critical thinking is a basic academic competence that students will take into the world with them when they leave each class and the institution. This is a high bar, however, because worldviews tend to be difficult to change. The set of presuppositions we carry around shapes our understanding of the world. Many of those assumptions might be true or false; we might recognize them clearly or be completely unaware of them. Either way, worldviews are often fixed; people tend to grab on to them for comfort, particularly when new ideas are presented. Critical thinking disrupts, at least temporarily, that sense of comfort and familiarity.

But what is critical thinking? There are many definitions, but at its most basic, *critical thinking is systematic, careful inquiry that follows the evidence wherever it leads*. Critical thinkers tend to be curious about why things are the way they are and want to understand how things got that way. They do not stop at asking simple factual questions and accepting whatever answer they are given. Critical thinkers keep an open mind, ask good questions—that is, questions that are well defined and lead to answers based on evidence. Critical thinkers can be swayed by the preponderance of evidence. They learn to sift through sources for those that are useful and those that are questionable. They identify false dichotomies, circular arguments, and rhetorical devices that can misdirect the reader.

The traits of developed critical thinkers are many. Are you curious and willing to sift through large amounts of information? Do you know how to sort and categorize that information, to determine what is useful to a particular argument and what might be secondary or irrelevant? Can you communicate effectively to explain and support your arguments in ways suited to particular audiences? Are you aware of your own biases? Do you aim to work from a place of objectivity and logic? Do you shun overgeneralization and embrace complexity? Religious studies classes almost always require you to practice each of these skills.

As explained at the end of the previous chapter, an academically critical stance on an issue is not a combative or aggressive stance. This word—"critical"—used in this way derives from the Greek for "to judge or discern," and it refers to careful evaluation in a range of endeavors. There are many formal disciplines that enshrine this word: biblical criticism, literary criticism, music criticism, art criticism, and film criticism are all approaches to bodies of work for the purpose of evaluating and judging the worth of that work. *Critical thinking is not negative or corrosive (as the word "critical" can seem to imply) but, rather, evaluative and productive: it is a way of using evidence to support argumentative claims.* A critical thinker looks for patterns and seeks to understand their significance within a complex web of factors. This requires a degree of temporary neutrality or "bracketing" in handling the evidence; a willingness to entertain ideas that might not be native or agreeable to you; and a sense of curiosity that drives inquiry.

Most religious studies courses by design will expose you to alternative beliefs, practices, and values that might be at odds with those you have learned through family and culture. Few courses require only memorization of ideas; most require students to assimilate and evaluate information, a task that seems daunting in introductory classes. The goal of many teachers is to help you move past the tendency to accept generalizations, stereotypes, prejudice, and rigidity of thought by helping you become aware of your own assumptions and biases. Your teachers aim to steer you away from emotional responses and unconsidered assumptions to rational, evidence-based conclusions. It is very possible that you will go into class with your own narratives about the history of Christianity, about what Jews do or do not do, about what Hindus might or might not believe. The disciplined academic work in religious studies aims to correct misperceptions and open minds.

In religious studies classes, students learn to think in certain ways about various phenomena, some of which actually happened (the deaths of 909 members of the Peoples Temple poisoned by cyanide-laced Flav-r-Aid in Guyana on November 18, 1978)[9]; some of which is believed by some people to have happened (e.g. that on the death of a Dalai Lama his being will be reincarnated in another person, who can be identified by High Lamas and Tibetan government officials); and some of which is purely abstract but recognizable in various forms (e.g. cruelty, hatred, wisdom, and religion itself). Unlike the so-called "hard" sciences, religious studies takes seriously claims that people make about both the material and immaterial worlds. As a student of religion, you must learn to think critically about a range of objects of study, some of which are merely conjectural to the outsider but which are central to the insider. Consequently, certain moves common to critical thinking, such as detecting fallacies in formal arguments, do not apply in all contexts, because "logic" or "truth" are not necessarily at issue.

As the opening quote from William of Baskerville suggests, the tension between learning what to think and how to think is ageless. He does not want to simply digest what he reads without question: he wants to subject his books to inquiry. A glance back at the medieval ideal of higher education gives us perspective on how expectations of students have changed. As we discussed in Chapter 1, in the days of the fictional William of Baskerville, students were taught what to think, a goal accomplished by teachers who placed emphasis on rote memorization and the replication of traditional ideas in conventional ways. New ideas were not prized; students were largely judged on their ability to express what had been expressed before. Even today, the testing that is so pervasive in K-12 schools tends to focus on memorization and facts. Standardized tests on the whole tend to opt in favor of assessing factual knowledge over assessing the processes behind building knowledge.

Today, however, college faculty who favor teaching critical thinking are often opposed to education that focuses on memorization, rote learning, and standardized assessments, all modes of education that were in favor until recent decades in higher education. Most college classes will require mastery of a particular set of content, but most will also ask you to do more than just learn "the facts." Not all religious studies classes focus on critical thinking. A survey of syllabi in religious studies indicates that many classes are still taught on a lecture/examination model, one that is unlikely to foster critical thinking skills explicitly. A focus on facts and concepts is important for developing a certain kind of religious literacy, but it is ill-suited to teaching critical thinking about those facts, particularly within a single semester. *For critical thinking to occur, you must have some degree of content knowledge, but content knowledge is never enough.*

A brief history of critical thinking

You can better understand what is expected of you in any class if you know why your teacher focuses on it. "Critical thinking" as a term was not in common use in higher education until the early twentieth century, and it only became common across institutions in the last few decades. Yet it has a history that is worth attending, because the habits of mind it requires have long been prized in academic study. Indeed, its roots are ancient, traced to the pedagogy of Socrates, who peppered his students with questions in order to allow them to understand, dismiss, or strengthen their views. Socrates wanted his students *to know why they believed what they believed*, and a key part of that understanding came from questioning their most dearly held assumptions and beliefs. Socratic questioning enabled a student to attain awareness and insight through the skilled guidance of a teacher. This method is a staple of many college classrooms, although students often mistake the method for laziness on the part of the teacher. You might find yourself frustrated by a teacher who asks more questions than she answers, but for many this is a technique to encourage higher orders of thinking. You might want a teacher to just tell you what she knows, but that approach can slow the complex process of developing critical thinking skills. Discussion is, in many classes, a key method for developing those skills.

For Socrates and his contemporaries, these sorts of dialogues were part of a commitment to question authority. Socrates' questions encouraged using relevant and reliable evidence, examining assumptions closely, and looking at implications of certain lines of thought in order to undermine unwarranted or outmoded beliefs and traditions. Authority for authority's sake held no power when it could be questioned on many fronts by those willing to do the work. This tradition of speaking truth to power continued on in the work of Plato and Aristotle as well as the Greek skeptics, who challenged appearances to uncover deeper truths.

Critical thinkers thus worked to challenge authority, although similar moves of critical thought could also be used to buttress existing authority. For instance, theologian Thomas Aquinas was a master of the scholastic method of posing a question, listing objections, and replying to those objections in systematic ways. Although theologian Aquinas's championing of reason in the thirteenth century was in service to the Christian church, his emphasis on evidence and the refutation of error became a staple of critical thinking curricula centuries later. His conclusions might have been those of the church, but he modeled a type of inquiry that many still use today.

Several other thinkers contributed to this legacy. The humanists of the fifteenth and sixteenth centuries, such as Erasmus, set about translating classical texts and opening them to critical analysis. In 1502 Francis Bacon published *The Plan for the Advancement of Learning*, in which he encouraged his readers to reject unquestioned authority and uncritical thought. Bacon and his intellectual heirs, including René Descartes and Thomas More, led the way for what we know now as scientific inquiry.[10]

The most direct ancestor of our understanding of critical thinking is the American philosopher and educational theorist John Dewey, who advocated "reflective thought," a kind of thinking requiring healthy skepticism, an open mind, and suspended judgment. For Dewey and his heirs in education today, critical thinking is active, in contrast to passive acceptance of the ideas of others. As he wrote in *How We Think* in 1910,

> The essence of critical thinking is suspended judgment; and the essence of this suspense is inquiry to determine the nature of the problem before proceeding to attempt its solution. This, more than any other thing, transforms mere inference into tested inference, suggested conclusions into proof.[11]

Dewey calls here for a sort of bracketing of personal judgments to allow space for thoughtful investigation that leads to meaningful insights. This requires slowing down in order to ponder the nature of a problem before leaping to an answer. You might find this difficult if you have been trained through timed and standardized tests. You might want an answer to be given to you rather than having to work an answer out for yourself. *Thinking well takes time and focused effort, but the habits you develop will be useful in whatever career you choose.*

Elements of Dewey's ideas continue on in all disciplines. Stephen Brookfield, an expert in adult learning and critical thinking, argues that "thinking critically—reflecting on the assumptions underlying our and others' ideas and actions, and contemplating alternative ways of thinking and living—is one of the important ways in which we become adults."[12] Becoming a thinking adult involves shaking the foundations of what one thought one knew, a process that brings with it a sense of disequilibrium and, for some, anxiety. Passively accepting what you are told can be comforting, but asking questions that might destabilize what is taken to be true can be upsetting. For all advocates of critical thinking, this discomfort is a necessary part of the process. Critical thinking stands in opposition to narrow-mindedness, naivety, conformity, and inconsistency in argumentation. It calls for clear, fair-minded, and active intellectual engagement. Critical thinking is harder than believing whatever you are told. But the payoff is great.

How to think critically

Critical thinking as a core value appears to be pervasive in higher education, although, as explained above, clear definitions of the phrase are rare. A 1972 study of 40,000 faculty members by the American Council on Education showed that 97 percent identified their most important pedagogical goal as critical thinking. Studies of incoming college students and conceptualizations of developmental stages tend to characterize first-year college students as dualistic (or black and white) thinkers who are very self-focused and have had little if any academic practice with structured critical thinking. You might notice your peers in class responding more emotionally than intellectually to complex issues. You might also see them mistake personal anecdote for evidence. These are common early stages of learning to distinguish critical thinking from other sorts of problem solving. They are where we all begin.

The simplest way to understand critical thinking is to break the phrase into its parts. *Critical thinking involves thinking.* This requires time spent considering, reflecting, and weighing issues, problems, and questions in a disciplined way. Thinking requires observation, collection, examination, and evaluation of evidence. It involves making judgments and connections. It involves asking thoughtful questions and positing hypotheses. The first half of the phrase is often misunderstood. As highlighted earlier in this chapter, "critical" in academia does not mean negative or combative, though critical thinking can produce negative conclusions. Learning to be critical means learning to make judgments by breaking a problem down to its parts and analyzing it based on other relevant factors. Being critical also involves being objective to the extent that is possible. One can only be productively critical from a distance.

Dr. Peter Facione, a philosopher who currently works as a consultant on strategic thinking, spearheaded the Delphi Report (formally titled "Critical Thinking: A Statement of Consensus for Purposes of Educational Assessment and Instruction"), which was published in 1990. The study provided an articulation of factors involved in critical thinking in its consensus statement. This sentence is complex and full of unfamiliar terminology, which will be explained below.

> We understand critical thinking to be purposeful, self-regulatory judgment which results in interpretation, analysis, evaluation, and inference, as well as explanation of the evidential, conceptual, methodological, criteriological, or contextual considerations upon which that judgment is based.

This statement, which is full of SAT-worthy vocabulary, is both idealistic and realistic. The contributors to the report know that critical thinking is within the grasp of those who wish to develop it even as they recognize the challenges of doing it well. The statement also makes clear that critical thinking is a set of practices as well as habits of mind. The ideal critical thinker is one whose predisposition is to examine all things thoroughly and carefully, using specific tools and keeping in mind particular considerations. We will examine each of these in turn, and you may be surprised to discover you already do some of these in your daily life without realizing.

There are some complex ideas in the quotation from the Delphi Report, above. The first part of that quotation includes the terms interpretation, analysis, evaluation, inference, and explanation. While those intellectual processes are listed in a sequence, in fact they often overlap and don't follow a strict order. *Interpretation* is a most basic level of decoding. Interpretation refers to understanding information and being able to communicate that information to others. People interpret things every day, such as a nutritional information chart on a cereal box, a pie chart in the newspaper, or a piece of mail that they identify as "junk." More exposure to a particular type of information generally increases one's literacy in interpreting that information. Someone who receives piles of credit card offers can decode the envelopes to determine which to open; someone who is limiting sugar will quickly compare a cereal with others without necessarily having to look at more than one box.

Interpretation is often inflected with the reader's conceptions and assumptions. One can interpret the intentions of another person in ways unimagined by that person. This is to be expected in any thoughtful consideration of an idea or action. Interpretation should not become completely subjective, however. Facts, evidence, and context should be brought to bear on any interpretation, alongside a recognition that individual perspectives matter. To claim that Cap'n Crunch is not loaded with sugar is wishful thinking that flies in the face of the facts on the label. A preference for Cap'n Crunch is fine, but claiming that preference is based on its low sugar content makes no objective sense.

Analysis supports interpretation. Analysis breaks a whole into parts to examine each alone, often with the goal of bringing them together again in some insightful way. Comparison (as described in Chapter 6 of this volume) is an analytical exercise. Analysis consists of labeling and categorizing each element of a whole in order to connect bits of information in useful ways and be able to explain those connections to others. To continue with the cereal example, one could examine boxes of cereal to answer "What sorts of marketing appeal to those who prefer sugary cereals?" An analysis of the cereal aisle would lead an observer to conclude that those who prefer sugary cereals are drawn to cartoonish, brightly colored boxes, while those who prefer "natural" cereals tend toward earthy colors and images of grains. There are outliers to this generalization, and there are questions to be asked about how this situation came about. At the level of analysis, however, one can examine what is there for possible types, categories, and conclusions.

Evaluation requires a certain level of knowledge within a particular context. Evaluation has to do with judging the validity or credibility of a source. It focuses on the worth or quality of a particular claim or source. This goes well beyond preference or subjective judgment: it is based on reasons and backed by evidence. Evaluation can come into play when one has decided to change up the cereal routine and find a cereal with higher whole grain content. To find that information and to compare with one's current cereal, one has to know how to read nutritional labels. More importantly, one has to know that those labels are required to list certain information that has been verified by experts. If one has reason to trust the scientists and nutritionists who enter that information, one can easily evaluate one cereal against another. This is more complicated, clearly, in the case of texts from various sources and no clear expert or authority validating the data.

Inference is making an intellectual leap to a conclusion from the evidence at hand. Inferences can be justified or unjustified, depending on the circumstance. Those who know a field well are more capable of making justified inferences, because they have a better sense of the context. Imagine standing in the cereal aisle of the grocery store in England, with no time to read nutritional labels. Which is a sugary cereal? Experience with cereal marketing in America will likely lead one away from the earth-toned, grain-decorated boxes and toward those in more garish colors with cartoonish characters on the box. The result might well be a surprise, but given what one knows of cereal packaging, it is a good bet the child-friendly box contains a lot of sugar.

Explanation is restating with clarity and added perspective when needed. Explanation pulls all of these elements together so that another person can follow along with an argument. When questioned at home about a cereal purchase, one might explain that "I am changing my diet for the better. I have chosen to stop buying Cap'n Crunch, which has 12 grams of sugar in each ¾ cup, in favor of Super Fiber Delights, which has no added sugar." When asked what prompted this change, the argument can be expanded to add perspective on this lifestyle change. Explanation is stating clearly what, when, where, how, and why, depending on the argument. It helps others see how any argument holds together.

The second part of the quotation from the Delphi Report, above, includes "evidential, conceptual, methodological, criteriological, or contextual considerations." "Evidence" is data, specific information that is relevant to the issue, question, or problem. Data is interpreted by the thinker through analysis and inference to reach a conclusion. But one needs to be clear about the type, amount, and validity of data available in any study. What counts as evidence depends on the question being asked. In the cereal example, the nutritional label and the size and weight of the box can provide testable data for certain questions; the artwork and fonts can be evidence for other sorts of investigations. The questions you ask determine the evidence that matters.

One also must account for any conceptual notions that might shape the study. *Concepts* are, most basically, ideas or thoughts, often in generalized form (such as "justice," "truth," or "beauty"). They are abstract and often open to interpretation. Many would say they think that "justice" is part of a democratic society, but when pressed to define "justice" they reach an impasse. Is justice an inherent right? If so, what does it consist of? The right to a jury of one's peers? To use a popular phrase, what constitutes "social justice"? Is social justice the same for everyone? Conceptual assumptions underlie all study, and the critical thinker should make those conceptual or theoretical biases as clear as possible. To continue with our example, "cereal" is a conceptual category that helps manufacturers and retailers sell a particular kind of product. There is no essential "cerealness" that defines a manufactured cereal, and there is no legal definition of the term. For some, cereal must be paired with milk; for others, cereal should go with yogurt. Some would argue that breakfast cereal in milk is best categorized as "soup." Either way, people tend to understand the concept of "cereal" without having to list every type.

Methodology also matters. A "method" is a system of rules and principles by which one conducts research in a particular field of study. The broadest categories of method are quantitative and qualitative, but there are many other methodologies in religious studies, such as historical-critical, ethnographic, phenomenological, and hermeneutical. Historical-critical approaches tend to be text- and context-based and are often set in a particular time and place or theme. Ethnographic studies involve living subjects observed and/or interviewed in their natural habitat. Phenomenological studies focus on religious experience and are often comparative across cultures. Hermeneutical studies focus on interpreting biblical texts. There are many subtypes of each of these methods. One could do a quantitative study of cereals' nutritional information and popularity; one could interview people in the store about their favorite cereals; one could visit a cereal factory and get the perspectives of the workers; or one could read texts from the mid-nineteenth century, when cereal was first invented, to trace the earliest development of breakfast cereals in America. Again, the method one chooses depends, in part, on the question one asks.

Criteriological considerations are those that help one narrow down a subject. What criteria are required for evidence to influence this particular investigation? If one were investigating the rise of sugary cereals, how would one proceed? Would it be a regional study of advertising or a more global study, necessitating a trip to the Museum of Brands, Packaging, and Advertising in London? What level of sugar constitutes "sugary"? Will the study look at the earliest phases of this trend or track those changes to today? Defining the criteria for any study is essential to focused and meaningful results.

Contextual considerations place the subject of study within a particular historical or cultural context. This kind of careful contextualization helps the thinker avoid blanket generalizations and trying to do too much. Context and criteria make research projects feasible and more easily understandable. If one is wondering about the types of products that are included in the category "breakfast cereal," one can approach the subject in several ways. A study that compares several local grocery stores might yield interesting results, particularly if some cereals are placed in the "international" aisle in some stores and not in others. This kind of local context can bring a focus to any study and can shed light on socio-economic and other factors that drive people to shop in particular locations. Other studies are limited by chronological parameters or by geographical or linguistic boundaries.

All of these elements play a part in thinking critically about any text or issue. As the extended cereal example indicates, people use these skills regularly in real life: we are already accomplished explainers, inferrers, evaluators, and analyzers in many areas. Walking through a particular example germane to the field and to public discourse will help illustrate how they all work together.

Test case: Creationism in public schools

Critical thinking is essential to doing the work of religious studies as well as to the work involved in setting public policy and making laws. The elements described above—interpretation, analysis, evaluation, inference, and explanation—are all part of reading and assessing any extended argument. People make claims all the time in the public sphere, and society only functions well when citizens are well informed about the issues under discussion. Critical thinking skills are essential in thinking through the complexities of any argument. Critical thinking in college can help you be a more effective citizen who can weigh the evidence and consider all sides of an issue, recognizing what is at stake and thoughtfully considering solutions.

Here we will move through the steps of critical thinking about issues surrounding teaching creationism in public schools. This subject, which is often in the news, could be taken up in an introductory general education course, in a course about Christianity in America, or in a course on creationism. Many school systems have faced challenges to their science curriculums by parents and others who think creationism should be taught alongside evolution in public school classrooms. It has been the subject of considerable debate in politics, law, and among religious groups. How would you go about thinking through this complex issue?

To use critical thinking skills in interpreting, analyzing, evaluating, and explaining this question, we will follow a simplified path from forming a question to reaching a considered, reflective conclusion that is supported by evidence (see Box 5.1 for a selection of uncritical statements alongside critical thinking questions). The specific question we are trying to answer is "Should creationism be taught in public schools?" Taking each of these elements in turn should help illustrate the steps in developing an analytical stance to the issue.

Identify the problem: This first step seems obvious, but it can be deceptively difficult. The question as posed is quite broad: Should creationism be taught in public schools? That breadth invites definitions and contextualization. The word "should" indicates an ethical question rather than one of practicality. "Can creationism be taught in public schools?" involves either a legal judgment or a judgment about the capabilities of teachers. "Should" muddies the waters a bit, as it calls for judgment based on evidence.

Other definitions are important, too. Which "creationism"? Creationism is most broadly defined as a belief that the universe is the result of divine creation, not natural processes. Yet there are several definable versions of creationism just in contemporary Christianity. Young-Earth Creationists believe the earth is less than 10,000 years old, while Old-Earth Creationists accept the findings of scientists that the earth is about 4.5 billion years old. Old-Earth Creationists have several notable subgroups, including Gap Creationists, Day-Age Creationists, and Progressive Creationists. In addition, those who believe in evolution but still hold to theistic origins and/or sustenance admit of their own subgroups.

There are "creationisms" in other religions as well, some of which also depend on the narrative in Genesis 1–3 for support. Islamic creationism is one such example. Creation narratives from cultures around the world posit multiple creator deities or describe natural processes at work in the creation of the world and humanity. Others, such as the Church of the Flying Spaghetti Monster, also known as Pastafarians, challenge the Genesis narrative by proposing an equally unverifiable narrative in which the Flying Spaghetti Monster created the world with His Noodly Appendages. In other words, defining "creationism" can be very complex, but a clear definition is pivotal to any constructive argument.

So how do we identify the problem? We do so partly by interpreting the question through definition and contextualization. This requires interpretation of the words being used as well as a consideration of the context in which the question has meaning and weight.

The next step is to **define any relevant context**. This requires us to identify the facts and circumstances surrounding the issue. This also requires interpretation: what are we looking at in this particular case? In most cases, we are looking at more conservative Christian groups challenging curricular decisions made in public schools. The broader context is American culture, which permits religious freedom of a particular sort in public life. Similar issues have arisen in many other countries around the world, but that is not the focus here. The more specific context is American public education, but state contexts can vary widely, with more conservative viewpoints more common in Texas and Alabama than in Massachusetts and California, for example. Prior legal decisions are also part of the context.

An even more specific context is that of the science classroom, where evolution is taught as the scientific theory of human origins. Some Christian creationists have called their stance "scientific creationism" or "creation science," labeling that can confuse or clarify, depending on your point of view. The most specific context might be an individual classroom, where a particular teacher might espouse a materialist view that excludes the validity of theistic views or quite the opposite. Either specific situation adds a new dimension to any inquiry, and specific test cases are often helpful in showing nuances of situation and possibility.

With the context defined, we can now begin to **evaluate choices**. Choices in this case are divided into two broad options: allowing theistic ideas into science classrooms or excluding them. To include theistic ideas, a science curriculum can still focus on evolution but admit some flaws in the theory; teach all creation stories from around the world, including satire like Pastafarianism and religious ideas such as those espoused in Raelianism (which sees our world as having been created by advanced beings from other planets and identifies those beings with the God of the Genesis account); teach fringe "scientific" theories, such as panspermianism, which holds that life on earth was "seeded" in various ways from space; teach a representative sampling of creation stories from around the world; or not address questions about the origins of human life at all.

On the other side of the argument, science teachers can refuse to mention or accept theological perspectives on the origins of the planet and of life. Other compromises are worth considering: allowing dissenting students to opt out of lessons about evolution or giving individual teachers the freedom to choose what to do in their classrooms. All of these options should be tested against existing laws and considered within particular contexts for legality and feasibility. What rights are individuals afforded in this context? What freedoms are permitted?

The next step is to **analyze options**. This is where analysis and evaluation come into play. It is also where criteriological and conceptual ideas should be made explicit. What is the best course of action, knowing what we know? Each thinker has a set of assumptions that shape thought and action, and this is a good point at which to make those clear. Science teachers might well have different starting assumptions than evangelical parents, and high school students might well start from a different baseline than laboratory scientists. A district court judge will examine the case with different eyes than a school principal. Each option outlined above should be weighed for feasibility and fairness. The baseline against which those options are considered should be made explicit: is the goal to provide equal voice to all sides? To protect the freedom of religious people? To promote democracy? To allow professional teachers the right to free speech in the classroom on issues pertaining to their training? To teach all sides of the controversy for students to weigh for themselves?

One of the final steps in critical thinking is to **list reasons explicitly**. Once a thinker has weighed the evidence within a particular context, he or she should be ready to justify making one choice over another. If the conclusion is to disallow the teaching of creationism in any form in public schools, the argument should make the reasons for that decision clear and specific. If the key value being weighed is intellectual freedom, the writer should explain why that is pivotal. This may sometimes seem obvious to you and not something that needs to be spelled out. Yet no reader can fully understand a logic that is not made explicit, so always spell things out (even if they are obvious to you). If you are asked to write a position paper on this subject, make it possible for your reader to follow your logic and the evidence you have chosen so they can assess the validity of your argument.

Box 5.1 Critical thinking questions

Uncritical statements	Critical thinking questions
All Roman Catholics in Northern Ireland are terrorists.	What sorts of evidence (if any) support this claim? How does one define "terrorist"? Is there a chronological frame for this claim? Can the word "all" ever be justified in this kind of claim?
Tide must be the best laundry detergent because that commercial said so.	Is it possible that claim is made for marketing purposes and is not supported by laboratory evidence? Why should you believe claims made in a commercial?
This is a lousy novel.	What are your expectations for a novel? Are those expectations different from those of contemporaries when the novel was written? What particular things (e.g. plot, language, characters) led you to dislike it? Are those elements perhaps necessary to the author's purpose?
Nobody should be vegetarian, because bacon is tasty.	Does the reason given here really support the conclusion? Why should the tastiness of any food have any effect on all people's dietary choices? What would the consequences be if this sort of thinking became public policy?

The final step in critical thinking is often overlooked. It is important to take some time to allow for **self-correction**. One often becomes compelled by a particular position and easily swayed by its allure. This can result in a skewed argument that fails to consider all sides of an issue. It is always worth taking the time to ask what might have been missed in the process of analysis and decision making. What premises and assumptions shaped the study? What biases or misunderstandings might need to be corrected? You might find this difficult to see in your own work but very easy to spot in others' arguments. As with any skill, the more practice you have at thinking through issues, the more easily you will be able to identify limitations and biases.

How to think critically in religious studies

All academic disciplines are ways of thinking, and thus critical thinkers in particular disciplines will adopt particular approaches. In philosophy, critical thinking focuses on the study of informal and formal logic. Critical thinking in English is often the study of rhetorical devices and persuasion. As John McPeck, author of several books on teaching critical thinking, argues, "Thinking, by definition, is always thinking about something, and that something can never be 'everything in general' but must always be something in particular."[13] If that is true, then *there is a particular way (or ways) of "thinking like a scholar of religion," a way that folds critical thinking deep within its profile even as it approaches the subject from multiple angles*.

Without experience in critical thinking, your natural initial reaction might be to respond in uncritical ways. Most people tend to think locally: "our" group is most often considered special and correct. This seemingly universal trait encourages mental habits that justify rigidity and defensiveness in the face of new information. Practicing critical thinking will enable you to become aware of and control this tendency, if present. Critical thinking asks thinkers to consider other ways of understanding things without necessarily accepting those understandings. Widow burning (*suttee*) in India might seem morally repugnant, but the goal of the religious studies student is to understand the culture that makes such a practice reasonable in its particular context. Critical thinking might call you to think through issues such as child marriage in certain small sects and denigration of Muslims in the American press, among many other things. Sometimes, practices that seem repugnant in other cultures are easier to consider than those close to home.

It is interesting to note that what faculty want to achieve in a given class or in the broader degree program may be at odds with your own expectations of the class. One influential study, the so-called Spellings Report, produced in 2005 by the US Commission on the Future of Higher Education convened by Secretary of Education Margaret Spellings and titled *A Test of Leadership: Charting the Future of US Higher Education*, showed that students and parents looked at higher education as a means to the end of a good job, while faculty saw the goal of higher education as skills in critical thinking and problem solving.[14] Although the two goals are not mutually incompatible, this divide is real, and you should be aware of it as you choose courses. A course with little obvious connection to training for skills in a particular job might well be the best training for critical thinking, a skill that is broadly applicable.

Student interest in spiritual growth in college is most fully explored in the Higher Education Research Institute (HERI) report titled "The Spiritual Lives of College Students: A National Study of College Students' Search for Meaning and Purpose."[15] This study presents a wide range of findings and notes the investment on college campuses in student services that cater to students' religious and spiritual needs. Students' strong interest in personal growth and religious involvement can come into conflict with teacher expectations in religious studies courses. *Students enrolled in an introductory survey course on world religions should not expect that the focus will be on their own experience*. After all, faculty members have their own private lives, in which they are religious or not religious, "spiritual" or not. For many, their own choices do not affect their expectations of students. Faculty in humanities disciplines are some of the most open to fostering students' spiritual and religious lives. Yet, again, those values are almost never part of assessing student intellectual and academic progress, as discussed in Chapter 3 on bracketing.

This disjunction between the curriculum and students' expectations tends to feed a misunderstanding that religious studies classes in particular aim at tearing down students' worldviews, that they are critical of religion in the negative sense. Religious studies faculty are trained in the academic study of religion, not, in general, in pastoral care, counseling, or spiritual growth. They are experts in helping students see other ways of viewing the world, to reconsider their intellectual commitments, and to become aware of why they believe what they believe. Teachers are committed to the idea that there are facts students must wrestle with and that there are stereotypes and generalizations they ought to shed. Teachers tend to believe that doing so will strengthen thinking skills and produce more able and thoughtful citizens. Students and parents sometimes bristle at the kinds of topics raised in religious studies classes. The goal, however, is not destructive; rather, teachers in religious studies aim to help students understand different ways of seeing the world.

Like many other students, you might find yourself resisting reading a text considered sacred by people outside of your own faith tradition. You might find yourself confused or even offended by the ideas in other people's sacred texts. That resistance is likely based on a mix of intellectual, religious, and emotional issues. Alternately, you might describe yourself as "spiritual but not religious" or atheist and thus might reject religious authority, refusing even to consider the ways religious authority matters to those in and out of any given faith tradition. Both attitudes get in the way of critical thinking. Teachers thus aim to help students unlearn habits of thinking that have become both routine and useful to them. *It is precisely these seemingly solidified habits of mind that get in the way of meaningful learning, so you might need to unlearn habits of thinking that have become routine and useful to you.*

As a multi-disciplinary field, religious studies approaches critical thinking from a variety of disciplinary perspectives: its faculty and students think anthropologically, archeologicially, historically, literarily, philosophically, and sociologically. The ways faculty express their understanding of critical thinking varies, with some being very explicit about expectations and others using the term with little explanation of what they mean. Syllabi might include certain key words and phrases in a section on learning outcomes: critical reflection, critical analysis, argument analysis, interpreting, applying, analyzing, inferring, synthesizing, conceptualizing, or "thinking about one's thinking" (also called metacognition). Others might refer to using relevant evidence, recognizing unstated values or assumptions, or evaluating arguments. You should be able to tell if a teacher is focused on teaching critical thinking skills if questions and not answers are a large part of the class dynamic.

These skills can be developed in several different ways in the course of a semester, and the topic of the class often drives the degree to which critical thinking becomes a learning outcome. Introductory "World Religions" classes tend to focus more on content than on critical thought, while classes that focus on ethical issues tend to focus more on critical thought than mastering a domain of content.

Faculty in religious studies have various ways to assess your critical thinking skills. Most recognize that basic literacy about facts and concepts is a necessary starting point for any critical thought. It is true that the world today is so interconnected electronically that an English-speaking student in Malaysia can find the temperature in Normal, Illinois, within seconds. Yet an informed conversation cannot happen when the parties involved start from wildly different premises. A person who works in the corporate world can pick up a newspaper and read the business section with greater acuity than a music teacher might. A person who works in medicine will read a recent journal article on cutting-edge research with greater understanding and insight than someone who works in a plant nursery. And a person who works with small children will likely have far more ability to read the signs and signals of children's needs and wants than someone who never spends time with children.

Accordingly, when a Southern Baptist student reads an article about the destruction of the *eruvim*, or Jewish ritual enclosures, in New York, she probably cannot parse the passage as deftly as can a scholar of Judaism. The article might explain how eighteen miles of translucent wires hung at least fifteen feet above the streets of Manhattan provide a symbolic "private" space in which Orthodox Jews can carry things on the Sabbath. She might learn that these wires must be intact for the Sabbath exemption to hold. Her confusion on reading this article could be due to several factors. For instance, the student may not have encountered the vocabulary or concepts before and may not fully understand them even after looking up definitions and looking at maps.

This student almost certainly will not understand the broader context of an *eruv* and its cultural and religious meanings without further study. Or she might have a personal reaction that interferes with understanding. It is easy to dismiss the behavior of "the other" without examining one's own, and new ideas are often hard to process. The student might well be frustrated at the strangeness of a prohibition on certain behaviors on the Sabbath, even as she uncritically accepts the prohibition of alcohol at weddings in her community. Critical thinking is only possible when one understands basic vocabulary and concepts, but it requires so much more.

Often that "much more" can only be discovered in the process of discussion with the professor and one's peers. Many teachers require discussion, either in class or online, that helps students dig deeper into a text or an issue. Box 5.2 shows a sample assignment, designed specifically to get students to think from multiple perspectives.

This type of thought experiment can be very helpful in getting students to consider various sides to a controversial issue. It also happens to mirror actual arguments made by religious, political, and ethnic groups through time. You might pick a side quickly and unthinkingly, choosing the side that seems "obvious" to you. A teacher might poll the class to see who holds each view and then require students to argue for the side they oppose. Or a teacher might allow students to argue for their "natural" choice, encouraging students to use specific examples to make their points. The focus in this discussion often comes down to questions about what assertions or actions are "rational," "ethical," and "justifiable." Such discussions are almost always eye-opening, as they give you the opportunity to learn about your own biases and assumptions, that you may not have realized you had.

As described briefly toward the end of Chapter 3, the best discussions will engage you and your classmates by prompting you to think out loud, a process that has been shown to increase retention of facts and understanding of concepts. Many discussions will not be so general; in fact, most discussions in religious studies classes will be based on readings assigned for that day

Box 5.2 In-class discussion

Discuss these statements with members of your group. Can you logically support either claim? Can you logically support the two claims together? Explain yourselves as thoroughly as you can in a brief paragraph. Remember to put all group members' names on your submission.

Statement #1: We, the members of our group, are rationally and ethically justified in our conception of things; for example, that when you are dead you are dead, that virtuous people can die young, that souls do not transmigrate, and that authors have a natural inalienable right to publish works critical of revealed truth.

Statement #2: They, the members of some other group, have a different conception of things [and are rationally and ethically justified in that worldview]; for example, that the spirits of dead ancestors can enter your body and wreak havoc on your life, that widows are unlucky and should be shunned, that a neighbor's envy can make you sick, that souls transmigrate, that you get the death and afterlife you deserve, and that a parody of scriptural revelation is blasphemous and blasphemers should be punished.

[Adapted in part from Richard A. Shweder, *Thinking Through Cultures: Expeditions in Cultural Psychology* (1991), excerpted at http://www.wsu.edu:8001/vcwsu/commons/topics/culture/culture-definitions/shweder.html]

in class. To make the most of the opportunity, prepare by reading closely, annotating the text, and taking notes about ideas and questions sparked by your reading.

As described in Chapter 4, that kind of preparation for class discussion involves reading skills that go well beyond passing one's eyes over the page. The key to evaluating any argument is a careful and sympathetic reading of each text on its own terms. When reconstructing, explaining, and analyzing a particular argument, make any reconstruction as strong as possible, even if the author's premise or conclusion seems wrong or misinformed. Generally the first step in doing this is to identify the thesis (sometimes, although not always, indicated by key words or phrases such as "in summary," "in conclusion," "therefore," "I conclude that"). Identify the question the author is trying to answer or the problem he or she is trying to solve. Then identify the explicit premises (sometimes, although not always, indicated by key words or phrases such as "because," "is implied by," "follows from the fact that"). Premises are any statements that support the conclusion (or might be thought by the author to support the conclusion). Any given reader might disagree with the particular premises chosen by an author; this does not, however, make those premises invalid or unworthy of note.

It is sometimes harder to determine the implicit premises of an author, because so-called "value assumptions" or ingrained ideas about the way the world works often remain unstated. As such, they can be hard to detect and might require some informed guesswork. This is also often where personal biases, stereotypes, and other unexamined assumptions can get in the way. Be sure that any implicit premises are consistent with the intentions of the author in his or her context, to the extent that can be determined.

Several common shortcuts make the process of critically thinking through an argument less effective. Sometimes a reader will accept an argument because he or she believes or rejects the conclusion, forgetting that even if the conclusion is demonstrably true or false, the argument itself may still be weak or strong. Other readers might quickly dismiss an argument as "mere opinion" instead of doing the work to make substantial and warranted criticism. Remarks such as "That's only your opinion" are often merely excuses for not doing the work of thinking through specific, reasoned criticisms. Always provide reasons, not reactions. Direct any criticisms to specific premises and, in doing so, make use of any relevant information.

Another common error is dismissing an argument based on standards that the original author either could not or would not consider. For instance, an argument on medicine made in the twelfth century should not be held to the same "scientific" standards as an argument made in the twentieth. Likewise, do not impose, for instance, Christian ethical standards on a secular or non-Christian moral treatise. You should always be aware of cultural and other biases as you examine the ideas of others, and that awareness is a key part of critical thinking. Awareness of contexts—both of your own and those of others—is essential to thinking critically.

One of the most common mistakes you could make is to think that there must be one absolute answer to any given problem. You will probably go through several stages of intellectual growth in college. You and your peers will progress from more black-and-white thinking to a more nuanced ability to accept complexity.[16] You will likely move from more simple factual knowledge to more advanced analytical and metacognitive skills. This is also how you learned things as a child: you began with simple identification and moved over time to analyze and relate and then to innovate or generate new ideas. Even the most dedicated cereal scholar began with the basics and worked his way to mastery. Such an individual might begin believing that Cap'n Crunch is the best cereal ever, without competition. Yet focused study of cereals might yield new insights and new abilities to compare, analyze, and hypothesize. The cereal scholar may or may not uphold the primacy of Cap'n Crunch at the end of such a process. But the reasons for the scholar's position will be clearer, fuller, and firmly based. This will happen to you, too, if you do the work required in your courses: your cognitive abilities will grow as you move into adulthood, and those skills will grow most quickly with practice.

For most college work, assessing an argument as simply "right" or "wrong" is insufficient. It is often more interesting and fruitful to pay attention to the ways an argument is constructed than to assess the "truth" of its conclusion. If we look, for instance, at William Paley's "watchmaker argument," we can see a particular logic at work that may or may not be acceptable today. Paley, an English theologian writing this vignette in the early nineteenth century, asks his reader to imagine walking across a field and kicking a stone. He notes that few walkers would question the age or design of the stone. He then asks his readers to imagine walking across a field and finding a watch. This, Paley argues, is an entirely other matter. The watch, he insists, practically demands the walker to take notice: the watch speaks volumes about design in a way the stone cannot. Paley then lays out an analogy in which the watch is to a watchmaker as the universe is to a universe maker. The function and complexity of the watch is akin to the function and complexity of the universe; consequently, both require an intelligent designer.

Students who believe in a divine creator find this a satisfying analogy. Of course a watch relies on complex mechanisms to achieve an astonishing result (particularly in the early nineteenth century, when Paley was writing). Yet the analogy breaks down in several ways. A watch is composed of parts assembled by one individual, perhaps, but produced by several. Does that mean that the universe was simply assembled by a non-human assembler who used parts from various sources? Some also question any analogy from human experience to divine characteristics. We can know who made the watchmaker. But who made the universe designer? These objections, among others, can be found by those willing to take the time to examine the argument in depth. Accepting the conclusion of any argument should not necessitate agreement with the ways the conclusion was reached.

Critical thinking beyond the classroom

Critical thinking is good in a society that values people's informed opinions. But how can you transfer those skills learned in college and specifically in the study of religion to issues in "real life"? There are two main approaches among thinkers who advocate for the effectiveness of critical thinking across disciplines: generalist and specifist.[17] Generalists argue for transferability of critical thinking skills because they boil critical thinking skills down to a set of systematic rules that can be applied in all contexts, regardless of discipline.[18]

Specifists argue for discipline- and context-specific critical thinking, because thinking is never completely abstract: it is always about something.[19] Critical thinking in religious studies is specifist, as it adheres to particular norms in the field even under a broadly interdisciplinary umbrella.

You might find this interdisciplinarity challenging even across religious studies courses. Several studies have shown that transfer of skills from one course to another is difficult for many students. It is likely that critical thinking skills function in the same way and that having one teacher who understands critical thinking from an anthropological lens might expect something different than a teacher who approaches study through literature. As Daniel Willingham notes in "Critical Thinking: Why Is It So Hard to Teach?", "Critical thinking is not a set of skills that can be deployed at any time, in any context. It is a type of thought that even three-year-olds can engage in—and even trained scientists can fail in."[20] In other words, knowing how to think critically in one area does not necessarily mean being able to think critically in any other. In fact, the areas in which we consider ourselves experts are sometimes those in which we are least able to think objectively and in measured ways.

The specifist approach recognizes that there are distinctly identifiable ways of "thinking like a scientist" and "thinking like a philosopher." It recognizes that while critical thinking is found in courses in all disciplines, it looks very different in biology than in history. This debate among philosophers, cognitive scientists, and educational leaders will continue on. Nevertheless, it is apparent to many in the field of religious studies that *there are certain ways of thinking like a religious studies scholar*. Those skills might overlap with those learned in other disciplines in higher education; nevertheless, they require a particular bracketing of belief and an ability to see the other side for what it is, not what one might like it to be.

Critical thinking is not particular to academia, nor can it only be learned in a college classroom. You probably use some aspects of critical thinking every day as you use knowledge from experience or new data to help make judgments and decisions. Liking a new song can lead to a new genre of music; reading the nutritional label on a box of cereal can lead to new breakfast (or dinner) choices. Nevertheless, the kinds of critical thinking expected of religious studies students aim at a particular end that will serve you well in the complex reality of life beyond college. Good students become thoughtful citizens, able to weigh evidence and make informed choices even in complex situations.

A course in religious studies should help you achieve a level of empathy and intellectual humility that will serve you well in interacting with all sorts of people. Mastery of data is ultimately less important than a flexibility and ability to respond to changing circumstances and new ideas. Critical thinkers are capable of divesting themselves of comforting, long-held ideas. They are able to place their own traditions and ideas in context with others, without judgment and without considering their own views as somehow above or beyond history.

John Dewey, a preeminent philosopher of education who is in some ways the founder of the modern critical thinking movement, insisted that critical thinking skills are beneficial not just to the thinker. He expanded the influence of critical thinking to the school, the community, and to democracy most broadly. This rings true if critical thinking comes down to making reasoned decisions about applicable evidence, forming acceptable questions, and developing ways of arguing for and against any position in full consideration of context. We believe that religious studies is ideally suited to fostering critical thinking, as comparison and close reading provide ample opportunities to make novel connections and consider new conceptual schemes.

Exercises and questions for further thought can be found at https://www.bloomsbury.com/cw/the-religious-studies-skills-book/skill-building-exercises/chapter-five/

6

Comparison

We have used comparison throughout this book as a strategy of presentation and analysis. In Chapter 2, for example, we compared three syllabi from introductory courses. We wanted to see what they might reveal about what teachers think the study of religion entails, how it relates to students' general education, and what types of skills it helps students refine. Similarly, in Chapter 4, we compared two different translations of the first *sura* of the Qur'an as well as multiple representations of the menorah first described in the biblical book of Exodus. The underlying assumption in each instance was that comparison could tell us things about the topic at hand that other approaches could not.

In fact, comparison is a fundamental feature of critical thinking. The author of a recent guide for K-12 teachers argues that "Without the ability to make comparisons—to set one object or idea against another and take note of similarities and differences—much of what we call learning would be impossible."[1] Think of something as apparently simple as ordering from a menu. Choosing one dish over another at least implicitly involves comparing things like taste, price, and fit with other items that might make up the entire meal. A similar process is involved in deciding which music to listen to: any listener quickly makes decisions about choosing certain genres, artists, and individual songs, all the while excluding other genres, artists, and songs. People think comparatively all the time.

Because it is such an important part of critical and analytical thinking, comparison is taught at all levels of education in the US. If you undertook compare and contrast exercises earlier in your education in K-12, you will, in some ways, be prepared for the kind of work that will be expected from you in college. But the focus of comparative exercises in college is often different from what typically happens in K-12 education. Developing a full list of similarities and differences is a preliminary step rather than the culmination of an exercise. In college, comparing and contrasting are processes that prepare you for more important, and difficult, tasks. Having compiled lists of similarities and differences, and even represented them in some graphic form such as a Venn diagram, students still need to answer the question: so what? That is, what can be learned from the pattern of similarities and differences? Comparison and contrast are *preliminary* ways of organizing information, but it remains to interpret that information. *Comparison and contrast are, therefore, not goals in themselves, but means toward an end.*

We are using "interpretation" here to denote the general process of making meaning. Interpretation begins when any observer comments on any collection of information. We refer again to Box 2.2 in Chapter 2, which details how to generate an argument through the processes of description, analysis, and interpretation. *Interpretation involves more than simply summarizing or restating the material at hand*, but accurate description serves as a necessary foundation for interpretation. *Interpretation is built upon careful analysis* of things like language, structure, and genre, but analysis on its own does not constitute interpretation. *Interpretation answers the question: what does it mean?* or *why does it matter?* Interpretation, therefore, is the point at which an observer *makes something out of* the particular material under consideration.

Interpretation occurs when an observer connects certain material to questions, theories, or problems that the observer wants to address. It involves putting the material into a new, and potentially illuminating, context. Interpretation turns the material at hand into an example of something greater than itself. In the act of interpreting, an individual observer exercises creativity by making new connections, asking new questions, proposing new hypotheses, or venturing new theories. While processes like summary and description put the material at center stage, interpretation puts the focus on the individual interpreter. For you as a student, interpretation is the chance to state a personal, but informed, understanding of the material, to make a point or advance an argument. Interpretations strive to persuade others to see the material in a new light. They provide both conclusions and the reasoning on which they are based. Your interpretation is your contribution to a scholarly discussion.

In Chapter 2 we noted that in college-level courses about religion you will often be asked to write persuasive or argumentative prose, either on examinations in the form of essay answers or in papers. We also cover these issues in Chapter 7. In the terms we have been using in this chapter that means that you will be asked to develop interpretations, frequently using comparison as a tool, and provide reasons for why your interpretations should be considered persuasive. You will need both to make an argument, in summary form as a thesis statement, and to provide reasons that support your case. Becoming adept at the intellectual processes involved in constructing and learning from careful comparisons can support the central task of crafting persuasive arguments in important ways.

Comparison has long been central to the academic study of religion (see Box 6.1). Consequently, the study of religion has a rich array of questions, problems, and theories that both depend upon comparisons and can be

Box 6.1 Some observations on comparison in the study of religion

"Whoever knows one, knows none."[a]

"Whoever does not know this religion, knows none, and whoever knows Christianity together with its history, knows all religion."[b]

"The historian of religions does not reach a comprehension of the phenomenon until he has compared it with thousands of similar or dissimilar phenomena, until he has situated it among them; and these thousands of phenomena are separated not only in time but in space."[c]

"Similarities and differences, understood as aspects and relations, rather than as 'things' are the result of mental operations undertaken by scholars in the interest of their intellectual goals. Comparison selects and marks certain features within difference as being of possible intellectual significance by employing the trope of their being similar in some stipulated sense."[d]

"Comparative analysis is not only intrinsic to the process through which we construct and apply categories in the study of religion, it can also serve as an important corrective to the strategies of domination through which we privilege certain categories and models over others in our academic discourse."[e]

"Comparativism here is not just the study of different religions set side by side or considered serially, not just a classification of types of religious categories, and not just a hermeneutic which reconstructs or universalizes 'the sacred' for an otherwise desacralized age. Rather, it is the basic, proper endeavor of religious studies as an academic field of inquiry—finding explanatory linkages and differentials among religious expressions at either regional or cross-cultural levels, and seeking to discover otherwise unnoticed relationships among religious data."[f]

"...comparison is the intellectual act of negotiating **sameness** and **difference** in a set of observations. More complexly, this act of negotiating sameness and difference leads to the recognition of *patterns* and to a subsequent *classification* of what has been observed. Most complexly, these classifications lead to a *theory* about the deep underlying structures that produce these particular patterns, that is, to a model of what might lie behind them."[g]

[a] Friedrich Max Müller, *Lectures on the Science of Religion* (New York: Scribner, 1872), p. 1. See Jeppe Sinding Jensen, *What is Religion?* (London: Routledge, 2014), p. 22.
[b] Adolf von Harnack, "Die Aufgabe der theologischen Fakultäten und die allgemeine Religionsgeschichte, nebst einem Nachwort (1901). Rede vom 3. August 1901," in *Reden und Aufsätze*, Band 2, ed. Adolf von Harnack (Giessen: Töpelmann, 1906), pp. 159–87 (168); see Jensen, *What is Religion?*
[c] Mircea Eliade, *Shamanism: Archaic Techniques of Ecstasy* (New York: Bollingen Foundation, 1964), p. xv.
[d] Jonathan Z. Smith, "The 'End' of Comparison," in *A Magic Still Dwells: Comparative Religion in the Postmodern Age*, edited by Kimberley C. Patton and Benjamin C. Ray (Berkeley: University of California Press, 2000), p. 239.
[e] Barbara Holdrege, "What's Beyond the Post: Comparative Analysis as Critical Method," in *A Magic Still Dwells*, eds. Patton and Ray, p. 87.
[f] William E. Paden, "Elements of a New Comparativism," in *A Magic Still Dwells*, eds. Patton and Ray, p. 190.
[g] Jeffrey J. Kripal, with Ata Anzali, Andrea R. Jain, and Erin Prophet, *Comparing Religions: Coming to Terms* (Malden, MA: John Wiley & Sons, 2014), p. 4, original emphasis.

addressed afresh by a process of comparison. In fact, the category of "religion" itself is founded on comparison. "Religion" is a synthesizing and generalizing concept that has been constructed out of multiple comparisons. When Judaism and Confucianism, Hinduism and Christianity, or any other entities are grouped together as "religions," the implicit claim is that they have sufficient similarities to merit being categorized together. The area of overlap provides a characterization, if not a definition, of "religion" in general. As students move back and forth between considering any necessarily provisional definition of "religion" and examining specific instances of human religious life, comparison is the tool that they use most frequently.

The academic study of religion has been bedeviled by questions about comparison. Scholars have asked whether comparison is necessary to forming statements about religion in general. They have argued about whether it is even necessary, how comparison should be undertaken, and precisely what procedures should be followed. They have also asked about the goals of comparison, whether they be to identify a common denominator for all religions, to discern what lies behind the diverse forms that religion takes, or even to decide which particular religions might be superior to others. In one way or another, comparison is central to all of those scholarly discussions.

In the nineteenth century, for example, F. Max Muller asserted concerning religions that "whoever knows one, knows none."[2] With that Muller thrust comparison to the forefront of the study of religion. But at the turn of the twentieth century, the Christian church historian Adolf von Harnack proposed a very different approach to understanding religion, claiming that "Whoever does not know this religion, knows none, and whoever knows Christianity together with its history, knows all religion."[3] Yet even Harnack's focus on a single religion, through its emphasis on history, necessarily included comparisons of one era to another.

Later, in the second half of the twentieth century Mircea Eliade's comparative approach attracted a host of imitators, only to come under criticism later for, among other things, emphasizing similarities at the expense of differences in the comparison of religious phenomena.[4] Both the application and the critique of Eliade's comparative method raise the question of the purpose of comparison. Is it to identify and at least implicitly emphasize similarities? Or is it to identify and emphasize differences? In our view *comparison is most instructive and effective when it holds the double recognition of both similarities and differences in tension*. Moreover, comparison is most instructive when it ventures an account, interpretation, or explanation of the pattern of similarities and differences that an observer has identified.

Comparison, therefore, ideally unfolds in three complementary phases. The first phase involves making a full inventory of similarities between or among the items being compared. That inventory provides a reason for conducting the comparison. For example, fish and bicycles are things that exist in our world and may even be possessed by the same individual. But beyond that there is not much about them that can be identified as similar. Apples and oranges, however, and despite the common saying that warns against comparing them, have many points of similarity. They both grow on trees; they are both fruits; they are both edible; they are both likely to be available for purchase at the local grocery store, and so on. Graphically, phase one of a comparison looks like that shown in Figure 6.1.

Phase one of a comparison produces a single column of identified similarities. To make a comparison worth undertaking, there needs to be a

FIGURE 6.1 *Similarities.*

sufficient number of similarities. We acknowledge, however, that what counts as "sufficient" may be particular to a given act of comparison and may be to some extent a matter of personal judgment. No matter what, if a preliminary look only finds similarities, then there is no worthwhile comparison to be done because the items being compared collapse into identity. If two things are exactly the same, there is not much comparison that can be done. On the other hand, if there are no similarities to be found, then it is hard to see why comparison would be worthwhile.

Anyone who ventures a comparison needs to consider the level of generality at which it is being done. As we noted before, apples and oranges are definitely comparable, in many ways. Comparing apples and apples, or oranges and oranges, would involve making finer distinctions. For example, Granny Smith apples are both similar to and different from Macintosh apples. Similarly, navel oranges are both similar to and different from blood oranges. In any case, *what makes a comparison worth doing is the question it is designed to answer*, or at least address. Comparing apples to oranges would address a broader question or problem—say, concerning which fruits contribute most to a healthy diet. Comparing Granny Smiths to Macintoshes, on the other hand, might address a question about which kinds of apples have a longer shelf life.

Developing a preliminary inventory of similarities is the first phase of comparison. Once that first phase is completed, the second phase of comparison takes over. We acknowledge that in actual practice phases one and two will likely overlap and that one could develop lists of similarities and differences at the same time. We distinguish them here, however, for the purpose of clarity. In the second phase the focus is on differences. This is

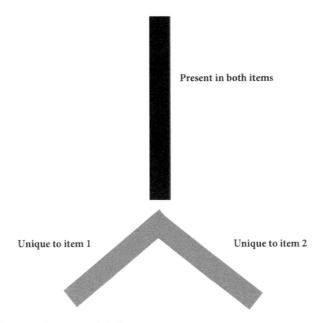

Present in both items

Unique to item 1   Unique to item 2

FIGURE 6.2 *Similarities and differences.*

where Venn diagrams, or other graphic organizers, might come in. We use a different form of graphic representation, and the reason will become clearer when we describe the third phase. Graphically, the addition of phase two to phase one looks like that shown in Figure 6.2.

Where the top of that figure identifies similarities, the bottom, with its two diverging segments, lists the differences. The inverted Y figure shows similarities and differences at a quick glance. By putting them in relation to each other, the diagram suggests that the similarities and differences are not random but they actually constitute a pattern. We think that this form of diagram effectively captures that emphasis. There are relations among the similarities, among the differences, and between the similarities and differences. Those patterns are what need to be addressed to move the comparison beyond a simple listing of similarities and differences. They need to be accurately described, carefully analyzed, and then interpreted by offering an account of why they occur and what that might mean. This is where comparative assignments in college differ from many of those in K-12 education, which often stop with the identification of the similarities and differences. College-level exercises in comparison emphasize the interpretation, accounting for, or explanation of the pattern of similarities and differences that the process of comparison can uncover.

Figure 6.3 adds the third phase of comparison to the previous two.

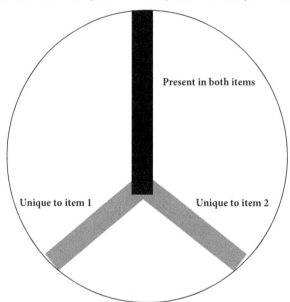

FIGURE 6.3 *Accounting for similarities and differences.*

In Figure 6.3, the encompassing circle represents the interpretation of the pattern of similarities and differences that lies within it. It is the point of the comparison. The encompassing circle depicts the argument, or at least hypothesis, about what the pattern of similarities and differences means or why it matters. It is the answer to the question: so what? Different observers might well come up with not only different lists of similarities and differences but also different accounts of what they might mean or why they might matter. That is another indication of what we have emphasized throughout this book. *Studying religion in college is about making and assessing arguments.* Particularly with the rise of electronic technologies that provide virtually instant access to information, *the collegiate study of religion cannot simply be about the acquisition of information*, the assembling of facts. It has to involve both making sense of and making sense with information, no matter how it is acquired. The process of comparison can make important contributions to the construction of persuasive arguments.

A simple comparison between two texts

In many ways there is no substitution for practicing the skills of close reading and critical thinking that undergird the construction of comparisons. As with the other skills we have focused on in this book, you can get better at comparison by practicing the three phases that we have outlined. In what follows, we will guide you through a comparison of two short texts, emphasizing the questions that might be asked rather than the answers that they might receive.

The first text comes from the Christian Scriptures, specifically the sixth chapter of the Gospel according to Matthew, verses 9 through 13. Matthew's gospel is generally thought to have been composed around 80–85 CE by an anonymous author. Only much later was it attributed to Matthew.[5] It may well be familiar to students who are practicing Christians or who have a Christian background. The second text may be less familiar. It, too, comes from a sacred scripture, but one that has been composed much more recently. The second text appears at the end of the first chapter of *Science and Health with Key to the Scriptures*. It was composed by Mary Baker Eddy, the founder of Christian Science, in the nineteenth century and is accepted by Christian Scientists throughout the world as the central text of their religious movement. Here are the texts:

Our Father in heaven,
    hallowed be your name.
Your kingdom come.
Your will be done,
    on earth as it is in heaven.
Give us this day our daily bread.
And forgive us our debts,
    as we also have forgiven our debtors.
And do not bring us to the time of trial,
    but rescue us from the evil one.[6]

Our Father which art in heaven,
    Our Father-Mother God, all-harmonious,

Hallowed be Thy name.
    Adorable One.

Thy kingdom come.
    Thy kingdom is come; Thou art ever-present.

Thy will be done in earth, as it is in heaven.
    Enable us to know, —as in heaven, so on earth, —God is omnipotent, supreme.

Give us this day our daily bread;
  Give us grace for to-day; feed the famished affections;

And forgive us our debts, as we forgive our debtors.
  And Love is reflected in love;

And lead us not into temptation, but deliver us from evil;
  And God leadeth us not into temptation, but delivereth us from sin, disease, and death.

For Thine is the kingdom, and the power, and the glory, forever.
  For God is infinite, all-power, all Life, Truth, Love, over all, and All.[7]

Comparison phase one: Similarities

In order to organize an inventory of similarities, we return to some of the points of focus we have used before. At the level of language, for example, how are the two texts similar? Do the texts have words in common? Are there words in one text that are similar to, but not exactly the same as, the words in the other text? Whether you use a graphic organizer or not, it might be helpful at this point to make a quick list of both the words that are the same and the words that are similar. That exercise could also be done for both phrases and whole sentences. Eventually, the similarities are what would constitute the top portion of our diagram of comparison, the single bold line.

At a preliminary phase, at least, it is helpful to maintain a distinction between things that are actually the same and things that are similar in some ways but different in others. In terms of our graphic representation, words, phrases, or sentences that are identical could occupy the top of the figure while things that are similar would occupy the bottom portion. In common language, the distinction between identical and similar is often blurred. Think of someone saying, "I have exactly the same shirt, except mine is blue" or "I'll have the same, except with a salad instead of French fries." Both statements depend upon comparisons. But in those examples, "same" actually means "similar," rather than literally the same or identical.

The rhetoric of everyday speech often collapses similarity into identity, but comparisons undertaken for academic purposes need to be conducted much more carefully. It is precisely the interplay of similarities and differences that needs to be accounted for. Does, for example, the person in the first example only buy blue shirts in order to make the process of choosing a daily outfit as simple as possible? Or has that person undertaken a color analysis that matches complexion, certain colors, and a particular season as the key to looking one's best?[8] Is the person in the second example trying to eat healthier food? Or is the rejection of French fries instead a matter of distaste for salty, fried foods? Beginning with a clear and precise inventory of things that are identical or similar paves the way for answering such questions, or at least for forming hypotheses about them, in the third phase of comparison.

Similarities, as we have noted before, can also occur on a structural level. In Chapter 2 we showed how one translator laid out the first *sura* of the Qur'an in poetic form, while another translator printed it as prose. The structural differences in presenting what appears to be the "same" passage provide the observer with something that needs to be accounted for. In the example above, how can the structure of each individual text be described? Are there any similarities between the two structures? If so, what are they? Are the structures of the two texts best described as the same, similar, or different?

Other structural questions might be asked about the positions of each text within the longer works of which they are part. Just knowing that the first text is part of chapter six of the Gospel according to Matthew provokes questions about how the short passage might be related to the rest of the chapter, the entire book in which it is found, and the collection of books of which the Gospel of Matthew is a part, among other things. Since the second text comes at the end of the first chapter of *Science and Health with Key to the Scriptures* similar questions about the relation of the passage to the wholes (e. g. chapters, larger sections, the entire work) of which it is part might profitably be raised.

Other similarities between the two texts might also be noted. Some of them would depend on an awareness of the broader contexts of each text, such as the few details that we mentioned in introducing them above. What might it suggest that each of the texts is part of a holy book? Do the similarities between the two texts suggest that they are somehow related? If they are, how? Who is speaking in each of the texts, and in what context? Might the voice behind the text, the voice reciting "Our Father in heaven" or "Our Father which art in heaven," provide an indication of how the text is supposed to be used? The more you become aware of the contexts in which each of the two texts can be located, the more you will be able to frame questions about them.

Comparison phase two: Differences

In many ways, the procedures for this phase of comparison are very similar to the procedures followed in the first phase. The second phase of comparison also involves making a full inventory of the differences between, or among, the items being compared. Again, the identification of differences may involve making judgment calls. In our example, on the level of phrases, are "Our Father in heaven" and "Our Father which art in heaven" more similar or different? What freight do the two additional words in the second text carry? Does "which art" substantially alter the meaning of the phrase in question? It seems easy enough to offer a negative answer to that question. The figure ("Our Father") and the location ("in heaven") remain the same in each instance; the additional words really do not add much to the phrase. On the level of language, however, there do seem to be differences which may well be significant. The first occurs in the second line of the second text. For someone who has read the first text, the second line of the second text comes as a potential surprise. Grammatically, "Our Father-Mother God" appears to be a phrase designed to clarify the opening phrase in the first line, "our Father." An observer, however, could easily claim that the phrase does more than clarify. The addition of "Mother" upsets the gender expectations initially established in the first text and apparently describes "God" as having both male and female characteristics. Since there is no hint of such a concept in the first text, close reading would seem to have identified a substantial difference between the two texts.

Beyond the substance of the short phrase under consideration, there are other features of the second text that constitute differences. Most notable, perhaps, is that virtually every other line is printed in italics. In the first text none of the lines are printed in that manner. When a textual effect is used frequently, it is likely to be important. *Repetition indicates significance.* In this instance, structure also indicates significance. First, one line appears in regular print, then, the next one appears in italics. The pattern is repeated through the second text. Since that textual feature does not appear in the first text, it may well be worth further comment.

Attention to both structure and language reveals something additional about the two texts. The lines that appear in regular print in the second text are the ones that come closest to mirroring the language of the first text. After the first line of the first text and second line of the second text, which we have already discussed, come two rather similar second lines. The first text has "hallowed be your name," while the second one has "hallowed be Thy name." Three words are exactly the same and occur in the same order. Where the first text has the more contemporary and colloquial "your," the second text has the more archaic and formal "thy." The first text does not capitalize possessive pronouns related to the "Father," but the second one does. The two lines can thus be judged to be substantially similar, in terms of both their language and their place in the overall structure of their home texts.

What marks a substantial difference in the second text, however, is the introduction of the italicized (and capitalized) phrase, "Adorable One" of the second text. Since that line repeats a structural feature that had already been noticed in the second line, it raises the question of whether there might be a pattern to the text. The next six lines confirm the existence of such a pattern. In the second text, no line that mirrors the language of the first text exists without being followed by an italicized phrase or sentence that has no direct parallel in the first text. Both the structure and language of the second text, therefore, confirm the impression that the italicized portions of the second text contain the most significant differences between it and the first text. It remains, then, for the observer to develop some account that interprets the pattern of similarities and differences.

Comparison phase three: Accounting for patterns of similarity and difference

We have emphasized before that an effective comparison needs to identify items that have a sufficient number of things in common to make the effort at comparison worthwhile and instructive. That is why comparing apples and oranges makes more sense than comparing fish and bicycles. But, unless an observer is primarily in search of very fine distinctions, such as those between Granny Smith and Macintosh apples or even between different varieties of Granny Smiths, the items being investigated need also to display sufficient differences to make the comparison interesting. What makes a comparison worthwhile, instructive, and interesting is largely in the eye of the beholder. It is something that has to be argued for. An imagined (or real: e.g. your peers in a course and/or your teacher) audience needs to be persuaded.

As we have stressed, comparison and contrast are preliminary procedures, designed to help you collect and organize information. They set the stage for more important, and complex, procedures. Specifically, the third phase of comparison involves making sense, somehow, of the pattern of similarities and differences that has been identified.

For the two texts in our example, we might ask on the level of language why there are so many similarities (virtually every line of the first text is echoed in the second) yet some many pronounced differences (beginning with the italicized portions of the second text). Such questions drive observers back to the texts themselves but also to their contexts and backgrounds. In order to make the best use of information about contexts and backgrounds, a reader might formulate a set of largely historical questions, for example, Which text came first? Do the similarities suggest that one text may have incorporated parts of the other? Simple contextual information nails down the temporal relations between our two examples. The Gospel according to Matthew was likely composed toward the end of the first century CE; *Science and Health* was composed some 1,800 years later, at the end of the nineteenth century CE.

If one text made use of the other as raw material, it was Mary Baker Eddy who used the Bible, not vice versa.

In accounting for similarities and differences, though, one question inevitably leads to another. If Mary Baker Eddy adopted the Lord's Prayer from Matthew 6, why did she do it? The key would likely be found in the differences that close reading has revealed. Where did those differences come from and what were they supposed to accomplish? We have established that the most numerous, and therefore likely significant, differences come in the italicized portions of the second text. Where did they come from? The history of the composition of *Science and Health* indicates that they came from Eddy herself, to express her particular understanding of the biblical text.

In the case of our second example, it appears that Eddy chose to insert her interpretation of the Lord's Prayer directly into the biblical text itself, offering her clarifications line by line. That, at least, answers where they came from. What led her to believe that her words could actually clarify those of Scripture, or even stand authoritatively alongside it, would, however, be another question. It would lead the investigator into the origins and history of Christian Science, to comparing the re-purposing of the biblical text that Eddy undertook to what might have been its original purpose, among many other things. But we cannot pursue those interesting questions here. When the inquiry opens up into such detailed and complicated questions, it has clearly left the initial exercise of comparison and contrast far behind. But the comparison fueled the other, more complex, questions that can be pursued only after the identification of similarities and differences has laid the groundwork. Phase three of a comparison cannot be undertaken until the first two phases have been completed.

We think that you can follow a procedure similar to the one we have outlined above in any comparison that may be part of an assignment. There are, of course, things that would make matters more complicated. For our example we chose two short texts. The first was only ten lines long, while the second was six lines longer. Longer texts would make for a more complex comparison. Comparing three or more items would also complicate the process. So would comparing items with multiple complex elements, such as the annual Muslim pilgrimage to Mecca (the *hajj*) and the Hindu Kumbh Mela pilgrimage in India.[9] Comparing elements of material culture such as Tibetan prayer flags and Vodou spirit flags,[10] the Meiji Shinto shrine in Tokyo and St. Peter's basilica in Vatican City,[11] or the temple devoted to the Hindu deity Hanuman in Port of Spain, Trinidad and the Mormon temple in Salt Lake City, Utah,[12] would also constitute more complex efforts at comparison.

The more complex the comparison, the more daunting it may seem. Even if you end up comparing complex items with other equally complex items, the process we have outlined facilitates breaking the entities being compared into their constituent parts. Whether the items being compared are two short texts or multiple highly complex rituals of pilgrimage, *the basic procedures remain the same*. Before starting, you should determine why you are making the comparison in question, especially if the reason for conducting the comparison has not been specified in the assignment, and what you hope to find out. Phase one of the comparison will enable you to determine if the chosen items are sufficiently similar to make a comparison worthwhile. Phase two, in a complementary fashion, will enable you to begin to identify not only a list but also a pattern of similarities and differences. Then, phase three ushers in the more difficult, and rewarding, process of accounting for or interpreting what you have found.

The more complex the comparison, the greater the need for effective ways of organizing what an observer has found. Fortunately, the academic study of religion has developed over time a number of intermediate categories, between the very general "religion" and the very specific information provided by individual religious people, to facilitate comparison. Those intermediate categories can help students organize large amounts of information by providing guidelines for both organization and analysis. Take one of the examples mentioned above. Both the *hajj* and the Kumbh Mela festival are described as pilgrimages. Pilgrimages themselves are a kind of ritual and a specific kind of rite of passage. All three of those categories—ritual, pilgrimage, and rite of passage—can contribute to the organization, analysis, and interpretation of information.

For example, identifying a set of actions as a pilgrimage creates certain expectations. A pilgrimage will involve a journey that takes individuals away from home, to a sacred spot, and then home again. Scholars have done a lot to identify and analyze the characteristic features of that three-part structure, which is common to all rites of passage. The middle period, when pilgrims are away from home and concentrated at a sacred place, has come under specific scrutiny. Ideally when individuals are immersed in a group of like-minded pilgrims, they are changed by their experiences. They then return home as different people in some identifiable ways.

Just those few comments suggest that scholarly thinking about rituals in general, about rites of passage, and about pilgrimages in particular can help students organize their comparative observations. For example, you might use the threefold structure of leaving home, being at a sacred place, and returning home to organize the lists of both similarities and differences between the Muslim *hajj* and the Hindu Kumbh Mela. In the form of our inverted Y diagram, this would look like that shown in Figure 6.4.

Using categories A, B, and C would probably not exhaust either the similarities or the differences between the two pilgrimages. But it would help you keep track of at least some of them by introducing sub-categories

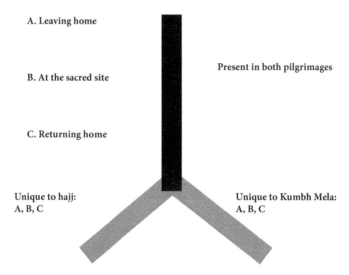

A. Leaving home

B. At the sacred site

C. Returning home

Present in both pilgrimages

Unique to hajj:
A, B, C

Unique to Kumbh Mela:
A, B, C

FIGURE 6.4 *Comparing pilgrimages.*

into each of the lists. It is entirely possible that categories A, B, and C could be further subdivided. Under "leaving home," for example, it might be asked whether the departure is mandatory or voluntary; whether the ritual occurs annually or with some other frequency; and who pays for the pilgrims' expenses, among many other things. In addition, other concepts borrowed from scholarly analysis could also be used to further sub-divide each of the two lists.

The introduction of sub-categories into the lists of similarities and differences moves them from being undifferentiated accumulations of individual observations toward becoming the building blocks of more complex analytical statements. It makes each individual subsection easier to work with by reducing the scope of things that need to be included in each sub-category. It also, as in our example above, sets individual subsections into tentative relationships with each other. Those relationships can then be explained further once the individual sub-categories are populated.

Comparison undertaken in this way, then, is much more complicated than simply "tak[ing] note of similarities and differences." It is a complex intellectual process that involves not only the identification of similarities and differences but also a dialogue with relevant scholarly literature that can help the observer formulate categories and sub-categories that not only help the observer organize information but also lead to at least tentative attempts to identify and characterize the relationships among discrete categories of information. In the end, not only the patterns of similarities and differences but also the relationships between and among them are what need to be accounted for.

Comparing multiple scholarly statements

As we have stated before, scholarly arguments often unfold over too many pages to make a fully developed comparison feasible here. We can, however, build on the brief example that we used in Chapter 4, where we subjected William James's well-known definition of religion to a close reading. In this example we will map out a comparison of three different definitions of religion. This comparison will give a preliminary indication of how to compare more than just two items. Two of the definitions will come from founding figures of the academic study of religion, William James and Émile Durkheim. The other definition comes from a popular recent introductory textbook on religion in America that has gone through multiple editions. In formulating her "working definition" of religion, Catherine Albanese had the benefit of being fully informed about more than a century of attempts at definition.

Our goal is not to have you choose the definition you prefer. Though that may be an unintended consequence of this exercise, our selection is necessarily very partial. There are quite a lot of definitions of religion. Instead we want to focus on two things. First, we argue that secondary sources like definitions of religion and the broader arguments of which they are part can be subjected to the same type of comparison that we have used to investigate primary sources. Second, we want to show briefly the increase in complexity that is entailed in comparing more than two items.

Let us lay out the definitions themselves first. In each instance we will retain the textual effects, such as italics, that occur in the original. As we stated in Chapter 4, William James proposes that "religion, therefore, as I now ask you arbitrarily to take it, shall mean for us *the feelings, acts, and experiences of individual men in their solitude, so far as they apprehend themselves to stand in relation to whatever they may consider the divine.*"[13]

Not long after James delivered the Gifford Lectures during which he outlined his definition of religion, in 1912 the French sociologist Émile Durkheim ventured his own definition. In his massive book *The Elementary Forms of the Religious Life* Durkheim proposed that *"a religion is a unified system of beliefs and practices relative to sacred things, that is to say, things set apart and surrounded by prohibitions—beliefs and practices that unite its adherents in a single moral community called a church.*"[14]

Finally, in the fifth edition of *America: Religion and Religions* Catherine Albanese offers this "working definition" of religion. She suggests that

"**Religion** here can be seen as *a system of symbols (creed, code, cultus) by means of which people (a community) locate themselves in the world with reference to both ordinary and extraordinary powers, meanings, and values.*"[15]

Although we can still use the graphic organizer that we have used throughout this chapter, some alterations will be necessary. Since the first phase of comparison focuses on developing an inventory of similarities, we can use the original drawing (see Figure 6.5).

In this case, the single, bold line would represent things that all three definitions have in common. For example, each of the definitions purports to define "religion"; each focuses on the human dimensions of religion (something that we discussed early in Chapter 2); each discusses relationships between the human and something more than human (the "divine," the "sacred," "extraordinary powers").

An added complication in this comparison of three items, however, is that there may be similarities between items 1 and 2, but not 3, between 1 and 3, but not 2, and between 2 and 3, but not 1. This underscores the fact that the greater the number of items being compared, the greater the number of columns will be in the diagram. Graphically, for a comparison of three items, the diagram would look like that shown in Figure 6.6.

Another way to represent the comparisons in the first three columns above would simply be to repeat the two-item comparison chart three times, once for each pair of items.

However they might be organized graphically, here is a brief example of some elements of comparison. In our current example, all three definitions at least mention the importance of action. James focuses on the acts of individuals; Durkheim focuses on practices that help form a community, and Albanese's cultus and code involve actions. Some similarities, however,

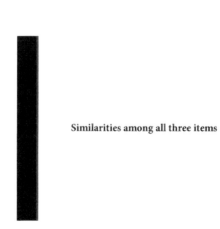

Similarities among all three items

FIGURE 6.5 *Similarities in a comparison of three things.*

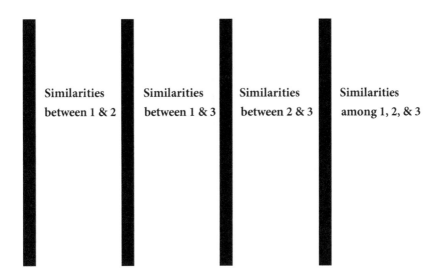

FIGURE 6.6 *Patterns of similarity in a comparison of three things.*

occur between only two of the three. For example, definitions 1 (James) and 3 (Albanese) have in common an explicitly provisional nature. James wants his readers "arbitrarily" to accept his definition in order to see what kinds of insights it might produce. Similarly, Albanese asks her readers to view hers as a "working definition" or short, descriptive statement about religion. She explicitly acknowledges that it "does not tell us what the substance, or core, of religion is, but it tells us how religion works (to deal with boundaries), and it tells us what forms (creed, code, cultus, community) it takes."[16] Further, both definition 2 (Durkheim) and definition 3 (Albanese) focus on the religious community. For Durkheim the formation of a single moral community is the function of religion; for Albanese the community is the primary religious actor.

Those brief examples indicate how a comparison of three items can quickly get more complicated than a comparison of two. There are more decisions to be made, more observations to record and organize, more possibilities to consider. Because of that, it is even more helpful to introduce some sub-categories to help organize the information. The same would hold for the second phase of comparison, which focuses on differences. As with the simpler, two-item comparison, in this case the listing of similarities inevitably leads to the specification of differences. Simply noting, for example, that definition 1 and definition 3 share something also implies that definition 2 does not share it. That is, definition 2 is different from the other two definitions in at least one way.

The differences among the definitions could be schematically arranged in parallel columns (see Figure 6.7).

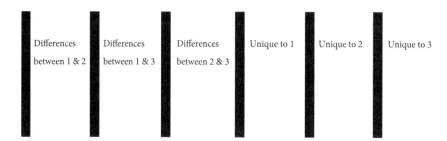

FIGURE 6.7 *Patterns of difference and uniqueness in a comparison of three things.*

As that diagram shows, the enumeration of differences is also more complicated when three, or more, items are being compared. The first three columns on the left focus on recording differences between pairs, while the next three columns aim at describing what is distinctive to each of the three items.

This way of recording differences, when coupled with the prior identification of similarities, can be particularly helpful in discerning patterns. For example, both definition 2 (Durkheim) and definition 3 (Albanese) have a strong focus on the community. That similarity starkly contrasts to definition 1 (James), where the focus is emphatically on "individual men in their solitude." Overall, James shares less with Durkheim and Albanese than Durkheim and Albanese share with each other. Among the three, he is generally the outlier. For example, his concern with the interior life ("feelings," "experiences") is not shared by the other two. Similarly, if one reads further in *The Varieties of Religious Experience* one quickly learns that James has little interest in ritual and community life, things which feature prominently in both Durkheim's and Albanese's definitions.

Phase three of comparison would pursue insight into why the particular patterns of similarities and differences among the three definitions might have occurred. In our earlier exercise of comparing two primary texts, we mentioned that one might look at the contexts and backgrounds of the texts in order to develop analytical and interpretive ideas. In this example, one might look to the role that each of the three definitions plays in the overall work of which it is a part. What prior observations and arguments, for example, led James to focus on "individual men in their solitude"? What assumptions and analysis led Durkheim to decide that "religion must be eminently collective"?[17] How explicitly is Albanese indebted to Clifford Geertz when she states that a religion is "a system of symbols," since the same phrase begins Geertz's own definition?[18]

An observer might also focus, for example, on the disciplinary backgrounds of each of the authors. It could be argued that James's work in both philosophy and psychology inclined him toward a focus on the individual. By contrast, Durkheim's work as a founder of modern sociology inclined him toward a focus on social groups, such as religious communities. Albanese, in that light, seems to have located herself more in the tradition of Durkheim, and his successors, than in the tradition of James. Many more questions, of course, could be asked. As a comparison becomes more complex, more things will need to be accounted for, interpreted, or explained.

In this final example, we have just scratched the surface of what a comparison of definitions of religion, let alone the larger works of which they are part, could look like. We want, however, to re-emphasize a few basic ideas that apply to all acts of comparison no matter how simple or complex they may be. First, we strongly recommend the three-phase model of comparison outlined in this chapter. Effective and instructive comparisons need to develop full inventories of similarities and differences. Each of those inventories may be further organized by using a variety of sub-categories. But the most important part of comparison occurs in the third phase. In the third phase the observer steps back from the individual similarities and differences and attempts to discern patterns in them and then to offer an account of why and how those patterns have occurred. The importance of that third phase is why we have insisted that individual acts of comparison and contrast, such as those frequently assigned in K-12 classrooms, are only *preliminary* processes that aid in the collection and organization of information. The hard, creative, and intellectually rewarding work comes next.

Exercises and questions for further thought can be found at https://www.bloomsbury.com/cw/the-religious-studies-skills-book/skill-building-exercises/chapter-six/

7

Writing about Religion

Writing is an extension of thinking, and it is used extensively in higher education as an essential way to gauge student learning and to foster critical thinking skills. Until modern times, the term "writer" referred most often to someone who copied or compiled texts written by others. Some writers provided original work or commentary on others' works, but few were expected to produce original work. Indeed, "writer" used to mean scribe: one was a writer when one compiled notes or made comments on ancient texts. That is still part of writing, but writing in colleges and universities has become a key skill that reveals the cogency and accuracy of the writer's thoughts. Both speaking and writing give shape and clarity to one's thoughts. Others can only know what you think by what you say out loud or in print.

Writing is important to re-learning and reconsidering anything presented in class or in a reading. *Writing well is hard work.* You will likely find that behind every good paper you write is quite a bit of reading and thinking that aren't all captured in the final product. Writing a paper often amounts to much more than what one hands in for a grade: it is the culmination of a process of collecting, selecting, organizing, structuring, revising, and proofreading. This often means that parts you have labored over get tossed out or that the process of writing takes you in an unexpected direction. You might well discover a more nuanced or more accurate thesis after the process of writing seems to be over. In that case, you should revise the paper to feature the new thesis and thus present a more coherent argument. Sometimes, however, jettisoning any written work is difficult: you might want to hold on to all of the phrases you have labored over. But those bits of the learning process sometimes need to go. Above all, *writing is a non-linear process that is crucial to learning and analyzing information.*

Because writing is a way of judging student knowledge and progress, your academic papers should showcase the way you analyze and explain things.

That is why plagiarism is such a serious offense (see Box 7.1). All institutions of higher education impose heavy penalties on students (and faculty) who present the work of others as their own. Plagiarism is a form of cheating and lying that cannot be tolerated by degree-granting institutions, because each degree must be earned by each recipient. Plagiarism can result from presenting another's work as one's own by not correctly citing the source (or failing to cite at all) or through too closely paraphrasing another work. Every institution will have guidelines about plagiarism, and many faculty will include policies about plagiarism and cheating on their syllabi. You will do well to learn them and observe them carefully.

Box 7.1 Plagiarism

There are two main types of plagiarism, both of which involve presenting someone else's work as your own, whether they are words, ideas, or creative products.

INTENTIONAL PLAGIARISM: Copying another source word-for-word, without citing the source. This often results from a mix of laziness and hoping you won't get caught.

ACCIDENTAL PLAGIARISM: Using the ideas or words from another source without citing the source. This can happen because students don't understand what they are reading or analyzing, or because students don't clarify sources in their notes, or because they do not understand the conventions for citation.

Both types of plagiarism are serious offenses. Intention does not matter, because plagiarism of any type is fraud. At many institutions, plagiarism can be grounds for suspension or expulsion. Many teachers will fail any student who commits plagiarism, which are easily discovered by programs like turnitin.com, grammarly.com, and others.

You can avoid plagiarism in several ways:

- Learn how to paraphrase and cite all sources. Take complete notes so you will know which ideas are yours and which are not.
- Don't borrow writing from other students, as you often cannot verify the sources used. Do not submit papers purchased from websites or from a fraternity or sorority file.
- Never cut and paste material from a website without making sure you provide the full citation. Online materials are easy to steal, but the stealing is easy to trace.
- Above all, do the work. Plan ahead. College is about learning how to think critically and independently. Plagiarizing cheats you out of opportunities to learn those skills.

Some plagiarism is born from frustration. Students find writing challenging for many reasons. It is difficult to come up with interesting analytical and interpretive ideas, not to mention explaining them to others. Writing also tends to be harder for those who don't read regularly and for those who don't write often. Like any athlete in training, any writer must work consistently and progressively to improve. *There is no substitute for practice.* There is also no substitute for reading the syllabus and any assignments carefully for clues about expectations. Clarity about what a faculty member expects can help with focus and save you time and worry.

As with the other chapters in this book, you should use these suggestions as a guide. All of the descriptions below are generalizations based on common expectations. You should be careful to follow each instructor's specific directions for any assignments. Teachers differ in their preferences and emphases, so you should always read syllabi and assignments carefully and ask instructors when unsure.

Why so many writing assignments?

Reflection papers, book reviews, exam short answers, reading summaries, research papers, and annotated bibliographies are just some of the writing assignments encountered in religious studies classes. Teachers assign so much writing because writing is often the best way to examine and work toward improving a student's thinking and analytical abilities. What one knows cannot be known by others until you communicates it. How one communicates contributes to the receiver's ease or difficulty in understanding. After all, if you can't express what you know, it doesn't matter to your teacher that you know it. One way to express this is that "You do not know what you cannot show." Writing also requires revision and thus can help a teacher see measurable progress over time. There are many tasks involved in creating a successful written product, and practice is the only path to doing each of those things well.

Teachers tend to assign particular types of writing to gauge certain types of knowledge. Some assignments will solicit description or summary, which is a way to see how much knowledge a student has learned about a particular subject. Some assignments will ask for comparison and contrast. These assignments require the ability to provide summary or description alongside the more advanced skills of analysis and comparison. Papers in religious studies can be explanatory, argumentative, historical, descriptive, comparative, and exegetical (or a mix of these). They can be based on one source or many. They often require analysis and evaluation of significance, and they always require that complicated ideas be expressed clearly. They almost always require an argument, not meant as negative or confrontational but rather as a thoughtful, logical use of sources to make a point.

Although students do not always take advantage of it, one of the most valuable parts of any college education is receiving feedback from teachers, and written work is a common place to encounter extensive comments. As in other areas, teachers vary in their enthusiasm for written feedback. Some might use minimal marking, which generally means highlighting substantive and grammatical issues for the student to figure out. Some provide extensive line-editing, with suggestions (sometimes coded to fit an assigned grammar guide) for improvement. Some will give split grades for content and style, while others will provide one grade that accounts for both. Reading feedback from several professors over time will help you see common problems in your own writing, such as habits of misusing commas or of repeating particular words. Repeated comments about coherence can help a writer work on the overall structure of writing, while hearing from several teachers about spelling or punctuation issues should spur some work on those issues (and the informed use of spell check). Most campuses have writing centers designed to help students with all aspects of writing, and students should take full advantage of them when possible.

Employing evidence

The types of evidence appropriate to any argument in any course can range widely. Some teachers expect original survey data or interviews with peers, while others want to see students draw only from primary sources from the fourth century in translation. These differences are often disciplinary: biology papers rely on very different sorts of evidence than papers in English. Many students are puzzled when instructors ask for examples or more evidence in their papers. "How do you know this?" is a common marginal comment, as is "expand on this" and similar notes. Sometimes this is in response to a student using primarily personal experience as evidence.

Anecdotal evidence can be useful, but it is rarely sufficient in an academic paper. For example, one's own experience of meditation cannot be generalized into an account of what every meditating Buddhist experiences. To make that case would require much more substantial research and accumulation of evidence. Simply assuming that one's own experience is replicated by everyone else, across cultures and through time, is not persuasive. Comments from a teacher asking for more evidence generally mean that you need to work on strengthening the argument with relevant evidence from sources (outside of personal experience).

That said, you should be aware that evidence is neither self-explanatory nor free of bias. One of many charts from the Pew Forum on Religion and Public Life showing the relative religious literacy of groups of Americans says any number of things. As the headline makes clear, the researcher concluded that atheists, agnostics, Mormons, and Jews score best on a 32-question Religious Knowledge survey. But that conclusion is heavily dependent on the particular questions asked and the numbers or respondents polled, and it can ultimately raise more questions than it answers. A good researcher will delve further into the survey results, asking questions of the data in light of the information provided by Pew about the structure of the original survey (see Image 8).

This survey can answer certain questions a student might want to research. But other questions require other sources. A mainline Protestant minister is likely to turn to other sources to show how well educated her flock is. A student interested in how much children know about religion will not find the answers here. Likewise, the classic Chinese *Tao Te Ching* can be used to make some arguments and not others. It might help answer questions about gender roles or ideas about emptiness in the late centuries BCE in China, but it is unlikely to shed any light on how little religious Americans know about religion.

Moreover, in the field of the academic study of religion, no evidence is incontrovertible. Evidence is often biased, and writers choose evidence based on how useful it is for a particular argument. Facts are often facts-from-a-particular-point-of-view. The strongest papers make that transparent by

Atheists and Agnostics, Mormons and Jews Score Best on Religious Knowledge Survey

Average # of questions answered correctly out of 32

Total	16.0
Atheist/Agnostic	20.9
Jewish	20.5
Mormon	20.3
White evangelical Protestant	17.6
White Catholic	16.0
White mainline Protestant	15.8
Nothing in particular	15.2
Black Protestant	13.4
Hispanic Catholic	11.6

PEW RESEARCH CENTER'S
FORUM ON RELIGION & PUBLIC LIFE May 19-June 6, 2010

IMAGE 8 *Pew Forum statistics.*
http://www.pewforum.org/2010/09/28/u-s-religious-knowledge-survey/.

showing how a point of evidence that works to support an argument helps the reader follow the logic of that argument.

Ultimately, it is the job of any writer to choose the bits of evidence that fit a particular argument and explain the significance of that evidence to the reader (see Box 7.2). In a paper advocating education about religion in K-12 schools, for instance, the degrees of religious illiteracy among ostensibly religious groups might be drawn from the survey mentioned above and highlighted. In a paper about atheists in America, survey data which shows that atheists are more educated about religion than "religious" Americans can be used to flesh out a portrayal of a misunderstood group. In a paper about categories in religion scholarship, the same chart can be used to show the ways categories include and exclude as well as the ways we subdivide Christian groups and not others in surveys of the American religious landscape.

Box 7.2 Defining the thesis

A thesis is usually a sentence (sometimes two) that states the major point or claim of a piece of writing. A convincing thesis is supported by relevant evidence. College writing most often calls for a well-stated thesis developed with relevant evidence and examples.

All theses derive from questions, either those prompted by a teacher or those generated by a writer. *A thesis is an argument.*

A thesis is not a *topic*: "Things Bahá'ís do in worship."

A thesis is not an ill-informed *opinion*: "Bahá'u'lláh is the best prophet ever."

A thesis is not a *fact*: "Bahá'ís respect the teachings of a series of messengers, including Krishna, Zoroaster, Buddha, Jesus, and Muhammad."

A thesis is not a set of interesting *observations*: "Bahá'ís can be found all over the world, they focus on family life, and they work toward establishing universal peace."

A thesis is not a *question*: "Why do Bahá'ís consider Bahá'u'lláh the final messenger?"

A thesis is an *argument* that can be supported by evidence and examples.

Some theses are too broad: "All Bahá'ís are familiar with the Bible, because they accept Abraham as a messenger." How could you prove this with the evidence at hand? Beware of generalizations. Don't try to prove too much.

Some theses are too narrow: "Bahá'u'lláh and the Báb founded a lineage of leaders, although now the group is guided by the Universal House of Justice." What evidence besides simple facts would support this claim? How does this add to what can easily be looked up in Wikipedia?

The best theses are arguable based on accessible and relevant evidence: "Bahá'í focus on universal social advancement and world peace have encouraged a revolutionary growth in the education of girls and women." Quantitative and qualitative evidence from various locations can be used to support this claim.

"Bahá'í emphasis on communal life can overshadow the importance of self-direction of each individual." Refer to the writings of the founders and of current adherents.

"The Bahá'í's Nineteen Day Feast and Muslim's Eid Mubarak both show how food rituals shape religious communities." Foundational and ethnographic work provide ample evidence for this claim.

Evidence alone is insufficient, however. If all that were needed were evidence, academic papers might be reduced to bulleted lists of relevant data points. *Academic papers are meant to be cohesive arguments about the evidence, with carefully constructed prose that links ideas and ultimately answers the question "so what?"* A paper that seeks to show that Buddhist repression of the Muslim Rohingya minority in Myanmar derives from Christian values will be hard pressed to make its case without some impressive linkage of disparate information.

Citing sources

As described in Chapter 3, there are three types of sources (primary, secondary, and tertiary) useful in academic research. Those sources must each be acknowledged by any author who uses them, aside from issues of common knowledge. Most academic papers rely on other quotations and paraphrases from other written work for evidence. Some students quote too much and leave little room for their own analysis, while others don't quote enough and leave the reader wondering what is being hidden. Be wary of quoting when the original is not particularly striking or interesting; a well-worded paraphrase with citation should suffice in those cases.

There are exceptions to the general rule minimizing the number of quotations in a paper. If a paper is about rhetorical strategies or use of vocabulary, it is important to use direct quotation to illustrate those strategies. Sometimes a source will be unique and essential to the core argument of a paper or the reader needs a sense for the tone or flow of an original. In any of those cases, all quotations should be exact to the original (with care taken to point out any error in the original with the use of [sic] directly after the error to mark it, even when the "error" is a matter of style or preference, such as that for gender-inclusive language or uncommon [but not archaic] spelling).

As a general rule, you should provide at least one line of analysis for each line of quotation. Never let a quote speak for itself. Readers need to understand how you understand any quotation you choose to include. Imagine a case in which you are crafting a paper on dietary prohibitions in religions. You choose to use the following quote from Huldrych Zwingli, a contemporary of Martin Luther in the reformations of the sixteenth century: "If you want to fast, do so; if you do not want to eat meat, don't eat it; but allow Christians a free choice."[1] This short quote demands several points of explanation, depending on the focus of the entire piece and the audience for whom it is written. Historical context is critical: Zwingli wrote this in the wake of the 1522 "Affair of the Sausages," in which he and some fellow reformers defiantly ate meat during the traditional Lenten fast. This quote summarizes his feelings about church authority and individual conscience, and it says much about the ways reformers wished to challenge the status quo. This informal sausage-eating rebellion sparked the Swiss reformation in Zurich and led the way for what became the "radical" Reformation. Leaving that quote without context or interpretation can leave your reader wondering how it matters to any broader argument. Here, you can use it as an example of the ways a commitment to individual conscience can overrule religious authority in matters of diet.

Using sources well means, in part, being careful to avoid plagiarism (see Box 7.1 above). Doing so ensures that your ideas (and the ideas of others) are presented accurately. When taking notes from any source, always distinguish which of the information is direct quotation (with page number), which is paraphrase (always with citation in the style specified by your instructor), and which are independent thoughts that occur while reading. It is generally good practice to write down all bibliographical details about a book and to include page numbers on all notes, with ways to indicate if what one has written is a direct quote, a paraphrase, or one's own thoughts.

Take this passage copied directly from Colleen McDannell's *Material Christianity* as an example.

The artifacts, landscapes, architecture, and arts that make up material culture are not discrete units. Each of these interacts with the others to produce an array of physical expressions. Material culture is not static; it is constantly changing as people invent, produce, market, gift, or dismantle it. A natural product like water, for example, is transformed into an artifact when Catholics in France bottle it and priests ship it to the devout across the United States. Christian T-shirts do not merely appear on teenagers' bodies. They must be conceptualized, manufactured, advertised, and sold.[2]

It is clearly plagiarism to include this passage (or any part of it copied exactly) in one's own writing as if it is one's own, without quotation marks or citation. McDannell deserves the credit for the style and substance of her wording, so using this quotation requires full citation, with page number. Any such long quotation should be formatted as blocked and single-spaced.

Long blocked quotes can disrupt the flow of your argument. To avoid over-quoting, which tempts many students who are anxious about their own voice, you might want to present ideas from a more complex quotation in a simplified form. This choice can also be driven by space limitations or matters of style. One of the most valuable skills you can master is that of paraphrasing. Unlike summary, which generally covers a large range of material, paraphrase is used to present part of a text without direct quotation. The key to paraphrasing well is to retain the meaning of the original quote without stealing ideas or style from the original author. A good paraphrase maintains the meaning and sense of the original in a new form. A good paraphrase of the passage above might be, "Colleen McDannell argues that material culture is in constant flux, as objects are imagined and created continually." You might then give a few other examples in addition to noting McDannell's examples, in addition to citing the source for this insight in the style specified by your instructor. In doing this, you would be building on another's ideas while giving credit for the original insight to the original author.

Rules about paraphrasing are a bit less clear than those about direct quotation, and it is always advisable to err on the side of caution. You might paraphrase the original quotation above as follows:

> Material culture, which is made up of interconnected things like arts, architecture, artifacts, and landscape, is a constantly changing system. People are always inventing, manufacturing, and distributing things, like holy water for Catholics. Teenagers who wear Christian T-shirts should know those shirts were conceived of, produced, and sold to them.

This "paraphrase" amounts to plagiarism: it retains the meaning but also the basic wording of the passage (albeit with some thesaurus substitutions), which constitutes excessive adherence to the original. All direct phrases should be put in quotation marks with citation. Students should include page numbers when citing phrases from a longer quote, since the assertion is not original to the student.

As explained above, you should never let any quotation or bit of evidence speak for itself. A good rule of thumb is to provide at least one line of interpretation for every line of a quotation. Let's look at one of the lines from McDannell's quote above: "A natural product like water, for example, is transformed into an artifact when Catholics in France bottle it and priests ship it to the devout across the United States." To explain this to a reader, a student might write something like this: "McDannell is referring here to bottling and marketing of Lourdes water, which some Catholics believe is capable of producing miracles. This transatlantic trade allows Catholics in America access to the holiness and healing power of the water from this site, which to non-believers produces regular spring water." Such an explanation helps the reader better understand the quotation and allows the writer to add context while connecting the quotation more fully to the overall argument.

Quotations by themselves do not carry an argument. They ground an argument in the facts, but you must explain what you understand the facts to mean. You should then provide analysis, which goes beyond summary to show connections, implications, contradictions, or other important issues raised by the paraphrased information. The final step is to explain how this quotation or set of quotations support the particular argument being made. It is, above all, your responsibility to explain unclear words and phrases and to explain any quotations and their import for your reader. Any quotation taken out of context must be placed within its context. Both context and your interpretation of the quotation must be made clear to your reader.

Writing assignments

There are many different types of writing assignments, all of which help any teacher see that students have mastered skills, content, or approach (or two of those, or even all three). Some writing assignments are designed for students to "write to learn," and sometimes those assignments are not graded. This does not mean they are less important; indeed, some assignments that are just for the student can have the most impact on a student's intellectual growth. Other assignments are formal and the expectations for form and substance are high. Distinguishing among these types will help you navigate class expectations.

Prompts for writing assignments, whether they be on electronic discussion boards, examinations, or formal papers, generally include certain words that can help you understand what the teacher wants to observe in your writing. *Reading clearly and perceptively what an assignment requires is thus one of the first steps toward writing clearly and persuasively for a particular audience.* If the assignment aims to help the teacher assess content knowledge, the prompt will likely include words such as describe, define, illustrate, summarize, and explain. If the teacher wants to see that you can compare and contrast texts or rituals, the prompt will likely contain those words as well as relate and apply. Assignments looking for more applied interpretation generally include words such as evaluate, support, analyze, synthesize, argue for or against, and justify.

One example is a final paper prompt presented on the syllabus of RELS 3308: "Studies in World Religions," taught by Michael Zolondek at Florida International University in summer 2016.[3] The term-paper assignment directs students to choose one of three prompts, the first of which reads:

> Which of the religions you have studied seems to be most focused on behavior and deeds, and which on the cultivation of spiritual and moral character? Explain the reasons for such differences by exploring underlying sociological and historical themes.

The teacher is careful to note that students need to support their argument with evidence, which students might presume will come from sources presented during the course. This prompt is clearly asking for sorting information ("which") as well as some degree of analysis ("explain" and "explore"). A careful reading of the syllabus makes it clear that extra research will be required for these essays, including at least three outside sources (two of which must be "academic" and one of which must be a book). Savvy students will note these guidelines and the prohibition against using Wikipedia. They will pay attention to the three elements the teacher will focus on: research, style, and argument. And they will be sure to make what they know explicit in their answer, including consideration of "underlying sociological and historical themes," a part of the prompt that might be forgotten in the more straightforward process of pulling together evidence.

In most cases, teachers are looking for a cohesive argument (which is usually called a thesis or a claim), even in the most prosaic prompts. Rarely is a teacher looking for a list of regurgitated facts in a writing assignment. It is usually to your advantage to figure out how to make an argument (preferably a persuasive argument backed up by evidence) based on the given prompt. A good thesis is arguable, interesting, and original (with less emphasis on originality in undergraduate education as long as the exposition of the thesis is original to the student). This means that you do not need a completely new idea but rather should strive to justify the argument in your own way.

As we have mentioned, writing assignments are designed to gauge different things about your learning and skills. Some assignments call for simple summary of a reading; others aim at analysis through comparison; while other projects might require summary, interpretation, analysis, and a host of reading and research skills. Some writing prompts are given on exams while other are given in class; others still require sustained attention over a long period of time. The types explored here are organized roughly in order of complexity.

We present here several different types of writing in religious studies. These include the most common but are not the only types of writing you might encounter. As always, be sure to read your teacher's directions and any guidelines to understand any assignment in a course you are taking.

Note-taking and annotating

It is worth mentioning two types of writing that students do often but that are rarely explicitly taught: note taking and annotating. Taking notes in lectures or while reading is a skill that you can develop based on course expectations. *Listening to a lecture, following a discussion, or reading a text requires active engagement.* Each activity gives you an opportunity to learn to relate what you are hearing or reading to assimilate new information and relate that new information to what you already know. Taking notes can help you sift through information to sort out useful bits for particular questions or issues, although this can take some practice. Taking notes word-for-word makes it impossible to follow the thread of a lecture, while taking too few notes can result in disengaging altogether. As explained above, always distinguish in any notes which of the information is direct quotation (with page number), which is paraphrase (with citation as specified by your instructor), and which are independent thoughts that occur while reading.

Annotating is like note-taking in that it encourages interaction with the text. There are many styles of annotating, from highlighting meaningful passages to making notes in the margins. This is not a new practice: medieval monks used hand-drawn hands with fingers to point the way to important parts of lengthy texts. It is unlikely that you are reading well and closely if you are not marking the page as you go, in whatever way works best for you. You may wonder if you are marking a text correctly. Like so many other skills, text marking follows the demands of the course. If a teacher expects memorization of facts above all, facts should be highlighted for later review. If a teacher expects argument analysis, stages of the argument should be highlighted. If a research paper focuses on a particular use of a word or concept, annotations can highlight those mentions throughout a text. *Note-taking and annotation are essential skills that can provide a firm foundation for writing more complex papers and for informed participation in class discussions.*

Summary paper

These are usually brief writing assignments meant to show that a student has read and understood a text or an experience. A summary paper (sometimes called a précis or microtheme) generally comprises a restatement of the main idea of the piece and any essential supporting information. Summary is fairly straightforward. Each short description should include the main idea of the passage, explain the structure of the whole, and identify the supporting data. These are generally brief, with little to no room for quotation, citation, or even the standard introduction and conclusion. You will need to distinguish the important from the incidental, even when everything somehow seems important. Any good summary will answer basic questions, such as who? what? when? where? and how? Summaries are generally graded on completeness as proof that a student has done the work assigned.

Box 7.3 "Discussion starter" papers

This assignment aims to increase the level of student preparation and to give the teacher evidence of what students have been thinking about so that the teacher can pose productive questions and orchestrate discussion of disputed points of interpretation. So, this assignment lies at the intersection of careful critical reading, clear argumentative writing, and articulate argumentative oral presentation.

The Specific Assignment: Beginning with the second week of the term each student will be required to compose weekly "discussion starter" papers. This is "low stakes" writing; papers will receive some evaluative comments, but no grade. Each student must complete at least ten discussion starters during the semester, and students may not do more than one in any week. Strong performance on these papers can positively influence the final grade, since the contribution and discussion of "discussion starter" papers is a major form of participation in the course.

Due dates: Papers should be posted to the course website under the appropriate heading for the specific date and topic on which students are writing, *by 2:00* pm *on the day before class.* Late submissions may be subject to penalties.

Format: (1) pick a single passage of no more than 3 consecutive sentences that best summarizes the argument or raises the issues of that day's reading. In a brief essay of no more than 300 words explain that choice, its meaning, and its implications; (2) formulate 3 questions about the assigned reading and offer a brief (approx. 100 words) rationale for the importance of each question and its relation to the reading and our ongoing discussions. Include a word count at the end of each discussion starter. Students may be asked to summarize and comment on their discussion starter at the beginning of class.

Reading response

This is often a regular assignment throughout the semester that usually entails a summary of the reading with analysis and/or possible discussion questions based on the readings (see Box 7.3). This is not about what you "like" or "don't like" about the readings but about how the readings make you think about things in a new way. Teachers will often encourage you to engage with the text under discussion in relation to the ideas raised in class discussions and in relation to any ideas and/or texts encountered in other courses that might be relevant. Even brief reading responses should go well beyond "I liked this passage" or "I thought this was really boring." One common variation asks students to identify and explain the most important passage from a reading.

Journal writing

These assignments are often "low-stakes" work that tell a story to make a point. These are generally fairly informal (which does not mean conventions of grammar and punctuation can be ignored). Such assignments are usually designed to get you thinking actively and critically about the work you are doing in the course. It is fully expected that journal writers will pose questions that might not be answered or will leave some topics unexplored as they delve into others. Although "journal" might indicate to some an invitation to engage in emotional and spiritual issues, academic journals are usually more focused on tracking intellectual development.

Comparative essays

Comparison (see Chapter 6) invites the writer and reader to consider similarities and differences between texts or topics. Some assignments will ask for both comparison and contrast, while others will ask the writer to focus on similarities or differences. Some will ask you to compare historical periods, people, texts, objects, or ideas or theories. A simple comparison is fairly easy to construct: In *The Cat in the Hat*, Thing One and Thing Two are both mischievous characters who live in a box. It is difficult to show differences, as the Things are twins whose only clear differentiating characteristics are the numbers of their shirts. Comparison between texts becomes more complicated: "The Cat in Dr. Seuss' *The Cat in the Hat* shares several characteristics with Kokopelli, a trickster figure in some indigenous groups in the southwestern United States." A paper could then detail the ways each character sows chaos and uses magic.

Another example of a comparative paper would be to pick two arguments on the same topic. They can be clearly contradictory or complementary (or something in between). If they contain significant differences, you should explain and argue the two sides against one another. If it is possible to reconcile the sides, you should show how this can be done. If they can't be reconciled, you should say which side (if any) is correct, and why.

Position or persuasion paper

In some classes, you will be asked to take a position on an issue and defend that position with evidence that goes beyond personal experience or preference. Some teachers will distinguish clearly between argument and persuasion, with an argumentative paper judged on its use of logic and reason to make a point and a persuasive paper judged on its appeal to the reader's emotions (in concert with logic and reason). In most cases, a teacher will be looking for an argument that uses both persuasion and logic to convince the reader. In some types of religious studies classes, you will be asked to write a persuasive essay about ethical or legal issues (e.g. Should gene-editing be encouraged to allow us to produce more perfect children? or Should corporations be permitted a religious exemption for providing insurance covering birth control?).

Position papers can be difficult to write. In such assignments you are invited to present original insights in a clear, cohesive argument, supported throughout by evidence that supports the thesis. Such papers often cite authorities who bolster or question the argument, and they often consider alternative understandings in order to show the superiority of the paper's argument. Position papers are best when they explain to the reader how the argument holds together, how it makes the best sense of the available data, and how what it argues matters in a broader context.

Annotated bibliography

This is a list of sources relevant to a research project, in alphabetical order and proper citation format, that includes a brief description (1–3 sentences) and assessment of the source's relevance to the project at hand. Teachers will generally be directive about the number of sources and the length of annotation required. A teacher might assign an annotated bibliography as part of a research paper or as a separate project. In order to write an effective annotated bibliography, you must be able to write concisely and clearly and be able to read appropriate resources to assess their utility for a particular project. Each annotation is short, so every word counts. It is essential to actually read the sources before providing an annotation.

Primary source analysis

These papers generally deal with one or more primary sources and focus on a central issue that defines it or them. Primary source analyses often conclude with a question (or several) that gets at new issues or other avenues for thought. The goal of these papers is not to restate the arguments in any text but to analyze them. To help you escape the related temptations of simply describing, summarizing, and generalizing about texts, some writing assignments will be designed to work on a "microscopic" level that focuses on independent critical reading without the help of secondary sources. One example of this type of assignment might instruct you to type out a defined length of a passage from a primary source and to number every line. Your job is to develop a thesis that can be proven with evidence from within the passage. This requires the student to work on depth and detail rather than more grandiose claims. Annotation can support this type of paper.

In all primary source papers, you are expected to slow down to consider certain focused questions: Which words seem important? What do they mean? Why are they significant? What is the effect of the entire passage, read as an isolated source? How does the passage heighten, complicate, perhaps even obscure the author's meaning as displayed in the longer text from which any excerpt is taken? How does the form of the text highlight or obscure its function?

Book review

All good book reviews do more than simply summarize the topic of the book: good, useful book reviews interrogate the author's claim and assess how successful the author is at proving that claim. To that end, the bulk of the review should be a critical assessment of what the author has (or has not) accomplished. Depending on the prescribed length of the piece, the first (brief) paragraph should set the stage for the review by establishing the main points of the piece. For example, is the book a total disaster or something you would recommend? The second paragraph should provide a brief summary of the book, including content and organization. This is the place to mention the questions the author is pursuing and the sorts of evidence this author values in making his or her case. The purpose of this section is to orient the reader rather than to give a page-by-page or chapter-by-chapter description. The third and any subsequent paragraph(s) should focus on the author's central argument and your evaluation of it.

Beware of mistaking the general topic of the book for the central argument. The main argument is most often found in the introduction and conclusion, so a keen reviewer will refer to those when in doubt. Any review should examine the author's perspective or point of view in relation to other arguments in the same field. Is the author's view shaped by a particular ideology or worldview? Does that tendency weaken or strengthen this particular argument? Does the author use meaningful, relevant evidence? Does the author privilege a certain kind of evidence or way of viewing the evidence? Is the argument convincing? Why or why not?

Essays on exams

Examinations often include a written portion, requesting either short or long answers to specific prompts. The most all-encompassing prompts are found on final exams. Sometimes teachers will provide a set of questions from which the students choose, and sometimes the questions will be available in advance or provided as take-home prompts. Here are a few examples.

Describe and compare at least two creation stories we have read in this class. What characteristics do they share and how do they differ? What values do the stories seem to uphold and what questions do they seek to answer?

All religions must respond in some way to the world. This response can be negative or positive, antagonistic or accommodating; it can be welcomed or unwelcomed; and it can prompt changes in both thought and practice. How has Christianity adapted to different times and places? How have Christians defined themselves against other Christians and against "outsiders"?

Edward Said famously argued in *Orientalism* (1978) that there are "many Islams." After the attacks of September 11th, Said expanded on this idea in light of the attacks of 9/11:

Besides, much as it has been quarreled over by Muslims, there isn't a single Islam: there are Islams, just as there are Americas. This diversity is true of all traditions, religions or nations even though some of their adherents have futilely tried to draw boundaries around themselves and pin their creeds down neatly.[4]

Discuss Said's claim that there are "many Islams" in light of what you know about the history of Islam(s) and the form(s) of Islam(s) practiced in the world today. If you were a journalist, how would you go about showing your readers the truth or falsehood of Said's claim? How might an acknowledgment of this "fact" about Islam(s) change views of Muslims in American culture? What benefits do we derive from imagining religious traditions as coherent wholes?

These prompts invite a range of answers, all of which should be developed from the work assigned during the semester. Such essays are generally judged based on your use of materials assigned in the course. Teachers are looking for more than general thoughts about these subjects: they want to see students using evidence from class materials to make specific arguments.

Online discussion boards

Many courses now incorporate online discussion boards. Some of these are forums for sharing ideas and commenting on the readings. Others are more directed, with regular, specific prompts and expectations about how often students should post and in what way. Discussion boards appear to be informal, but most instructors require students to adhere to formal rules of academic writing and standard rules of civil discourse. The best posts wrestle with information and skills presented in the course and thus go well beyond personal opinion. *As with all written work, make sure you read the syllabus or assignment directions before launching into discussion participation.*

Fieldwork

Many aspects of religious life are lived, and some courses will require students to observe and chronicle their experiences with such lived religion. Introductory courses in religion or specific religious traditions often include a site visit as a requirement. These visits are often done in voluntary groups or alone, but sometimes they are a class trip. Sometimes a teacher will expect a report or comparative essay based on the site visit or multiple visits to the same site. The best papers will contain description along with some analysis of the phenomena observed. Be sure to keep your observations academic; in other words, describing snake handlers as "really cool" doesn't tell readers much about the theology behind snake handling, and dismissing a particular group as "crazy" is absolutely not justifiable. Those sorts of uncritical judgments tell the reader much more about the writer than about the group in question.

Research papers

A research paper is an extended argument supported by primary and secondary sources. Some teachers will give suggestions for possible research areas, but most often students are expected to devise research topics and questions of their own. If a topic or area of focus is not assigned, you should aim to pick a topic that interests you and that is feasible with readily available sources.

Many interesting questions do not lend themselves to an undergraduate research paper. Some are simply too straightforward: What percentage of the world's population is Sunni Muslim? The resulting paper could be a single number with a brief explanation of how that number was reached. Others are far too complicated: How does the entire corpus of Sufi Mubyī al-Dīn Ibn 'Arabī compare to the entire corpus of Christian Thomas Aquinas? Always choose a question that can be answered with the sources and the time available. Most research papers are written within the span of a semester, so a manageable topic is essential. Not all topics lend themselves to research by an undergraduate: delving into prehistoric guesswork, cognitive science debates, and psychoanalytical arguments by a student who has never studied those topics is bound to fail. Topics that lend themselves to counter-arguments can be especially interesting.

Being able to devise an appropriate question for a research paper is a complex but essential process. Good questions are essential to good research. An example of a question that could be either too broad or too specific might be "What do Muslims believe?" This question could lead one to a fascinating study of Muslim beliefs as evidenced in texts from various Muslim contexts around the globe or it could lead one to a list of core tenets expected to be held by Muslims universally. It could produce a library full of books or a 500-word paper. The latter can be found in a few moments in a textbook or online, while the former would take language skills, texts, and time that no undergraduate has readily at hand. A similar example would be "How has Judaism developed since its inception?" That question is so broad as to be unmanageable: it requires the student to identify a point of inception and to account for many different types of development, from ritual to cultural to institutional, not to mention the anachronistic use of "Judaism" as if it were a discrete phenomenon. A more focused study on a particular community at a particular time would yield more interesting insights.

Moreover, some theses are not arguable because they are too obvious or too general. To argue that the Torah is a central set of texts for Jews is not original and not even open to reasonable argument. In general, questions that deal with "how?" or "why?" within a specific geographical or chronological frame lead to more persuasive papers. For instance, How do indigenous peoples in the Northwest explain the beginning of the world? Or, Why are early Christian churches modeled on Roman basilicas? More advanced classes generally require even more specific questions. Questions that focus on "what?" often fall flat, although certain types of historical questions (for instance, "what factors led to the rise of Sikhism in the fifteenth century?") can yield interesting insights. In contrast, "What do Sikhs believe?" is probably not focused enough for an original research paper, nor does it encourage work in primary sources.

There are two ways to approach research based on primary sources: start with the primary sources and read secondary material next, or start with secondary perspectives and then launch into the primary material. Some primary texts are the focus of volumes of commentary and analysis, while others are comparatively unstudied. Most undergraduates start with more general studies, but certain topics can seem overwhelming if they are the subject of a vast secondary literature. Another drawback to extensive reading in secondary sources is that they can bias reading, potentially closing down avenues of interest and possible insights because they steer thoughts in a particular direction. Sometimes it is best to jump in to Meister Eckhart's sermons or the *Tao Te Ching* to formulate thoughts before being swayed by the thoughts of others. Many papers are written around a single primary source with the support of related secondary sources. Others are written around many primary sources that are related in some way the writer makes clear.

General reference works are helpful for orientation, but a strong research paper will always consider recent scholarly articles (peer-reviewed studies published in journals) and monographs (detailed studies of focused topics) in the field. Those sources will indicate the ongoing discussions and debates in the field and will provide clues to what questions are considered, thus far, answered and unanswered. In general, looking back at least five years is good; ten years is better, and 20 years or more is best to get a sense for the arc of scholarship on any chosen topic.

Once a general topic has been chosen, a research paper should focus on a subtopic or subquestion that is more manageable. This requires some reading to be able to identify important insights and ideas. Research papers generally begin with a general topic and a related question, to a more specific question that is answered in a thesis statement. A general topic for an informative paper might be "Zoroastrian ideas about death." A more specific topic might be rituals surrounding death, particularly how they relate to the *dakhmas* or "Towers of Silence." A specific research question might be "How have practices around treatment of the Zoroastrian dead in India changed since the vulture population has declined?" A thesis built around that question might be as follows: "Practices around death in Zoroastrian communities in India have shifted to allow solar collectors to decompose bodies in the absence of vultures, thus maintaining the faith's core principle of not defiling the elements." A more narrow question will lead to a set of primary sources that the student can analyze to reach a conclusion.

You will usually have initial expectations or hypotheses about your topic, and you may find those expectations and hypotheses are often narrowed and even contradicted through extended study. Sometimes this will encourage you to move the project in a different direction than first imagined. That is fine, as long as that is where the evidence leads. By the time you begin to write up this argument, you should be able to frame a clear thesis statement that can be defended with evidence. The ultimate goal of any research is to follow the evidence and then to present that research to others, arranged in a way that is accessible and convincing.[5]

Structuring arguments

In most academic writing, you will be expected to present arguments supported by evidence. There is no foolproof way of structuring an argument, although students unfamiliar with the basics would do well to follow some sort of template. Many papers include an introduction, an exposition, a critical evaluation, and a conclusion. The introduction does just that: it introduces the topic as stated in an assignment or as determined by the writer. The introduction should include the thesis the paper will defend and should briefly outline the argument that will support the thesis, discuss the position being presented or the issues that the paper will discuss, and state the plan for the paper.

Following the introduction will be exposition, in which the writer lays out the argument, being careful to treat sources fairly. This explanation of the argument should include direct and indirect citations from the sources. At every step of the argument, the writer should provide transitions (see below) to clarify the logical progress of the argument. An essay should also involve critical evaluation, in which the writer examines problems with the argument and how the argument is, nevertheless, the best account for the data at hand. The conclusion should restate the thesis along with a very brief outline of the basic issues explained in the exposition section. The conclusion is the final place for the writer to defend his or her critical evaluation of the sources as the most plausible.

Whatever specific assignment is being undertaken, it is crucial to write simply. Use transition words (e.g. because, given this argument, therefore, nevertheless, on the other hand, it follows that). Use "signposts" to help readers know where they are in any argument (e.g. "Finally, the factor that most shaped the development of X…" or "This argument will proceed in three stages. First…"). Be clear about when the voice is from the author of the paper of from another (the propriety of the use of "I" in academic papers is generally determined by individual teachers). Write in the present tense (even if some of the individuals discussed are long dead). Above all, you should say what it means as clearly as you can. Any given reader might not know much about the topic, and that should be borne in mind. Some professors want their students to imagine that their readers are all stupid, mean, and lazy;

others will expect students to write for an informed, interested audience. In either case, writing as if to a group of skeptics can help you strengthen any argument.

Bear in mind that all essays should have a reason for existing. A text that simply restates facts that can be found elsewhere is of limited value. Lists of facts and statistics constitute evidence, but they don't, on their own, form an argument. A thesis cannot stand on its own authority, as it requires evidence to support its assertions. An assertion without evidence goes nowhere, except for those who already agree with it. Consequently, certain types of argument are impossible to prove. Arguing for a particular interpretation of the Book of Mormon as "right" will not likely persuade outsiders, in large part because such an argument cannot be proven. *Writing an essay involves both telling and showing, and the best showing is specific and directly related to the argument.* Evidence from primary and secondary sources, not simple assertion, will help prove a thesis. Aim to make your writing persuasive, even if your argument will never completely settle the question being addressed. You can, however, stake a claim to providing an interesting and cogent perspective on the question.

You should also consider possible counter-evidence and objections to your thesis and respond to them as is feasible given paper length. Imagining what an informed reader in the field might say to challenge an argument can help you strengthen your argument. A nuanced argument that identifies its own weaknesses is actually stronger than one that ignores them. One book that can help students learn how to handle evidence and write in their own voice is *They Say, I Say: The Moves That Matter in Academic Writing*, by Gerald Graff and Cathy Birkenstein.[6] This book lays out the steps of argument analysis and construction in straightforward, useful ways. It also helps students understand how to own their authorial voice.

One standard outline for persuasive writing follows the Aristotelian idea of "tell them what you're going to tell them; tell them; and then tell them what you told them" (see Box 7.4). Provide your reader with a structure and roadmap that guide them through the steps of your argument, and never assume your reader agrees with your conclusions. Your job is to provide sufficient reasons in the form of well-presented evidence for them to agree.

Common writing errors

The most common mistakes students make in writing papers can be summarized under three general categories. First, before they even begin to write, students often overlook the importance of reading the sources

Box 7.4 Proposed paper outline

Introduction

- Introduce the topic as stated in the assignment.
- State the thesis in one clear sentence.
- Briefly outline the argument that will support the thesis and state the plan for the paper.

Exposition

- Lay your argument out fairly, despite your own point of view.
- Support any argument with citations (direct or indirect) from the text.
- Make each step of the argument(s) as clear as possible.

Critical Evaluation/Analysis

- Describe the strengths and weaknesses of the argument.
- Explain how this argument is stronger than others.

Conclusion

- Restate the thesis of the paper (reworded from the first paragraph).
- Restate the basic issues that were explained in the second section (exposition).
- Reiterate the reasons why your argument is reliable and worth considering.

The pattern suggested above is not meant to be definitive but to be instructive. Papers and other assignments unfold in different ways for many reasons. This structure tends to eliminate many of the misunderstandings readers might have.

closely and thoughtfully. The task of writing becomes easier when one has a grasp of what one is writing about. Students who write impressive research papers have put in many hours of reading to reach their conclusions. Second, students fail to develop a single, clear, coherent thesis that is supported by the source(s) they are considering. Remember that a statement of topic (e.g. "In this paper I will compare the accounts of creation in Genesis 1–3 and in *Enuma Elish*") is emphatically not a thesis. A thesis expresses an argument in summary form. Again, asking good questions will lead to interesting answers that can be expressed as academic arguments. Third, students tend to rely too much on summarizing the text(s) in question and thus downplay their own analysis. A good research paper goes beyond summary to say something more, and it goes beyond lengthy direct quotations in favor of interesting analysis.

Very few first drafts are worthy of submission for a grade. In the process of revision you should throw out bits and pieces that turn to be irrelevant or ill-fitting for a particular argument. It is helpful to separate higher order concerns from lower order concerns in revising any paper.[7] Higher order concerns can include focus and a thesis; structure that is conducive to a message and any relevant data; and a sense of the audience and purpose for the work. Lower order concerns include punctuation, grammar, sentence style, and word choice. All final drafts should be subject to close editing and proofreading, with special care given to formatting of bibliographical information. Proofreading a final paper should go well beyond running a spell check. Suggestions for catching errors and infelicities include reading the text aloud or having someone read it aloud, which can help you hear mistakes that aren't apparent when you read silently. You might try reading your work backwards word by word to find errors.

Higher order concerns

The most important element of any paper is a well-conceived thesis. Does the paper present a clear thesis within an introduction that explains to the reader the structure of the argument to come? Does the evidence fit the argument? In a longer paper, are there subheadings to clarify the structure of the argument? In all papers, are there sufficient guides to transition and logical structure for the reader? Does the paper speak effectively to its proposed audience? Does it accomplish its purpose (see types of writing above)? Does it answer "so what?" or explain to the reader why the argument matters? *Answering "so what?" helps show that you have made a contribution to a scholarly discussion.*

One of the most important parts of revision is making certain that the real thesis has not snuck in at the end. It is common for writers to "discover" a stronger thesis after the process of writing, and it is then incumbent on the writer to revise and adjust the paper accordingly, so that the thesis appears at the outset of the essay. If you find yourself discovering a more persuasive thesis at the "end" of writing, take some time to revise and thus strengthen your entire paper.

Higher order concerns can be addressed in the following ways:

- Devise a thesis that can be proven with evidence from classwork or original own research (not from what the writer just thinks is true).

- Define all terms, well beyond dictionary definitions. How have scholars defined the term? How is the term being used in this context? A writer should explain what particular meaning is being applied in a particular context.

- Provide citations for all words and ideas that are not the writer's own, even if those ideas are not directly quoted or are paraphrased in the paper.

- Consider the audience. Does the teacher want the writer to assume that the reader has no knowledge of the field or topic? Or does she expect each student to write as an expert to experts?

- Avoid focusing on straightforward information or plot summary to the exclusion of analysis.

- Don't leave quotations unexplained (in general, any explanation of a quotation should be at least as long as the quotation itself).

- Don't reject an argument without providing an informed reason (in other words, don't simply write "This interpretation is wrong" without providing an explanation backed by evidence).

- Avoid making personal professions of faith or belief (unless that is explicitly what a teacher expects).

Mid-level concerns

Some issues are more complex than grammar and punctuation and matter enormously to clarity and grace in writing.

- Provide topic sentences at the outset of paragraphs as well as transitions throughout the piece to show where the argument is going and to provide moments of summary and reflection. Use transition words to signal moves and to link ideas within an argument (e.g. because, given this evidence, therefore, nevertheless, on the other hand, it follows that). These act as "signposts" that help a reader know where he or she is in any argument.

- Avoid personal (also known as *ad hominem*) attacks, such as "Hume was clearly an idiot." There are other ways to show Hume's thought was, to the writer's understanding, faulty, and there are better ways to handle a prejudice that "these rituals are only done by superstitious, primitive people."

- Avoid hyperbole (e.g. "This is the world's best exposition on wombat moral reasoning") or complimenting an author (e.g. "Otto is the most brilliant theorist ever"). Avoid words such as "absolutely," "always," "clearly," and "never," unless necessary and supported by evidence. Nothing is clear until you make it clear.

- Avoid self-denigration (e.g. "a humble first-year student could never hope to grasp the complexity of the Upanishads").

- Don't start or end any paper with an overly general statement that cannot be proven or that pushes the evidence too far (e.g. "Humans have pondered these immortal questions since time immemorial" or "Men will always ponder the meaning of life" or something starting with a phrase such as "Throughout history" or "All people believe").

- Don't start a paper with a dictionary definition ("Webster's defines 'wombat' as…") or by quoting Wikipedia. Never rely on or feature encyclopedic sources in college work.

Lower order concerns

There are many useful guides to style and grammar both online and in book form, and all students wishing to excel at college-level writing would do well to consult such books regularly. One classic is Strunk and White's *Elements of Style*, which succinctly presents grammar and punctuation issues and their solutions in a brief volume.[8] This volume is worth a look if your teacher points out problems such as subject-verb disagreement, dangling participles, mixed verb tenses, overuse and underuse of commas, misuse of semicolons, and inconsistency in capitalization, hyphenation, italicization, and treatment of numbers in one's writing. Joseph Williams's *Style: Lessons in Clarity and Grace* is an invaluable volume for more advanced writers.[9] There are also many reliable sources from college and university writing centers available on the internet.

Before handing in a paper, review it one final time for each of the following issues.

- Give a paper a title that indicates its subject and tone. A clever or amusing title can be a bonus, not a necessity (and being too clever can often backfire). Here are some examples of poor titles: "Adam and Eve Eat the Apple!" or "Random Thoughts on Genesis."

- Avoid unnecessary words and phrases, such as "the fact that" and "in order to" and "There is/are." Almost all prose is better without those phrases. Avoid too many qualifiers (such as "somewhat", "very") unless they actually help contextualize the data.

- Avoid jargon, which is disciplinary-specific, overly technical wording that is often only understood by insiders to a particular field. Jargon often substitutes clarity, both in the original source and when it is used in student papers. If jargon is unavoidable, be sure to define it for the reader.

- Use inclusive language (e.g. "humankind" instead of "mankind") when possible. This extends to any wording that contributes to discrimination of any sort.

- Write in simple, declarative sentences. Do not mistake grammatical complexity for profound thought.

- Use the thesaurus with care. Going beyond your own vocabulary almost always leads to an awkward and fake-sounding argument. Why utilize "utilize" when one can use "use"?

- Do not use colloquialisms, short-hand expressions (especially email or texting short-hand), or most non-possessive contractions (e.g. don't, can't, let's, you'd) in formal academic writing. When in doubt, use the more formal option.

Writing well is hard work. It is, above all, a process of making meaning and transmitting that meaning to others. Teachers will differ in the types and formality of writing they expect in any given class. They will differ in the type and amount of feedback they provide on assignments. In all cases, reading and acting on feedback is essential to growing as a writer. If you are given a chance to revise a paper, be sure to learn the reasons for or rules behind the changes suggested. Simply knowing the grammatical and structural rules won't necessarily make you a better writer, just as knowing the rules of the road won't guarantee that you will drive safely. *Writing well takes time, practice, and patience.* Students in religious studies are given plenty of opportunity to learn how to write clearly, soundly, and persuasively. Take advantage of those opportunities.

Exercises and questions for further thought can be found at https://www.bloomsbury.com/cw/the-religious-studies-skills-book/skill-building-exercises/chapter-seven/

8

Beyond the Classroom

Toward the end of the first chapter of *In Defense of a Liberal Education*, Fareed Zakaria makes an interesting admission. Writing about how he came to the United States to attend college, he claims "I got very lucky and ended up going to Yale. I have no idea why they let me in or why I chose to go there."[1] Zakaria's statement is refreshing in its honesty. It also contrasts strongly with the severely over-engineered college searches that some high school students now go through. Zakaria emphasizes the intuition, guesswork, and sheer luck that influence college choices more often than many would like to acknowledge. But there are also students for whom the choice of a college is severely constrained, whether because of personal or family circumstances, financial considerations, or other factors. What all students have in common upon entering college, however, is that they generally face an array of choices that is distinctive to the US form of higher education.

In many European countries, by contrast, students enter university in order to study or "read" a single, specific subject. Through examinations and other means during their high school educations, those who will continue their education in universities are encouraged, or rather required, to focus upon a single subject, such as chemistry, history, or law, during their time at university. Their studies are thus "tracked" or directed in ways that do not happen in the US. Some students who begin college in the US may have their entire four years virtually mapped out for them due to their choice of major, especially in the sciences. But most will have ample time for experimentation according to their individual interests. Students like the young Fareed Zakaria, who may not have firm career plans or an already-formed deep attachment to a specific subject, can elect to take courses in a variety of fields.

The elective system is a distinctive feature of US higher education. It dates to the later nineteenth century. One of its strongest champions was the long-serving president of Harvard, Charles W. Eliot. During an 1885 debate with the president of Princeton, Eliot argued that "a well-instructed youth of eighteen can select for himself a better course of study than any college faculty."[2] Today, colleges and universities tend to side with Eliot, without generally promoting completely free choice to students. Typically, institutions both grant students some freedom of choice in their course work and channel their choices through various forms of distribution requirements, general education courses, and required courses in a major or concentration. Every institution has its own distinctive combination of requirements and electives. They range from very open curricula in which students can chart their own paths (with the advice of faculty and others) to highly prescriptive curricula, which may feature only a very few elective courses. Often there is a mix within a single institution, where requirements vary from one major to another.

As we have noted before, the study of religion is not currently a prominent part of the K-12 curriculum in the US. Accordingly, many students encounter it for the first time when they enter college. You might have been directed toward the study of religion by distribution or general education requirements as well as by the more straightforward factors that affect course choice, including scheduling, the reputation of the teacher among students, and the perceived degree of difficulty of the course. In some cases a course, even one specific course, in the study of religion may be required. But more often courses in the study of religion, along with other courses, can fulfill a requirement in global studies, US or international diversity, pre-modern studies, non-Western cultures, religion or philosophy, or some other category.

Three things, then, are particularly noteworthy about the study of religion in US colleges and universities. First, with the exception of some religiously-affiliated schools, *the study of religion in US higher education does not offer a career track for students who have already decided what they want to do with their lives.* That is markedly different from the European institutions that train religious education teachers for grades K-12. The lack of a direct link to a specific career that can be taken up immediately after graduation also exposes the study of religion to the criticism that it is frivolous or an indulgence that distracts students from equipping themselves with the skills necessary to earning a living.

One of the strongest examples of the criticism of higher education that is not directly linked to career preparation came from Florida Governor Rick Scott in 2011 when he vigorously advocated for pushing students toward STEM (Science, Technology, Engineering, and Mathematics) disciplines and away from subjects like Anthropology. Speaking specifically about public institutions, Scott said, "But just think about it: How many more jobs do you think there is for anthropology in this state? Do you want to use your tax dollars to educate more people who can't get jobs? I want to make sure that we spend our money where people can get jobs when they get out."[3] From that perspective, if studying a particular subject doesn't connect immediately to a job, it isn't worth studying, nor is it worth state funding. We strongly disagree.

Second, *by virtue of their frequent inclusion in distribution or general education programs, courses in the study of religion are institutionally identified as somehow serving goals beyond goals specific to the course.* Their very inclusion in such programs indicates that they are viewed as contributing value to students' education that is different from training for a specific job. General education or distribution programs typically take shape over a period of years. They are the products of often intense wrangling among faculty members (and sometimes student members of curriculum committees), who have both the best interests of students and the best interests of themselves and their own departments in mind. Such programs are inevitably compromises. Yet general education or distribution requirements do represent, however imperfectly, a vision of what graduates of their institutions need to know and be able to do. That vision typically addresses not only the need for job-ready skills but also the knowledge, attitudes, sensitivities, and capacities that help individuals become informed citizens and engaged participants in their communities.

Martha Nussbaum, in *Not for Profit: Why Democracy Needs the Humanities*, offers a bracing alternative to Governor Scott's emphasis on higher education as job-training. She argues that "Thirsty for national profit, nations, and their systems of education are heedlessly discarding skills that are needed to keep democracies alive. If this trend continues, nations all over the world will soon be producing generations of useful machines rather than complete citizens who can think for themselves, criticize tradition, and understand the significance of another person's sufferings and achievements."[4] Clearly, Nussbaum's conception of skills is very different from Scott's—and much more closely aligned with the claims that colleges and universities continue to make about the value of the education they provide. Where Scott is focused on the job-specific skills that can help college graduates gain a toehold in the marketplace, Nussbaum is more broadly concerned with the types of skills that can help college graduates become informed participants in democratic societies, no matter what jobs they hold. We would argue, though, that the types of skills on which Nussbaum focuses are also very useful in the working world.

Third, *courses in the study of religion are overwhelmingly populated by students with very little experience in the academic study of religion.* Even if you have participated in programs of religious education sponsored by a particular religious community, you are not likely to have encountered the specific emphases, approaches, and even subject matter of the academic study of religion. Unlike when you enroll in college-level introductory courses in History or English, for example, you are a double beginner when you embark on the study of religion in colleges and universities. Unlike History or English, the study of religion is rarely featured in the K-12 curriculum.

While you may be familiar with the conventions involved in, say, analyzing a poem or short story or in reading and interpreting historical documents, you likely have virtually no familiarity with the conventions of the *academic* study of religion. If you have studied religion in the context of religious education, you may be surprised to learn that courses in colleges and universities study religion in a markedly different fashion. While it may overlap to some extent, studying religion in an academic setting generally differs substantially from studying it in the context of religious education. When you take a first course in the academic study of religion you must begin to learn a set of conventions, attitudes, expectations, and approaches that you are likely not to have encountered in your previous schooling.

The three distinctive aspects of the academic study of religion that we have pointed to are most evident in courses at the introductory level. Those are the courses most likely to fulfill general education or distribution requirements. Such courses impose specific responsibilities upon both the faculty who teach them and the students who enroll in them. Because they are supposed to meet some goals that are extrinsic to the courses themselves, introductory courses need to make explicit the connections between their specific subject matter and the broader goals of distribution or general education programs.

We return to an example from Chapter 2. There we described how Gustavus Adolphus College, which is affiliated with the Evangelical Lutheran Church in America (ELCA), requires all students to take at least one course that substantially concerns the Christian religious tradition. That requirement both proceeds from and reinforces institutional identity at Gustavus. Consequently, Professor C. D. Elledge noted on his syllabus for his course on "The Bible" that it would cover not only how the Bible originated and how its individual books can be interpreted but also how those books and the Bible as a whole have been interpreted (by Christian readers among others) up to the present. The specific course goals link to the general educational goals of the institution. They set what students can learn in a specific course into a much broader context.

At an institution with a very different type of identity and mission, Missouri State University in Springfield, Professor Victor Matthews covers at least some of the same material in his course on the "Literature and World of the Old Testament" that Professor Elledge covers in "The Bible." But since his institution has a different mission, he uses similar material (texts from the Hebrew Bible or Christian Old Testament) to make a connection to a different sort of educational goal. In his syllabus Professor Matthews argues that his course's "application to the Public Affairs Mission of the University can be found in its efforts to educate students about the past so that they can build upon this heritage in making informed decisions about their own culture and the future direction of society."[5] Matthews' goal is not to form students' identity as Christians or to (re-)connect them to their tradition; instead, he is interested in helping them understand how the past (including the formative periods of the religious traditions of Judaism and Christianity) continues to shape the present.

Both examples show how the study of specific material in each course also serves broader educational goals that are linked to the identity and mission of each institution. They make broad statements about the *value* of the academic study of religion. They claim that the study of religion can make a contribution to the education of any student, regardless of the student's intended career. In that view, the value of the study of religion does not lie in its capacity to prepare students for immediate employment in a specific field directly after graduation. Instead, the value is ideally infused into every aspect of a student's life. *The academic study of religion provides students with both knowledge and skills that will be useful in whatever profession they choose, as well as in their lives as citizens and members of diverse communities.*

You can become aware of the connections between an individual course and broader educational goals both through careful reading of the syllabus and engagement with the material of the course. Having done that, you will be positioned to understand why the curriculum at your institution has directed you toward the academic study of religion, if it actually has. You will also be able to understand why the courses toward which you have been funneled take the forms that they do. Even if you have stumbled upon the academic study of religion with no impetus from a general education requirement, you would do well to figure out how a specific course might fit into your own course of study. At their best, when introductory courses make their connections to broader goals transparent and keep them in view throughout the semester, they can help you understand how the study of *any* specific subject can provide you with knowledge and skills that are relevant and useful beyond the confines of a specific course.

We believe that the value of the academic study of religion for students' lives beyond the classroom lies in both the type of knowledge and the kinds of skills that students can develop. Although we will treat them in sequence, knowledge and skills are not easily separable. As will become clear, we are focusing on the types of knowledge that cannot be easily retrieved by a quick search of the internet. Rather, courses in the study of religion provide the type of knowledge that comes from deep and sustained engagement with historical and contemporary sources from both familiar and unfamiliar contexts.

Knowledge

In recent years there has been a lively discussion among teachers of religious studies about what type of knowledge students need to acquire about religion in college courses. To a large extent, the debate was initiated in 2007 by Stephen Prothero's *Religious Literacy: What Every American Needs to Know—and Doesn't* as we have discussed in Chapter 3.[6] That book reached a much larger audience when it was noticed by various news and entertainment media. For a time, Prothero became the public face of the study of religion in the US.

The origins of Prothero's book lie in a short, factual test that he has routinely administered to his students. The answers that he received on that test over the years convinced him that "Americans are both deeply religious and deeply ignorant about religion."[7] Some of the answers that Prothero received are amusing at the same time that they are, to teachers of religion at least, alarming. Prothero also cites survey data, as well as some person-on-the-street interviews by Jay Leno, to show that the problem he sees is not by any means restricted to his students. A few highlights suffice to sketch the general picture. Prothero reports that:

1   Only half of American adults can name even one of the four Gospels.
2   Most Americans cannot name the first book of the Bible.
3   Ten percent of Americans believed that Joan of Arc was Noah's wife.[8]

The list goes on, and it doesn't yield any better results when the questions turn to other religious traditions.

The response thus seems simple. Students, as well as everyone else, need to learn some basic facts. The pure rehearsal of facts, however, does not make for a very interesting college course, nor is it a pedagogical approach that promises to keep students awake. The retrieval of facts is now only a few keystrokes away for anyone with access to a smartphone, tablet, or other computer. Learning facts will not in itself produce any kind of robust religious literacy. More is needed. And Prothero himself is aware of that.[9]

One promising way to promote religious literacy in college and university courses is to shift the emphasis from the *what* of religion (the kind of factual information that students can easily acquire) to the *how* of religion (what religion does for and to people; how it shapes their lives). As Diane L. Moore puts it, that kind of religious literacy "emphasizes a method of inquiry rather than specific content knowledge."[10] That is what Professor Burlein (see Chapter 2) is after when she proposes that one of the broad goals for her course is to help "students gain concrete information about the way religious beliefs and practices shape the world."[11] From that perspective, religious practices and beliefs, which in Professor Burlein's course are taken from Judaism, Christianity, and Islam, become the material that can be used to address a series of questions. Asking the questions yields knowledge, but that knowledge is not purely factual. It is instead knowledge about complex, interactive processes.

Although Professor Burlein directs students to look at monsters in Judaism, Christianity, and Islam, the value of that study is not simply that students will learn something specific about the monsters they investigate, but that they will then be able to ask questions about religion in general. Because the answers to such questions are developed through close reading, critical thinking, comparison, and conversation with both the teacher and fellow students, they are not the product of a few simple keystrokes. They are not raw facts, divorced from any context, but hard-earned insights that come from situating the raw facts in multiple contexts of possible significance. The type of knowledge in which Professor Burlein, and the academic study of religion, is interested has to be composed, argued for, tested, and revised in a process that lasts throughout the term—and well beyond.

From that vantage point, the classroom becomes a site for the provisional making and testing of knowledge of a specific sort. The readings provide the raw material, or the factual religious literacy, for students' and their teacher's attempts to make and test knowledge through asking questions, entertaining hypotheses, venturing comparisons, and trying out interpretations. Accordingly, class sessions would not be devoted to a simple review of the reading, which amounts to a rehearsal of factual religious literacy. Instead, class sessions move beyond making sense *of* the common reading toward making sense *with* it, by *using* it in various ways. *The goal of any class session should be for students to find more—more information, more angles of vision from which to investigate what they have read, more hypotheses about what it all means, more arguments about how to understand a particular example, more questions.*

For Professor Burlein, one general question is "What kind of thing can you learn if you try to understand different worldviews?" It is easy to see, therefore, how such broad questions fit into the types of goals that are expressed for distribution or general education requirements. On the evidence of her syllabus, Professor Burlein is less concerned with having students name the first book of the Bible, get straight the authors of the four gospels in the Christian New Testament, or identify the Qur'an as the holy book of Islam. Although factual accuracy is a necessary prerequisite to discussion, it is not the primary goal. She wants her students to understand how "religion shapes the world." In Nussbaum's terms, cited earlier in this chapter, she wants her students to discover how religion shapes "another person's sufferings and achievements." That type of knowledge or understanding, while it depends on a sufficient grounding in the facts of the matter, focuses primarily on processes rather than the facts themselves.

One underlying assumption of the approach that Burlein and Nussbaum share is that different religions, as well as different views of the same religion, shape the world in different ways. On a personal level, that is easy enough to understand. Your perceptions, preferences, and commitments are shaped by a variety of cultural and social factors. Any two people are very unlikely to have exactly the same taste in music, movies, food, and sports teams, for example, let alone understand their own and others' religions in exactly the same way. Rather, any two people are very likely to display a complex pattern of similarities and differences. Person A and person B may be united in their undying affection for Beyoncé but differ on whether to get Mexican or Indian food before the concert. Even if person A and person B agree on both their passion for Beyoncé's music and their love of shrimp fajitas, they may differ strongly on their willingness to camp out in order to get tickets for the first showing of the next installment of the "Star Wars" saga. When more items are added to the comparison, say persons C, D, and E, things get much more complicated. Our relations with others are always marked by both similarity and difference, no matter how similar—or how different—those others may initially appear.

The study of religion often focuses on recognizing, analyzing, and interpreting complex patterns of similarity and difference. Although the notion that our world is only becoming more interconnected and more diverse has become something of a cliché, it is nonetheless true. To be able to understand, and get along with, people who are different from yourself has never been more urgent. The academic study of religion can help you understand how people who are in some significant ways different from you view, understand, and act in the world. It provides an analytical perspective on their sufferings and achievements. The study of religion therefore gives you practice in recognizing, analyzing, and interpreting human differences and diversity. That is both a kind of religious literacy and a complex skill that will be useful for you in the rest of your life at work, at home, and in the community.

The ability to make sense of human diversity also fits well with the fundamental premises of a liberal arts education. In a simple sense, a college education has long been modeled on the maps that still appear in shopping malls, or more recently on computers. A dot, usually in red, locates the position of the user on the map. The user can then determine, with the help of the map, how to get to a desired location. Colleges both acknowledge the location of the user or student and point out in general terms the destinations that they want students to reach. They implicitly tell students, like the old mall maps, "you are here." But they confidently assure students, "you can get somewhere else." Students can become educated people, critical thinkers, effective communicators, engaged citizens in the globalized world of the twenty-first century, and, yes, attractive candidates for employment. To do that, colleges argue that students need to be able to situate their own experience in broader contexts. In simple terms, students need to learn how to situate their own "here and now" in terms of multiple "theres" (other cultures) and "thens" (other times).

College curricula, especially at the level of distribution requirements or general education, are fundamentally both historical and comparative. They implicitly assert that there is value in learning about, and from, others who are distant from you in space, time, or both. The academic study of religion is also fundamentally historical and comparative. It is therefore very well positioned to help you wrestle with human difference and diversity. In fact, that is one of its important contributions to any student's general education—and life after college. Courses like "What is Religion?," which consider multiple religious traditions, afford all enrolled students the chance to encounter views of the world that are different from their own. Even courses like "The Bible" and "Literature and World of the Old Testament," which some students might think treat very familiar topics, give students the chance to confront human diversity because they focus on texts that are thousands of years old and thus originated in very different social and cultural circumstances.

Colleges and universities proclaim that they are devoted to preparing students to function as engaged citizens in a globalized world marked by ever-closer relations among geographically distant cultures and a growing diversity within the US itself. The study of religion can rightfully claim that it helps you develop the ability to understand what happens when individuals and groups encounter difference and diversity. Students who study religion learn something about how to understand, and even respond to, the sufferings and achievements of others. That is something that can continue to inform their lives as individuals, community members, citizens, and workers in tangible ways.

That kind of knowledge is practical, though not in the fashion that Governor Scott had in mind when he belittled the value of a degree in Anthropology. It is practical because students who attend college in the first quarter of the twenty-first century will almost inevitably go on to take positions in a workforce marked by cultural, ethnic, and religious diversity; to live in communities with people from multiple cultural heritages; and to help determine the course of a nation that has been decisively shaped by immigration since its inception. Students who will work, live, and vote alongside others who are both like and not like them can therefore realize practical benefits from the academic study of religion.

Skills

Colleges and universities frequently claim that they will enhance students' skills. Hofstra University, for example, provides a particularly full list of skills that it aims to develop. Its mission statement claims that the university's broad-based education "develops students' analytical and critical thinking, strengthens their communication skills (oral and written), promotes cross-cultural competencies and provides information literacy and technological skills that prepare students to become lifelong learners."[12] Clearly, that is a heavy load of goals for a single course.

In Hofstra's College of Liberal Arts and Sciences, students must fulfill various distribution requirements which are designed, at least in part, to help them develop the skills that the university has decided are essential for an educated person. Students must take nine hours of coursework in each of the humanities, the sciences, and the social sciences. In addition, they must take three credit hours of coursework that is somehow "cross-cultural" and three credit hours of interdisciplinary studies. The intention is apparently that over those thirty-three credit hours of coursework, students will have multiple opportunities to practice analytical and critical thinking, communication skills, and the other skills and competencies that the college wants them to have.[13] They can then hone those skills in the rest of their courses.

Such a focus on skills is not restricted to Hofstra by any means. It is encountered in virtually every institution of higher education in the US. It is therefore imperative for the study of religion to be clear about what skills it can help students develop. In his book mentioned at the beginning of this chapter, Zakaria does a good job of boiling down the skills that can be developed in a liberal arts education, of which the study of religion forms a part. He proposes that "one can always read a book to get the basic information about a particular topic, or simply use Google. The crucial challenge is to learn how to read critically, analyze data, and formulate ideas—and most of all to enjoy the intellectual adventure enough to be able to do them easily and often."[14]

In that characterization, reading becomes something much more than a search and retrieval mission in which a reader hunts for a specific fact and, having found it, abandons the search until the need for another fact arises. Reading is also much more than passing one's eyes over a page of text. Instead, reading is a complex way of entering into conversation with a particular text, and even with other texts that may be brought into consideration by the text on which the reader is focusing. In that conversation, readers have to pay close attention to what others have to say, why they are saying it, and on what evidence their claims are based. That is what Zakaria calls reading critically and what we call close reading, which serves as a foundation for critical thinking.

When you enter a conversation through reading, you will quickly find that others are already making claims about the topics that the text addresses. Those claims are themselves based on others' readings of specific information. Any conversation that an assigned reading displays is therefore complicated. It has multiple participants and each of them, including you, brings something distinctive. That is why Zakaria asserts that part of reading critically is the ability to analyze data. Further, the purpose of reading critically and analyzing data is to be able to formulate ideas, or, as we have put it throughout this book, to make arguments and to offer interpretations. Thus the type of reading to which Zakaria is referring is a complex skill. And it is difficult to identify any profession in which the skill of reading critically, including the ability to analyze data and formulate ideas, would not be helpful.

The critical reading that Zakaria recommends is definitely a skill that is cultivated in the academic study of religion. It is also related to another fundamental, and broadly helpful, skill. Another brief anecdote from Zakaria introduces it: "Over the course of that semester, I found myself starting the make the connection between my thoughts and words. It was hard. Being forced to write clearly means, first, you have to think clearly. I began to recognize that the two processes are inextricably intertwined."[15] To the processes of thinking and writing, we can easily add reading.

Reading closely and critically helps provide anyone with material to think about. Thinking about what you have read helps you form ideas. But for ideas to be recognized, let alone grappled with, they need to be communicated. That takes hard work. Zakaria is particularly focused on the hard work of writing. Written communication is disembodied. It cannot take advantage of many of the things that can help clarify oral communication, such as gestures, facial movements, dramatic pauses, and changes in intonation, among other things. Accordingly, clarity and precision are crucial to written communication. And in this case, as in so many others, practice makes perfect. Or at least it leads in that direction.

Writing in courses in the academic study of religion is not, then, simply a sadistic imposition on suffering students by cruel teachers. By assigning writing, teachers aim to give students opportunities both to clarify and then express their thoughts. Those opportunities can have a dual impact. First, they serve the purpose of the particular course by moving students from being passive recipients of knowledge to active creators of it. *You can only contribute your own ideas about the material of the class when you actually know what your ideas are.* Second, writing assignments provide practice in an essential form of human communication. Zakaria's general admonition applies to persuasive writing for college courses and to writing done in any profession: "No matter how strong your idea, you have to be able to convince others to get behind it."[16]

Writing in college courses provides valuable practice in communication. So does speaking. In whatever form they take—for example, asking or answering questions in class discussions or more formal oral presentations—classroom opportunities for oral expression have many of the same characteristics as assigned writing. They give you both an opportunity to participate effectively and creatively in the work of the course at the same time that they give you chances to practice a form of communication that is used in workplaces and communities. They are hardly frivolous exercises confined to obscure corners of the curriculum, as Florida Governor Scott seemed to imply. Speaking and writing are both essential to the work of individual courses and crucial preparations for many tasks that contemporary workers have to undertake. One effect cannot be separated from the other.

A similar claim could be made for many of the other skills that are cultivated in college courses in the study of religion. We won't rehearse a full list here. But consider the emphasis on information literacy or fluency as an example. Generally, information literacy involves the ability to recognize when and what kind of information is needed for a particular task and the capabilities to locate efficiently, evaluate thoroughly and accurately, use effectively, and communicate clearly the relevant information. There are few pursuits in which increased information literacy would not be helpful. Zakaria, for example, quotes the former CEO of the Seagram Company as asserting that there is one common skill that business leaders must have: "how to evaluate raw information, be it from people or a spreadsheet, and make reasoned and critical decisions."[17]

Such examples could certainly be multiplied. But the lesson is clear. Courses in the academic study of religion, and elsewhere in college and university curricula, can help students develop and refine skills that are relevant not only to particular courses but to students' lives as workers, community members, and citizens. The type of false dichotomy promulgated by critics such as Governor Scott simply does not hold up. Not only is the study of religion interesting; it is *useful*.

That usefulness comes about in part because colleges and universities themselves frequently set introductory courses in the study of religion into broader programs designed to provide students with a general education. When such courses make clear their relation to broader programmatic goals, both on the syllabus and through daily practice in the classroom, they provide clear indicators about how the specific work of the course will also help you develop the kinds of knowledge and skills that will serve you well in many other endeavors. It remains only for you to be able to grasp what those indicators are telling them, a task we hope is made easier by the suggestions in this book.

You don't have to want to become a religious studies researcher and teacher in order to profit from a course in the study of religion. The skills that you need to succeed in religion courses are also skills that will serve you well for the rest of your life.

Extra resources can be found at https://www.bloomsbury.com/cw/the-religious-studies-skills-book/skill-building-exercises/chapter-eight/

Notes

Chapter 1

1 Brief but detailed overviews of religion in public schools in America can be found in Joanne M. Marshall, "Nothing New under the Sun: A Historical Overview of Religion in U.S. Public Schools," *Equity and Excellence in Education* 39 (2006): 181–94. See also C. J. Russo, "Religion and Public Schools: A Forty Year Retrospective," *Religion and Education* 30, no. 2 (2003): 1–22.

2 Paul Boyer, "In Search of the Fourth 'R': The Treatment of Religion in American History Textbooks and Survey Courses," in *Religious Advocacy and American History*, edited by Bruce Kuklick and D. G. Hart (Grand Rapids, MI: Eerdmans, 1997), p. 114.

3 See the classic study of university epistolary life by Charles H. Haskins, "The Life of Medieval Students as Illustrated by their Letters," *The American Historical Review* 3, no. 2 (January 1898): 203–29.

4 Douglas Jacobsen and Rhonda Hustedt Jacobsen, *No Longer Invisible: Religion in University Education* (Oxford; New York, NY: Oxford University Press, 2012).

5 https://www.upenn.edu/about/welcome.

6 https://www.aarweb.org/sites/default/files/pdfs/Publications/epublications/AARK-12CurriculumGuidelines.pdf, p. i.

7 D. B. Fleming, "Social Studies Textbooks: Whose Priorities?" in *The Textbook Controversy: Issues, Aspects, and Perspectives*, edited by J. G. Herlihy (Norwood, NH: Ablex, 1992), pp. 55–60.

8 See R.R. Robinson's *Two Centuries of Change in the Content of School Readers* (Nashville: George Peabody College for Teachers, 1930), which tracks a precipitous decline in religious topics in school books around the turn of the twentieth century.

9 NCSS standards, http://www.educationworld.com/standards/national/soc_sci/. See more at: http://www.educationworld.com/standards/national/soc_sci/#sthash.v8pCN69m.dpuf.

10 Ten themes are highlighted in the framework, which include culture; people, places and environments; individuals, groups, and institutions; production, distribution, and consumption; global connections; time, continuity, and change; individual development and identity; power, authority, and governance; science, technology, and society; and civic ideals and practices. Read more at: Social Studies Education—OVERVIEW, PREPARATION OF

TEACHERS—National, Curriculum, Content, and Teaching—StateUniversity.com, http://education.stateuniversity.com/pages/2433/Social-Studies-Education.html#ixzz3rbPR6SVm.

11 http://www.socialstudies.org/positions/study_about_religions.

12 "Religion in the Public School Curriculum: Questions and Answers," *Journal of Law and Religion* 8, no. 1/2 (1990): 310. "Religion in the Public School Curriculum: Questions and Answers" was disseminated widely by NCSS and other sponsoring organizations. The full document can be found at www.religiousfreedomcenter.org.

13 See AAR statement, "Teaching About Religion: AAR Guidelines for K-12 Schools," https://www.aarweb.org/about/teaching-about-religion-aar-guidelines-for-k-12-public-schools.

14 John R. Thelin, *A History of American Higher Education* (Baltimore: Johns Hopkins Press, 2004), p. 18.

15 Edward E. Domm, "Teaching Undergraduates," *Journal of Bible and Religion* 13, no. 3 (1945): 155.

16 http://www.bestcolleges.com/database/ and http://collegemajors101.com/.

Chapter 2

1 See Barbara Walvoord, *Teaching and Learning in College Introductory Religion Courses* (Oxford: Blackwell, 2008).

2 See Timothy Renick et al., "The Religion Major and Liberal Education—a White Paper," *Religious Studies News* (October 2008): 21–24, available at https://www.aarweb.org/about/teagleaar-white-paper.

3 See Joanne Maguire Robinson, "On the Natural History of the Syllabus," paper delivered at American Academy of Religion Meeting, San Antonio, TX, November 2016.

4 See https://www.wabashcenter.wabash.edu/resources/syllabi/. The Wabash Center maintains a searchable collection of more than 1,800 syllabi.

5 See http://www.hofstra.edu/about/about_glance.html.

6 http://bulletin.hofstra.edu/content.php?filter%5B27%5D=RELI&filter%5B29%5D=&filter%5Bcourse_type%5D=-1&filter%5Bkeyword%5D=&filter%5B32%5D=1&filter%5Bcpage%5D=1&cur_cat_oid=86&expand=&navoid=10757&search_database=Filter.

7 Ann Burlein, "RELI 10: What is Religion?" in the Wabash Center Syllabus Collection, https://people.hofstra.edu/Ann_Marie_Burlein/REL_10/whatreligion.html. All quotations are taken from the syllabus.

8 https://gustavus.edu/religion/.

9 https://gustavus.edu/general_catalog/current/gradreq#THEOL.

10 See http://homepages.gac.edu/~celledge/Rel-110.htm. All quotations are taken from the syllabus.

11 https://gustavus.edu/general_catalog/15_16/gradreq.

12 For a brief guide to metacognition see Nancy Chick, "Metacognition," https://cft.vanderbilt.edu/guides-sub-pages/metacognition/.

13 See http://publicaffairs.missouristate.edu/About.htm.

14 http://www.missouristate.edu/GeneralEducation/whygened.htm.

15 Ibid.

16 https://www.wabashcenter.wabash.edu/syllabi/SyllabiMatthewsREL101.pdf. All quotations are taken from the syllabus.

17 http://www.missouristate.edu/generaleducation/.

18 http://www.missouristate.edu/GeneralEducation/whygened.htm.

19 For a lucid exposition of what constitutes a thesis statement see http://writingcenter.unc.edu/tips-and-tools/thesis-statements/.

20 See https://people.hofstra.edu/Ann_Marie_Burlein/REL_10/whatreligion.html. All quotations come from this document.

21 This retains her original emphases.

Chapter 3

1 Lisa Miller, "Religious Studies Revival," *Newsweek*, September 12, 2010.

2 A. W. Astin, "The Spiritual Life of College Students: A National Study of College Students' Search for Meaning and Purpose," in *Spirituality in Higher Education* (Los Angeles, CA: Higher Education Research Institute at UCLA, 2004); Rick Kennedy, *Faith at State: A Handbook for Christians at Secular Universities* (Downers Grove, IL: InterVarsity Press, 1995); Damon Mayrl and Freeden Oeur, "Religion and Higher Education: Current Knowledge and Directions for Future Research," *Journal for the Scientific Study of Religion* 48, no. 2 (2009): 260–75; Christian Smith and Patricia Snell, *Souls in Transition: The Religious and Spiritual Lives of Emerging Adults* (Oxford: Oxford University Press, 2009); Trent Sheppard, *God on Campus* (Downers Grove, IL: InterVarsity, 2010); Vachel W. Miller and Merle M. Ryan, *Transforming Campus Life: Reflections on Spirituality and Religious Pluralism*, Studies in Education and Spirituality, Vol. 1 (New York: P. Lang, 2001); Lois Calian Trautvetter, "Undergraduate Perspectives About Religion in Higher Education," in *Encountering Faith in the Classroom: Turning Difficult Discussions into Constructive Engagement*, edited by Miriam Rosalyn Diamond (Sterling, VA: Stylus, 2008), pp. 33–47.

3 Robert A. Orsi, "The 'So-Called History' of the Study of Religion," *Method and Theory in the Study of Religion* 20, no. 2 (2008): 134–35.

4 See Chapters 4 and 6 for analysis of some definitions of religion.

5 James C. Livingston, *The Anatomy of the Sacred: An Introduction to Religion*, 2nd ed. (New York: Macmillan, 1993), p. 11.

6 Karl Marx, "Critique of Hegel's 'Philosophy of Right'," in *Karl Marx: Selected Writings*, ed. Lawrence H. Simon (Indianapolis, IN: Hackett, 1994), p. 28.

7 Rodney Stark and William Bainbridge, *The Future of Religion: Secularization, Revival, and Cult Formation* (Berkeley, CA: University of California Press, 1985), p. 432.

8 https://religion.ucsd.edu/undergraduate/courses/topics/reli101-syllabus-sp15.pdf. See the essays on a similar assignment by Chad Bauman et al., "The 'Make Your Own Religion' Project," *Teaching Theology and Religion* 19, no. 1 (January 2016): 99–110.

9 http://pewforum.org/Other-Beliefs-and-Practices/U-S-Religious-Knowledge-Survey.aspx.

10 http://www.pewforum.org/quiz/u-s-religious-knowledge/.

11 Stephen Prothero, *Religious Literacy: What Every American Needs to Know—and Doesn't* (San Francisco, CA: HarperCollins, 2007), p. 1.

12 http://www.pewforum.org/files/2007/12/protheroquiz.pdf.

13 Prothero, *Religious Literacy*, esp. Part 2 (pp. 73–154).

14 https://www.princetonreview.com/college-majors/244/religious-studies.

15 Neeta P. Fogg et al., *College Majors Handbook* (St. Paul, MN: Jist Publishing, 2004), p. 473.

16 See, for instance, a report by the World Economic Forum, https://widgets.weforum.org/nve-2015/chapter1.html.

17 The College Entrance Examination Board, *Book of Majors 2018: All-New Seventh Edition* (New York: Macmillan, 2013), p. 503.

18 Ibid.

19 https://new.oberlin.edu/arts-and-sciences/departments/sociology/documents/syllabi/2015-2016/SOCI%20303%20Greggor%20Spring%202016.pdf.

20 https://religion.ua.edu.

21 https://hope.edu/academics/religion/.

22 See Sarah Imhoff, "The Creation Story of Religious Studies, or How We Learned to Stop Worrying and Love Schempp," *Journal of the American Academy of Religion* (March 2016): 466–97.

23 http://www.digitalhistory.uh.edu/disp_textbook.cfm?smtID=3&psid=4087.

24 http://live-wabash.pantheonsite.io/syllabi/SyllabiMatthewsREL101.pdf.

25 http://live-wabash.pantheonsite.io/syllabi/SyllabiMatthewsREL101.pdf.

26 http://live-wabash.pantheonsite.io/syllabi/k/Kelhoffer/New_Testament_8Spring2007.pdf.

27 http://www2.kenyon.edu/Depts/Religion/Fac/Adler/Reln101/syl101.pdf.

28 http://www2.kenyon.edu/Depts/Religion/Fac/Adler/Reln101/syl101.pdf.

29 https://www.wabashcenter.wabash.edu/syllabi/w/wiggins/christianity-wiggins.htm.

30 https://www.wabashcenter.wabash.edu/syllabi/a/altany/rst305/rst305-0201.html.

31 https://www.csun.edu/~hcfll004/genesisq.html.

32 https://webcache.googleusercontent.com/search?q=cache:BHrZ0d9dLWgJ:h
    ttps://facultyinfo.unt.edu/mirror/jmp0309/schteach/SEX%2520AND%2520TH
    E%2520BIBLE%2520syllabus-1.doc+&cd=11&hl=en&ct=clnk&gl=us.

33 See, for instance, Stephen D. Brookfield and Stephen Preskill, *Discussion
    as a Way of Teaching: Tools and Techniques for Democratic Classrooms* (San
    Francisco, CA: Jossey-Bass, 2005) and Donald L. Finkel, *Teaching With Your
    Mouth Shut* (Portsmouth, NH: Boynton/Cook, 2000).

34 James Lang, *Small Teaching: Everyday Lessons from the Science of
    Learning* (San Francisco, CA: Jossey-Bass, 2016).

35 Vladimir Nabokov, *Pnin* (New York: Vintage, 1989), p. 155.

Chapter 4

1 See Jonathan Z. Smith, "The Necessary Lie: Duplicity in the Disciplines,"
   in *Studying Religion: An Introduction*, edited by Russell T. McCutcheon
   (London: Equinox, 2007), pp. 73–80.

2 For a review of scholarly theories of the origins of the Qur'an see A. J.
   Droge, *The Qur'an: An Annotated Translation* (Sheffield, UK: Equinox, 2013),
   pp. xi–xxxvli.

3 Such arguments often appeal to Qur'an 43:3: "Surely We have made it an
   Arabic Qur'an, so that you may understand." See Michael Sells, *Approaching
   the Qur'an: The Early Revelations* (Ashland, OR: White Cloud Press, 1999),
   pp. 2–3, 21–28.

4 A. J. Arberry, *The Koran Interpreted* (New York: Touchstone Books, 1955).

5 Many English translations of the Qur'an are available online and some sites
   offer side-by-side comparisons of different translations. See, for example,
   http://quranbrowser.org/.

6 Droge, *The Qur'an*, p. 1.

7 See Sells, *Approaching the Qur'an*, p. 43.

8 Ibid.

9 Droge, *The Qur'an*, p. 1.

10 Sells, *Approaching the Qur'an*, p. 43.

11 See Droge, *The Qur'an*, p. 1.

12 Ibid.

13 Ibid.

14 See Steven Fine, *The Menorah: From the Bible to Modern Israel* (Cambridge,
    MA: Harvard University Press, 2016).

15 https://www.templeinstitute.org/about.htm. Not writing out the name of God
    fully, in this case replacing the "o" with a dash, is an indicator of respect for
    the divine name that is practiced by many Jews.

16 https://www.templeinstitute.org/history-holy-temple-menorah-1.htm.

17 http://www.sgi.org/about-us/gohonzon.html.

18 Ibid.

19 http://www.nichirenlibrary.org/en/wnd-1/Content/45#para-2.

20 http://www.sgi.org/about-us/videos/chanting-nam-myoho-renge-kyo-a-pronunciation-guide.html and http://www.sgi.org/resources/video-and-audio/how-to-chant/gongyo-a-pronunciation-guide.html.

21 https://www.youtube.com/user/SGIVideosOnline.

22 http://www.sgi.org/about-us/videos/how-to-chant1.html.

23 See https://www.sgi-usa.org/study-resources/core-concepts/the-gohonzon/diagram-of-the-gohonzon/.

24 Williams James, *The Varieties of Religious Experience* (New York: Mentor Books, 1964), p. 42, original emphasis.

25 Ibid., p. 6.

26 See Peter J. Elbow, "Methodological Doubting and Believing: Contraries in Inquiry," in *Embracing Contraries: Explorations in Learning and Teaching* (New York: Oxford University Press, 1986), pp. 254–304 and idem, "The Believing Game: A Challenge after Twenty-Five Years," in *Everyone Can Write: Essays Towards a Hopeful Theory of Writing and Teaching Writing* (New York: Oxford University Press, 2000), pp. 76–80.

27 Elbow, "Methodological Doubting and Believing," p. 257.

Chapter 5

1 Umberto Eco, *The Name of the Rose*, trans. William Weaver (Boston, MA: Houghton Mifflin Harcourt, 2014), p. 338.

2 https://www.grinnell.edu/about/mission.

3 https://www.unr.edu/liberal-arts/about/mission-statement.

4 http://catalog.threerivers.edu/content.php?catoid=2&navoid=70.

5 See, for instance, Richard Arum and Josipa Roksa, *Academically Adrift: Limited Learning on College Campuses* (Chicago: University of Chicago Press, 2011).

6 Ken Bain, *What the Best College Teachers Do* (Cambridge, MA: Harvard University Press, 2004).

7 Ken Bain, *What the Best College Students Do* (Cambridge, MA: Harvard University Press, 2012).

8 Studies of critical thinking within religious studies include Richard Penaskovic's *Critical Thinking and the Academic Study of Religion* (Atlanta, GA: Scholars Press, 1997) and Barbara Walvoord, *Teaching and Learning in College Introductory Religion Courses* (Oxford: Blackwell, 2008).

9 Rebecca Moore, "Drinking the Kool-Aid," *Nova Religio* 7, no. 2 (2003): 92–100.

10 http://www.criticalthinking.org/pages/a-brief-history-of-the-idea-of-critical-thinking/408.

11 John Dewey, *How We Think* (Mineola, NY: Dover, 1997), p. 74.

12 Stephen Brookfield, *Developing Critical Thinkers: Challenging Adults to Explore Alternative Ways of Thinking and Acting* (San Francisco, CA: Jossey-Bass, 1987), p. x.

13 John McPeck, *Critical Thinking and Education* (New York: St. Martin's Press, 1981), p. 4.

14 https://www2.ed.gov/about/bdscomm/list/hiedfuture/reports/pre-pub-report.pdf.

15 http://www.spirituality.ucla.edu/reports/index.htm.

16 See, for instance, literature on Bloom's taxonomy arising from the original study in B. S. Bloom, M. D. Englehart, E. J. Furst, W. H. Hill, and D. R. Krathwohl, *The Taxonomy of Educational Objectives, Handbook I: The Cognitive Domain* (New York: David McKay Co., 1956).

17 Tim John Moore, "Critical Thinking and Disciplinary Thinking: A Continuing Debate," *Higher Education Research and Development* 30, no. 3 (2011): 261–74.

18 See John Schlueter, "Higher Ed's Biggest Gamble," *Inside Higher Ed*, June 7, 2016, https://www.insidehighered.com/views/2016/06/07/can-colleges-truly-teach-critical-thinking-skills-essay.

19 E.g. Daniel Willingham, "Critical Thinking: Why Is It So Hard to Teach?" *American Educator* (Summer 2007): 8–19.

20 Ibid., p. 9.

Chapter 6

1 Harvey F. Silver, *Compare & Contrast: Teaching Comparative Thinking to Strengthen Student Learning* (Alexandria, VA: Association for Supervision & Curriculum Development, 2010), p. 6.

2 Friedrich Max Müller, *Lectures on the Science of Religion* (New York: Scribner, 1872), p. 1. See Jeppe Sinding Jensen, *What is Religion?* (London: Routledge, 2014), p. 22.

3 Adolf Von Harnack, "Die Aufgabe der theologischen Fakultäten und die allgemeine Religionsgeschichte, nebst einem Nachwort (1901). Rede vom 3. August 1901," in *Reden und Aufsätze*, Band 2, ed. Adolf Von Harnack (Giessen: Töpelmann, 1906), pp. 159–87 (168); see Jensen, *What is Religion?*

4 See, for example, Mircea Eliade, *Patterns in Comparative Religion* (New York: Meridian Books, 1971). For a set of essays on comparison in conversation with Eliade and Jonathan Z. Smith see Kimberley C. Patton and Benjamin C. Ray, eds., *A Magic Still Dwells: Comparative Religion in the Postmodern Age* (Berkeley, CA: University of California Press, 2000).

5 See Bart D. Ehrman, *The New Testament: A Historical Introduction to the Early Christian Writings*, 4th ed. (New York: Oxford University Press, 2008), p. 102.

6 Matthew 6:9-13 in the NRSV translation; https://www.biblegateway.com/passage/?search=Matthew+5-7&version=NRSV.

7   Mary Baker Eddy, *Science and Health with Key to the Scriptures* (Boston, MA: The Christian Science Publishing Company, 1917), Chapter 1; http://www.christianscience.com/the-christian-science-pastor/science-and-health/chapter-i-prayer.

8   See, for example, http://www.thechicfashionista.com/your-best-perfect-colors.html.

9   See http://www.bbc.co.uk/religion/religions/islam/practices/hajj_1.shtml and http://www.kumbhmelaallahabad.gov.in/english/index.html.

10 For examples of each see https://tibetanprayerflag.com/ and https://theculturetrip.com/caribbean/haiti/articles/vodou-flags-between-the-terrestrial-and-the-spiritual/.

11 See https://commons.wikimedia.org/wiki/Category:Meiji_Shrine and http://www.vaticanstate.va/content/vaticanstate/en/monumenti/basilica-di-s-pietro.html.

12 See http://www.rishiray.com/dattatreya-temple-and-85-ft-hanuman-murti-in-carapichaima/ and https://www.lds.org/church/temples/salt-lake?lang=eng.

13 William James, *The Varieties of Religious Experience* (New York: New American Library, 1958), p. 42; italics in original.

14 Emile Durkheim, *The Elementary Forms of Religious Life*, trans. Carol Cosman, abridged with an introduction and notes by Mark S. Cladis (Oxford: Oxford University Press, 2001), p. 46; italics in original.

15 Catherine Albanese, *America: Religion and Religions*, 5th ed. (Boston, MA: Wadsworth, 2012), p. 10; italics in original.

16 Ibid.

17 Durkheim, *Elementary Forms*, p. 46.

18 Albanese, *America: Religion and Religions*, p. 10; see Clifford Geertz, "Religion as a Cultural System," in *The Interpretation of Cultures* (New York: Basic Books, 1971), p. 90. Geertz's definition is "(1) a system of symbols which acts to (2) establish powerful, pervasive, and long-lasting moods and motivations in men by (3) formulating conceptions of a general order of existence and (4) clothing these conceptions with such an aura of factuality that (5) the moods and motivations seem uniquely realistic."

Chapter 7

1   Huldrych Zwingli, *On Freedom of Choice in the Selection of Food*, excerpted in Denis R. Janz, ed., *Reformation Reader: Primary Texts with Introductions* (Minneapolis, MN: Fortress Press, 2008), p. 186.

2   Colleen McDannell, *Material Christianity* (New Haven, CT: Yale University Press), p. 3.

3   http://religion.fiu.edu/courses/courses-archive/summer-2016/rel3308-rvbb-zolondek.pdf.

4 Edward Said, "Islam and the West are Inadequate Banners." Guardian, September 16, 2001. Online at https://www.theguardian.com/world/2001/sep/16/september11.terrorism3. Last accessed June 25, 2018.

5 Extended explanations of the information given here can be found in Wayne C. Booth, et al., *The Craft of Research*, 4th ed. (Chicago, IL: University of Chicago Press, 2016.)

6 Gerald Graff, *They Say, I Say: The Moves That Matter in Academic Writing*, 2nd ed. (New York, NY: W. W. Norton and Co., 2010).

7 Thanks to Jan Rieman for her helpful outline of this subject for her students.

8 William Strunk, Jr. and E. B. White, *The Elements of Style*, 3rd ed. (New York: Macmillan, 1979).

9 Joseph M. Williams and Joseph Bizup, *Style: Lessons in Clarity and Grace*, 12th ed. (New York, NY: Pearson, 2016).

Chapter 8

1 Fareed Zakaria, *In Defense of a Liberal Education* (New York: W. W. Norton & Company, 2015), p. 36.

2 As quoted in Andrew Delbanco, *College: What It Was, Is, and Should Be* (Princeton, NJ: Princeton University Press, 2012), p. 83.

3 See https://stateimpact.npr.org/florida/2011/10/20/explaining-florida-gov-scott-war-on-anthropology-why-anthropologists-win/. The same essay offers a critique of Scott's reasoning: "According to federal Bureau of Labor Statistics data, job prospects for anthropologists are nearly as strong as they are for the math and science graduates Scott prizes." See also Rachel Newcomb, "To Governor Rick Scott: What Anthropologists Can Do for Florida," https://www.huffingtonpost.com/rachel-newcomb/to-governor-rick-scott-wh_b_1008964.html.

4 Martha C. Nussbaum, *Not for Profit: Why Democracy Needs the Humanities* (Princeton, NJ: Princeton University Press, 2016), p. 2.

5 https://www.wabashcenter.wabash.edu/syllabi/SyllabiMatthewsREL101.pdf. All quotations are taken from the syllabus.

6 Stephen Prothero, *Religious Literacy: What Every American Needs to Know—and Doesn't* (San Francisco, CA: HarperCollins, 2007).

7 Ibid., p. 1.

8 See ibid., p. 30.

9 See Stephen Prothero, Eugene V. Gallagher, Thomas Pearson, Joanne Maguire Robinson, and Martha Ellen Stortz, "Conversation with Stephen Prothero," *Teaching Theology and Religion* 12, no. 3 (2009): 208–21.

10 Diane L. Moore, *Overcoming Religious Illiteracy: A Cultural Studies Approach to the Study of Religion in Secondary Education* (New York: Palgrave MacMillan, 2007), p. 57.

11 http://bulletin.hofstra.edu/content.php?filter%5B27%5D=RELI&filter%5B29 %5D=&filter%5Bcourse_type%5D=-1&filter%5Bkeyword%5D=&filter%5B 32%5D=1&filter%5Bcpage%5D=1&cur_cat_oid=86&expand=&navoid=107 57&search_database=Filter.

12 https://www.hofstra.edu/about/about_mission.html.

13 See http://bulletin.hofstra.edu/preview_entity.php?catoid=86&ent_ oid=4634#BA.

14 Zakaria, *In Defense*, p. 61.

15 Ibid., p. 73.

16 Ibid., p. 77.

17 Ibid., p. 90.

Index